YOUR

LIFE

IS

WORTH

LIVING

YOUR

LIFE

IS

WORTH

LIVING

YOUR
LIFE
IS
WORTH
LIVING

50 LESSONS TO DEEPEN YOUR FAITH

FULTON SHEEN

Foreword by Bishop Robert Barron

IMAGE

New York

Published in the United States by Image, an imprint of the Crown
Publishing Group, a division of Penguin Random House LLC, New York.
crownpublishing.com

IMAGE is a registered trademark and the "I" colophon is a trademark of
Penguin Random House LLC.

Library of Congress Cataloging-in-Publication Data
Names: Sheen, Fulton J. (Fulton John), 1895–1979, author. | Davidowitz,
    Esther B., 1934– editor.
Title: Your life is worth living : 50 lessons to deepen your faith / Fulton
    Sheen.
Description: New York : Crown Publishing Group, 2019.
Identifiers: LCCN 2018029925 (print) | LCCN 2018041687 (ebook) |
    ISBN 9781984823298 (e-book) | ISBN 9781984823281 (pbk.)
Subjects: LCSH: Christian life—Catholic authors. | Catholic
    Church—Doctrines.
Classification: LCC BX2350.3 (ebook) | LCC BX2350.3 .S543 2019 (print) |
    DDC 248.4/82—dc23
LC record available at https://lccn.loc.gov/2018029925

ISBN 978-1-9848-2328-1
Ebook ISBN 978-1-9848-2329-8

Printed in the United States of America

Cover design by Sarah Horgan

10 9 8 7 6 5 4 3

CONTENTS

FOREWORD

BY BISHOP ROBERT BARRON

The book you're about to read is the closest thing we have to a *Summa Sheeniana*, a summary of Archbishop Fulton Sheen's teachings on the Christian faith. Much of the wisdom contained in Sheen's radio programs, television shows, sermons, classroom presentations, retreat talks, books, and lectures is synthetically presented here. The essays gathered in this book are written transcripts of audiotapes that the greatest Catholic evangelist of the twentieth century made in 1965, when he was seventy years old. What you hear is the confident voice of an old pro, a master teacher who had been plowing the evangelical and apologetic field for some forty years.

As I reread these chapters, I was struck by three qualities that Fulton Sheen had in spades: he was smart; he had a comprehensive vision; and he possessed one of the most active analogical imaginations in the history of the Church. Permit me to say something simple about each one of these. Archbishop Sheen had a magnificent intellectual formation in Catholic philosophy and theology, culminating in his rare *agrégé* postdoctoral degree from the Catholic University of Louvain. Moreover, he taught for many years at the

Catholic University of America in Washington, D.C., and he composed a number of academically sophisticated texts. Thus, when he turned to a wider audience, he did not engage in crude or simplistic popularization; rather, he brought to his task considerable intellectual firepower. In the course of *Your Life Is Worth Living,* he mentions and quotes, among many others, Thomas Aquinas, Aristotle, Cicero, John Henry Newman, Confucius, George Bernard Shaw, Isaac Newton, Martin Heidegger, Carl Jung, Shakespeare, and T. S. Eliot. How we need this sort of urbanity and intellectualism in our age of dumbed-down Catholicism!

Second, he demonstrates in this book, and indeed throughout his work, a marvelously integrated understanding of the mysteries of the Christian faith. We have entered, sadly in my judgment, into an era of hyperspecialization in theology. According to the cliché, we have many theologians and philosophers who know more and more about less and less. But Sheen ranges widely and comfortably over the whole arena of Catholic thought, speculating on creation, the Incarnation, the doctrine of God, the Trinity, theological anthropology, Grace, Sin, Redemption, the Resurrection, the blessed Mother, the Papacy, and the Mystical Body. And he doesn't simply cover this extraordinarily wide terrain. He shows the interconnections among the various topics, how, for instance, the Church is the prolongation of the Incarnation across space and time and why the virginity of Mary is an indicator of the truth of the Incarnation; how a correct understanding of sin leads to a correct understanding of the Cross, et cetera. In so doing, he practices the art of truly systematic theology, and he manages therefore to make the faith satisfying both to the intellectual and to the aesthetic sensibility of his reader.

The third and, to me anyway, most remarkable quality evident in these essays is the author's gift for finding analogies, comparisons, and illustrations to explicate the Christian mysteries. It is a commonplace among teachers that the key to all effective instruction is building bridges from the known to the unknown. And this process happens largely through analogy: every effective teacher, from kindergarten through graduate school, says some version of "This principle I'm trying to teach you, well, it's like this other principle you already understand." I don't know anyone in the great tradition of Christian preaching, catechesis, or theologizing who exercises this analogical method with greater skill than Fulton Sheen. Examples abound within this book: the seven sacraments are like white light that breaks into colors when passed through a prism; grace lifts us to a higher form of life, just as an animal absorbs a plant into its life and a plant lifts chemicals into its life; Mary's sinlessness is like a lock separating foul waters from pure; the Holy Spirit is the sigh of love breathed out by the Father and the Son; the Mass is like a drama repeated by a traveling troupe of players; and so on. These comparisons and images seem to tumble out of him, but I imagine that they were invented and then refined by Sheen over many years of popular communication.

One might get the impression that, given my enthusiasm for Fulton Sheen, I think we should simply go back to his method and content in our work of evangelization, but that would be mistaken. We must certainly learn from him, but we also must follow him in creatively engaging the culture of our own time. In a way—and I speak from a good deal of practical experience here—evangelization is a much harder task today than it was in Sheen's time. This is because the good archbishop could assume a remarkably broad cultural

consensus around many issues moral, philosophical, and
even religious. The very fact that huge numbers of non-
Catholics avidly followed him testifies to this truth. But
this consensus has largely evanesced today. And this is why
a simple repetition of his ideas, images, and comparisons
might not be effective for the contemporary audience. But
we should indeed endeavor to be as smart as he was, as
boldly comprehensive and synthetic as he was, and willing
to exercise our analogical imagination with something of
his flair and creativity.

PREFACE

This is the story of a friendship born through the writings of Fulton J. Sheen. I discovered Archbishop Sheen in the summer of 1981. After I graduated from the United States Military Academy at West Point, retired Army Colonel Richard F. Aschettino befriended me. He had completed a master's degree in philosophy and had written his thesis on Sheen. "Asch" introduced me to Sheen's writing, and I was immediately taken by the archbishop's gift of communication and read thirty of his books within twelve months.

During 1982, while searching for other books by Sheen, I purchased a copy of recordings he had dictated in 1965. The original title of this record set was *Life Is Worth Living*. Although the recordings shared the same title and format as the popular television program, this oral compendium was completely unrelated and was produced eight years after the show went off the air, at the conclusion of Vatican II. The television program format presented a new message to a general audience each week, not necessarily religious and not always related to the previous show, but always with the hope of drawing one soul closer to God. This work advances that of the television show. Sheen builds on each lesson and draws the individual soul into a personal relationship with Christ.

The recordings were made in the privacy of Sheen's New York City residence. Without the use of notes, the work flowed from his heart, drawing on forty-five years' experience as a priest. Each topic ran about twenty-five minutes. To illustrate his points, he used many stories from his own life, in addition to referencing over 450 scriptural passages and many noted poets and authors.

Socrates said, "The best flavoring for drink is thirst." Sheen's vast appeal was due to the fact that he related to people of all religious backgrounds. He received thousands of letters as a result of his radio and television ministries, with only a third coming from Catholics. This work was an attempt to quench the immense spiritual thirst of people from around the world. The international demand for Sheen's message went beyond his capability to fulfill each individual request. He created this vinyl encyclopedia to respond to the needs of the hundreds of thousands who wrote for personal direction. As Christ worked the miracle of multiplication to feed the five thousand, Sheen, using modern technology, created a work of multiplication that has fed and continues to feed so many lives. He was a great teacher and priest, and the world was his parish.

Many people have assisted in the development of *Your Life Is Worth Living*. Thanks to Reverend Monsignor Thomas Gervasio, who gave me instruction in the Catholic faith and encouraged my use of the recordings of Archbishop Sheen. Thanks to the many priests who assisted in providing the Latin, French, and Greek translations, especially Reverend Monsignor James Mulligan, S.T.L. A special thanks to Esther B. Davidowitz, who undertook the difficult task of editing the original transcripts. We were most fortunate to have the inspired editorial assistance of Professor Alfred S. Groh as grammarian. Siena Finley, R.S.M., Professor Kenneth D. Hines, Edwina Ustynoski, Paul Buckalew, Elizabeth Reinartz, and Laurie Siebert shared their Catholic wisdom. Thanks to Sister Pat Schoelles, S.S.J., Sister Connie Derby, R.S.M., Bob Vogt, and Patrick Mulich at St. Bernard's Institute in Rochester, New York, who made available the Bishop Sheen Archives during the summer of 2000. Most of all, thanks to my wife and family, who had infinite patience and faith through the course of this project. God love you!

Jon Hallingstad
Germansville, Pennsylvania
JUNE 10, 2001

PART I

GOD AND MAN

What do you have that was not given to you?

And if it was given, how can you boast as if it were your own?

(1 CO 4:7)

If it be a terrible thing to fall into the hands of the living God,

It is a more terrible thing to fall out of them.

—FULTON J. SHEEN

THE PHILOSOPHY OF LIFE

Peace be to you. There are two ways of waking up in the morning. One is to say, "Good morning, God," and the other is to say, "Good God, morning!" We are going to start with the second.

People who wake up that way have an anxiety about life. Life seems rather absurd to them, and considerable literature is being produced today on the absurdity of life. One of the best expressions of that absurdity is a novel with two factories, on either side of a river. One factory took great big stones, smashed and ground them into powder, and shipped the powder to the other side of the river, where the other factory turned them into great big boulders. Then the boulders were sent back to the first factory and so the routine continued. This is a literary expression of the way people regard life today.

One finds this absurdity expressed in a play by an existentialist who pictured three people in hell. Each one wanted to talk about himself, his own aches and his own pains. The others were only interested in their own aches and pains. Finally, when the curtain goes down, the last line is "My neighbor is hell!" which is the way some people live.

Along with this sense of absurdity there is also a drift. Many minds are like Old Man River; they just keep floating along, no goal, just a kind of an arrow without a target, pilgrims without a shrine, journeys at sea without any kind of a port. What is the common conclusion of people who wake up and say, "Good God, morning"? To them, life has no meaning; it is without purpose, goal, or destiny.

I remember when I first went to Europe to study as a young priest. I was taking courses during the summer at the Sorbonne in Paris, principally in order to learn French. I dwelled in a boardinghouse that belonged to Madame Citroën. I was there about a week when she came to me and said something, but it was all French to me. You get so angry in Paris because the dogs and horses understand French, and you don't! There were three American schoolteachers living in the boardinghouse, and I asked them to act as interpreters. This is the story that came out.

Madame Citroën said after her marriage, her husband left her, and a daughter that was born to them became a moral wreck on the streets of Paris. Then she pulled out of her pocket a small vial of poison.

She said, "I do not believe in God, and if there is one, I curse Him. I've decided since life has no meaning and is absurd, to take this poison tonight. Can you do anything for me?"

Through the interpreter I said, "I can if you're going to take that stuff!"

I asked her to postpone her suicide for nine days. I think it is the only case on record of a woman postponing suicide for nine days. I never prayed before as I prayed for that woman. On the ninth day the good Lord gave her great grace. Some years later on the way to Lourdes, I stopped off in the city of Dax, where I enjoyed the hospitality of Monsieur, Madame, and Mademoiselle Citroën.

I said to the village priest, "Are the Citroëns good Catholics?"

"Oh," he said. "It's wonderful when people keep the faith all during their lives."

Obviously, he did not know the story. So it's possible to find one's way out of this absurdity.

Let's come to a question which interests all psychiatrists and all of us, "What is the difference between a normal and an abnormal person?" A normal person always works toward a goal or purpose; the abnormal person looks for escape mechanisms, excuses, and rationalizations to avoid discovering the meaning and purpose of life. The normal person sets for himself a goal. A young man may want to be a doctor or a lawyer, but beyond that there is something else.

Suppose you ask, "What do you want to do after you become a doctor?"

"Well. I want to marry and raise children."

"And then?"

"Be happy and make money."

"And then?"

"Give money to my children."

"And then?"

There comes a last "And then?" The normal person knows what that "and then" is. The abnormal person is locked up within the barrel of his own ego. He's like an egg that's never been hatched. He refuses to submit himself to divine incubation in order to arrive at a different life than he has.

What are some of the escape mechanisms of the abnormal person? If he wants to go from New York to Washington, he isn't concerned about Washington; he's concerned about giving excuses why he doesn't go to Washington. A common escape mechanism for the abnormal person is a love of speed. I believe that an excessive love of speed or, should I say, a love of excessive speed, is due to the want of a goal or purpose in life. So they do not know where they are going, but they certainly are on their way! There may even be an unconscious, or half-conscious, desire to end life because it is without purpose. Another escape can be sex, as well as throwing oneself into business in an abnormal kind of way in order to have the intensity of an experience atone for a want of goal or purpose.

One very famous psychiatrist, Dr. Carl Jung, said that after twenty-five years of experiences dealing with mental patients, at least one-third of his patients had no observable clinical neurosis. All of them were suffering from a want of the meaning and purpose of life, and not until they discovered that would they ever be happy. The vast majority of people today are suffering from what might be called an existential neurosis, the anxiety and the problem of living. They ask, "What is it all about?" "Where do I go from here?" "How do I find it?"

You may be thinking, now I'm going to tell you to get down on your knees and pray to God. No, I'm not. I may say that a little later, because people who have an existential neurosis are too far away from that for the moment. I'm offering two solutions: the first, go out and help your neighbor. Those who suffer from an anxiety of life live only for themselves. Their minds and hearts have been dammed up. All of the scum of the river of life makes the heart and mind a kind of a garbage heap, and the easiest way out is to love people whom you see. If we do not love those whom we see, how can we love God, whom we do not see? Visit the sick. Be kind to the poor. Help the healing of lepers. Find your neighbor, and a neighbor is someone in need. Once you do this, you begin to break out of the shell. You discover that your neighbor is not hell, as Sartre says, your neighbor is part of yourself and is a creature of God.

A father brought his young son to me, a conceited young delinquent, who had given up his faith and was bitter with himself and everyone whom he met. Following our visit the boy ran away from home for a year. The boy came back just as bad, and the father brought him to me asking, "What should I do with him?" I advised him to send his son to a school outside the United States. About a year later the boy came back to see me, requesting, "Would you be willing to give me moral support for an enterprise I have undertaken in Mexico? There is a group of boys in the college where I am who have built a little school. We have gone all around the neighborhood and brought in children to teach them catechism. We have also brought a doctor from the United States, once a year for one month, to take care of the sick people of the neighborhood."

And I asked, "How did you become interested in this?"

He replied, "The boys went down there during the summer and I joined them."

He recovered his faith, morals, and everything else in his neighbor. It is the poor, indigent, needy, sick, fellow creatures of God, who give to us great strength. Some years ago there was an Indian who went into Tibet. He went in to do evangelizing in that non-Christian country with a Tibetan guide. During the trip they got very cold crossing the foothills of the Himalayas and sat down, exhausted and almost frozen. This Indian, whose name was Singh, said, "I think I hear a man moaning down there in the abyss!"

The Tibetan said, "You're almost dead yourself, you can't help him!"

Singh said, "Yes, I will help him."

He went down and dragged the man out of the abyss and carried him to the nearby village and came back completely revived from that act of charity. When he returned he found his friend, who had refused to aid the neighbor, frozen to death. Therefore, the first way to escape the anxiety of life is to find your neighbor.

The second way is to leave yourself open to experiences and encounters with the divine which will come to you from without. I say leave yourself open. Your eye does not have light. Your ear has no sound or harmony. Food of your stomach comes from outside. Your mind has been taught. A radio pulls in unseen waves from the outside. Allow yourself to receive certain impulses that come from without which will perfect you. No matter how far away you are from what I'm talking about, they will still come.

I remember inviting a woman to see me who had just lost her eighteen-year-old daughter. She was very rebellious and had no faith whatever.

She said, "I want to talk about God."

I said, "All right, I will talk about Him for five minutes, and then you talk about or against Him for forty-five, and then we will have a discussion."

I was talking about two minutes when she interrupted

me. She stuck her finger under my nose and said, "Listen, if God is good, why did He take my daughter?"

I said, "In order that you might be here, learning something about the purpose and meaning of life."

And that is what she learned.

I am suggesting you will not just reason yourself into the meaning and purpose of life; you will act yourself into the meaning and purpose of life by breaking the shell of egotism and selfishness and cleaning the windows of your moral life to allow sunshine in. You would not be seeking God if you had not already, in some way, found him. You are a king in exile with a kingdom. We will tell you more later on.

2

CONSCIENCE

A man of the theater came to see me and related to me this story. One night after a show he was talking to a number of theatrical people backstage who asked, "Are you Catholic?"

He said, "I used to be, but I have done considerable reading in comparative religion, psychology, psychiatry, and metaphysics, and I had to give it up. Nobody could answer my questions."

Someone suggested, "Why don't you go to Bishop Sheen, have him answer your questions?"

He said, "So here I am and I have a number of questions I would like to put to you."

I said, "Before you ask a single question, you go back to your hotel and get rid of that chorus girl you're living with. Then come back and ask the questions."

He threw up his hands, laughed, and said, "Oh, certainly! I'm trying to fool you just like I fooled myself."

I saw him a short time later and asked, "You are still off the track, aren't you?"

He said, "Yes, but I have not thrown away the map."

Here was a perfect example of someone covering up conscience. Conscience carries on with us a kind of an unbearable repartee. We are very different from other creatures regardless of how much we insist on similarities. What makes us different is that we can reflect upon ourselves. No stone can ever turn a part of itself on another part. No page of a book can so completely be absorbed in another page of the book that it understands that page. But we humans have the power of looking at ourselves in a kind of image. We can be pleased with ourselves; we can be angry with ourselves. It is possible for us to have all kinds of tensions which do not happen to animals. You will never see a rooster or a pig with an Oedipus complex. No animal ever has a complex. Scientists have induced ulcers in some animals, but humans introduced them. The animal left to itself never feels this tension. We feel a tension between what we are and what we ought to be, between the ideal and the fact. We are somewhat like a mountain climber; we see the peak way up at the top to which we're climbing, and down below we see the abyss into which we might fall at any time.

Why does conscience trouble us this particular way when it does not trouble the rest of creatures? Think of how many abnormal ways there are of avoiding our consciences. Sleeping tablets and alcoholism are just a few ways of avoiding this unbearable repartee. Have you ever noticed how pessimistic some people become? They are always expecting rain on the day of the picnic. Everything is going to turn out to be a catastrophe. Why do they have this attitude? In their own hearts and souls they know the way they are living and violating their conscience deserves an unfavorable judgment. Thus, they bring back judgment upon themselves and are always awaiting the electric chair. Their judgments are influenced by pessimistic attitudes.

Another psychological manifestation of conscience avoidance is hypercriticism. The neighbor is always wrong! Have you ever noticed the letters that are sent to the newspapers? They begin by criticizing their neighbor.

"The trouble with my husband is . . ."

"I cannot stand my wife because . . ."

"My son is stubborn . . ."

The poor neighbor never can do anything good in the ordinary affairs of life.

Why this hypercritical attitude? Abraham Lincoln once gave the right answer to it. He was going into a hospital in Alexandria during the Civil War at a time when presidents were not well known. His press secretary had not circulated his photographs! As Lincoln entered the hospital, a young man ran into him and sent him sprawling on the floor.

He shouted at Lincoln, "Get out of the way, you big, long, lean, lanky stiff!"

The president looked up at him and said, "Young man, what's troubling you on the inside?"

And so with hypercriticism, we are conscious of a real sense of justice, yet constantly have to be righting everybody else. For example, we cannot go into a room where there is a series of pictures, and one is two inches awry, without straightening out that picture. We want everything in order. We want everything in order except ourselves.

There are more serious escapes from this unbearable repartee. Human nature has always acted in the same way. Let us go back to Shakespeare. In his great tragedy *Macbeth*, Shakespeare, long before we had any of the profound findings of psychiatry, described a perfect case of psychosis and a perfect case of neurosis. It was Macbeth that had the psychosis; Lady Macbeth, his wife, had the neurosis. Do you remember the story? In order to obtain the throne they had Duncan, the king, and Banquo, Macbeth's rival, murdered. Conscience bothered Macbeth so much that he developed a psychosis, and he began to see the ghost of Banquo. He imagined he saw him seated at a table. The dagger that killed the king was constantly before him: "What is this dagger before my eyes?" (2.1). Imagination was the projection of his inner guilt. Note the great wisdom of Shakespeare in pointing out that whenever there is a revolution against conscience, then skepticism, doubt, atheism, and complete negation of the philosophy of life follows. Macbeth reached a stage where to him life was just a candle and had no meaning:

> Tomorrow, and tomorrow, and tomorrow
> Creeps in this petty pace from day to day,
> To the last syllable of recorded time,
> And all our yesterdays have lighted fools
> The way to dusty death. Out, out, brief candle! (5.5)

Skepticism, agnosticism, and atheism do not have rational foundations. Their foundations are in the moral order with a revolt against conscience.

Look at Lady Macbeth; her guilt was manifested in a neurosis. The maid said of Lady Macbeth that she washed her hands sometimes for as long as a quarter of an hour (5.1). There was a sense of guilt in her, and instead of washing her soul, as she should have done, she projected it to her hands. She said, "All the perfumes of Arabia will not sweeten this little hand" (5.1).

I was instructing a young woman, and she had finished fifteen hours on tapes and records. After the first instruction on confession she said to my secretary, "I'm finished. No more lessons. I do not want to hear anything more about the Catholic Church."

My secretary phoned, and I said to have her finish the other three on the subject of confession and then I would see her. At the end of the three she was in a veritable crisis, screaming and shrieking, "Let me out of here! I never want to hear anything about the Church again!"

It took about five minutes to calm her down.

I said, "Listen, there is absolutely no proportion between what you have heard and the way you are acting, so there has to be something else. Do you know what I think is wrong? I think you've had an abortion."

She said, "Yes!"

She was so happy that it was out. Her bad conscience came out as an attack upon confession; the truths of faith were not the problem. Often we find that an attack upon religion satisfies an uneasy conscience for the moment.

Conscience is something like the United States government, which is divided into three branches: legislative, executive, and judicial. The legislative: Congress makes laws. The executive: the president witnesses to the conformity of law in action. The judicial: the Supreme Court judges that conformity. All of these are inside of us.

First of all, we have a Congress. There is a law inside saying: "Thou shalt, thou shalt not." Conscience makes us feel good after a good act, and wrong makes us feel bad. Where does this law come from? From myself? No. If I made it, I could unmake it. Does it come from society? It does not, because sometimes conscience praises me when society condemns me; and sometimes conscience condemns me when society praises me. Where does the executive side of conscience, which judges whether or not I have obeyed the law, come from? It says, "I was there; I saw you!" Others will say, "Pay no attention to it!" One knows very well one must! One also knows the motives that inspired the act.

Finally, conscience judges us and gives praise for certain actions. We feel somewhat the same happiness and joy we would from being praised by a father or mother. We feel the same sadness and unhappiness as when condemned by a father or mother. There must be someone behind conscience, the divine Thou, that is the standard of our life. Most of the mental problems we suffer today are due to a mental revolt against this law which is written in our own hearts. When people return to conscience, peace and happiness come back. Life is very different. What we are after is peace of soul.

The conscience tells us when we do wrong, so we feel as if we'd broken a bone on the inside. A broken bone pains because the bone is not where it ought to be; our conscience troubles us because the conscience is not where it ought to be. Thanks to the power of self-reflection, we can see ourselves, particularly at night. As someone once wrote, "Every atheist is afraid in the dark." And it's a gentle voice, saying, "You are unhappy, this is not the way." Your freedom is never destroyed. You feel the sweet summons and ask, "Why is it not stronger?" It is strong enough if we would listen.

God respects the freedom He gave us. You may have seen a Holman Hunt painting of our blessed Lord knocking at an ivy-covered door with a lantern in his hand. Holman Hunt was criticized for that painting. The critics said there was no latch on the outside of the door, which is right. It was conscience; the door is opened from the inside!

3

GOOD AND EVIL

No one is born an atheist or a skeptic, one who doubts the possibility of ever discovering truth. These attitudes are made less by the way one thinks than by the way one lives. If we do not live as we think, we soon begin to think as we live. We suit our philosophy to our actions, and that is bad.

Let me tell you the story of an atheist in London, England. I used to do considerable work in St. Patrick's Parish, in Soho Square. One Sunday morning I came into the front of the church to read Mass, and found a young lady standing in front of the communion rail haranguing the congregation. She was saying, "There is no God! There is too much evil in the world! Reason cannot transcend sense! It is impossible to prove His existence!" "Every night," she said, "I go out to Hyde Park. I talk against God. I circulate England, Scotland, and Wales with pamphlets denouncing a belief in the existence of God."

As I reached the communion rail, I said to her, "Young lady, I am very happy to hear you say you believe in the existence of God."

She said, "You silly fool, I don't!"

I said, "I understood you to say just the contrary. Suppose I went out every night to Hyde Park and talked against twenty-footed ghosts and ten centaurs. Suppose I circulated England, Scotland, and Wales, denouncing a belief in these ghosts and in these centaurs. What would happen to me?"

She said, "You would be crazy! They would lock you up!"

I said, "Do you not put God in the same category as these fantasies of the imagination? Why would I be crazy attacking them and you are not crazy attacking God?"

She said, "I don't know. Why?"

I said, "Because when I attack these phantoms of the imagination, I am attacking something unreal, but when you attack God, you are attacking something as real as the thrust of a sword. Do you think we would have any such thing in the world as prohibition unless there was something to prohibit? Could there ever be anticigarette laws unless there were cigarettes? How can there be atheism unless there is something to atheate?"

She said, "I hate you!"

I said, "Now you've given the answer."

Atheism is not a doctrine, it is a cry of wrath.

There are two kinds of atheists. There are simple persons who have read a smattering of science and concede, probably, there is no God; but the other type of atheist is militant, such as the communist. They really do not deny the existence of God, they challenge God. It is the reality of God that saves them from insanity. It is the reality of God that gives them a real object against which they may vent their hate.

After discussing the attitudes any soul may take in the face of proofs, we will investigate the knowledge of God. How does God know? God knows by looking at Himself just like an architect. We know by looking at things. Before an architect puts up a building he can tell you the size, location, height, and the number of elevators because he is the designer of the building.

God is the cause of the very being of the universe. An architect looks into his own mind to understand the nature of that which he has designed. A poet knows his verses in his own mind, so God knows all things by looking at Himself. He does not need to wait for you to turn a corner before He knows you are doing so. He does not see little boys putting their fingers into the cookie jar and conclude they are stealing. Everything is naked and open to the eyes of God. There is no future in God. There is no past in God. There is only the present.

Suppose you walked through a cemetery in which you saw a succession of gravestones belonging to the same family. The first gravestone was inscribed: EZEKIEL HINGENBOTHAM, DIED 1938. Then you walked a little further and saw another tombstone reading: HIRAM HINGENBOTHAM, DIED 1903. A few steps more: NAHUM HINGENBOTHAM, DIED 1883; still further on: REGINALD HINGENBOTHAM, DIED 1861. These tombstones would indicate a succession of events that happened in space and time. Suppose you flew over the cemetery in a plane; then you would see all at once. That is how history must look to one who is outside of time.

Imagine you are looking at a motion picture reel that has the full story. Suppose the motion picture reel were conscious. If it were, it would know the whole story. But, if you and I were to know the whole story, we would have to wait until that film was unrolled upon the screen. We would only know successively what the reel knows all at once. That is the way it is with the knowledge of God.

God knows all things because He is Creator; thus, every

single thing in the world was made according to a pattern existing in the Divine Mind. Look around and see a bridge, statue, painting, and a building. Before any of these things began, they existed in the mind of the one who designed or planned them. In like manner, there isn't a tree, flower, bird, or insect in the world that does not correspond to an idea existing in the Divine Mind. The pattern has been wrapped up in matter. What our knowledge and science do is to unravel and unwrap this matter to rediscover the ideas of God. Because God put His ideas or patterns in things, we are assured of the rationality and purposefulness of the cosmos, which makes science possible. If there were no human or angelic minds in the universe, things would still be true because they correspond with the idea existing in the mind of God.

We cannot bring up a subject like the knowledge of God without meeting certain difficulties. One of the most obvious ones is "If God knows all things, He knows what is going to happen to every single soul in the world. He knows whether I am going to be saved or I am going to be lost. Therefore, I am predetermined." This argument was used a few centuries ago and was part of the philosophy of Eastern peoples.

To understand the knowledge of God you must make a distinction between foreknowledge and predetermination. The two are not identical. God does foreknow everything, but He does not predetermine us independently of our will and merits. Suppose you knew the stock market very well. Having superior knowledge of business conditions, you said a stock would be selling ten points higher than it is now within six months. Suppose six months later it actually sold ten points higher. Would you have predetermined and caused it to be ten points higher? There were other influences, were there not, besides your superior knowledge?

To make it still more concrete: In the early colonial days of this country, a farmer set out for the town to make some purchases. He went a short distance, came back, and told his wife he had forgotten his gun. His wife was a perfectly good determinist and argued this way: "Either you are predestined to be shot by the Indians or you are not predestined to be shot by the Indians. If you are predestined to be shot by the Indians, the gun will do you no good. If you are not predestined to be shot by the Indians, you will not need your gun."

The husband said, "Suppose I am predestined to be shot by the Indians on condition I do not have my gun."

In like manner, God knows all things, but He still leaves us with freedom. How can God influence you and still leave you free? Consider various kinds of influences. First, turn a key in a door. There is the impact of something material on something material and the result is the opening of a door. There is another kind of an influence. In the springtime you plant a seed in the garden. The sun, moisture, atmosphere, and chemicals in the earth all begin to exert an influence upon that seed. It's certainly not the same kind of action that's turning the piece of steel in a lock. There are tremendous capacities for growth in that seed, and what most awakens the seed to growth is something invisible, namely, the sun.

Now, go a stage higher. Consider the case of a father talking to a son, trying to influence him to become a doctor. What actually influences the son is some invisible truth as well as the deep love of the father for the son, and of the son for the father. What love actually does is to bring out in the son a free act. The son is not obliged to do exactly what his father wants. He is free to do the contrary. But truth and love have so moved him that he regards what he does as the very perfection of his personality. Later on he may say, "I owe everything I have to that conversation I had with my father. I really began to discover my true self." In some such mysterious way as this, God works upon your soul. He does not work like a key in a lock. He works less visibly than a father does on a son, but there are the same mysterious words: you and I. God is the very embodiment of love. Love inspires you to be what you were meant to be, a free person in the highest sense of the word. The more you are led by God's love, the more you become yourself, and it is all done without ever losing your freedom.

That still leaves another great problem, namely, the problem of evil. You may ask, "If God is power and love, why does He create this kind of world and why does He permit evil?" We are not going to give a complete explanation of evil. We will only give certain indications of why it is possible.

Let us begin with a question: "Why did God make this kind of world?" You must realize this is not the only kind of a world God could have made. He might have made ten thousand other kinds of worlds in which there would be no pain, struggle, or sacrifice. But this is the best possible kind of world God could have made for the purpose He had in mind. Notice the distinction we are making. For example, a little boy says to his father, who is a distinguished architect, "I want you to build me a birdhouse for sparrows." The architect designs a birdhouse. It's not the best house he could make, but it is the best house the architect could design for this purpose, namely, to build a house for sparrows.

What purpose did God have in making this world? God

intended to build a moral universe. He willed from all eternity to build a stage on which people with character would emerge.

He might have made a world without morality, virtue, or character. He might have made a world in which each one of us would have sprouted goodness with the same necessity as the sun rising in the east and setting in the west. But He chose not to make a world in which we would be good as fire is hot and ice is cold. He willed to make a moral universe that by the right use of the gift of freedom, people with character might emerge. What does God care for things piled into an infinity of space, even though they be diamonds? If all the orbits of heaven were so many jewels glittering as the sun, what would their external but undisturbed balance mean to Him in comparison with a single character which could take hold of the tangled strands of a seemingly wrecked and ruined life and weave out of them the beautiful tapestry of sacredness and holiness? The choice before God in creating the world, therefore, lay between creating a purely mechanical universe, people who were automatons and machines, or creating a spiritual universe in which there would be a choice between good and evil.

Granted, God chose to make a moral universe in which there would be character. What was the condition of such a universe? He had to make us free. He had to endow us with the power to say yes and no, and to be captains of our own fate and destiny. Morality implies responsibility and duty, but these can exist only on condition of freedom. Stones have no morals because they are not free. We do not condemn ice because it is melted by heat. Praise and blame can be bestowed only on those who are masters of their own will.

It is only because you have the possibility of saying no that there is so much charm in your character when you say yes. Take the quality of freedom away from anyone and it is no more possible for him to be virtuous than it is for the blade of grass which he treads beneath his feet. Take freedom away from life and there would be no more reason to honor the fortitude of martyrs than there would be to honor the flames which kindle a pile of sticks.

Is it any impeachment of God that He chose not to reign over an empire of chemicals? If God has deliberately chosen a kind of empire to be ruled not by force, but by freedom, and if we find His subjects are able to act against His will as stars and atoms cannot, does this not prove He has possibly given to those human beings the chance of breaking allegiance so there might be meaning and purpose in that allegiance when freely chosen?

Here we have a suggestion as to the possibility of evil. It's bound up with the freedom of man. Man, who is free to love, is free to hate. He who is free to obey is free to rebel. Virtue in this concrete order is possible only in those spheres where it is possible to be vicious.

A man can be a saint only in a church in which it is possible to be a devil.

You say, "If I were God, I would destroy evil!" If you did that you would destroy human freedom! God will not destroy freedom. If we do not want any dictators on this earth, certainly we do not want any dictators in the Kingdom of heaven. Those who blame God for allowing man freedom to go on hindering and thwarting His work are like those who see smudges and errors in the student's notebook. They would condemn the teacher for not snatching away the book and doing the copy himself. Just as the object of the teacher is sound education and not the production of neat and well-written notebooks, so the object of God is the development of souls and not the production of biological entities. You ask, "If God knew I would sin, why did He make me?" God did not make any of us as sinners, we make ourselves! In that sense, we are creators. The greatest gift of God to man, short of grace, is the gift of human freedom and the power to love Him in return.

4

THE DIVINE INVASION

A woman once wrote to me about her brother, saying he was dying in a hospital and had been away from the sacraments for about thirty years. She said not only had he led a bad life, but he was an evil man. There is a difference between being bad and being evil. A bad man steals; a bad man kills. An evil man may do none of those things, but he seeks to destroy goodness in others. Well, this was an evil man. He did much to corrupt youth and circulated all manner of evil pamphlets among the young to destroy both faith and morals. The sister of this man wrote, "About twenty priests have called on him, and he threw them all out of the hospital room. Will you please go?" Last-resort Sheen, I am!

I visited him this particular night and stayed about five seconds because I knew I would fare no better than anyone else, but instead of just making one visit, I made forty. For forty straight nights I went to see this man. The second night I stayed about ten to fifteen seconds, and I went up five to ten seconds every night, and at the end of the month I was spending ten or fifteen minutes with him, but I never once broached the subject of his soul, until the fortieth night. The fortieth night I brought with me the blessed Sacrament and the Holy Oils, and I said to him, "William, you are going to die tonight."

He said, "I know it."

He was dying of cancer, but cancer of the face, one of the most loathsome sights you ever saw.

I said, "I'm sure you'll want to make your peace with God tonight."

He said, "I do not! Get out!"

I said, "I'm not alone."

He asked, "Who's with you?"

I said, "I brought the good Lord along. Do you want Him to get out, too?"

He said nothing. So I knelt down alongside his bed for about fifteen minutes, because I had the blessed Sacrament with me. I promised the good Lord that if this man would show some sign of repentance before he died, I would build a chapel in the southern part of the United States for the poor people, a chapel costing $3,500. Not much of a chapel? No, but an awful lot of money for me.

After the prayer I repeated again, "William, I'm sure you want to make your peace with God before you die."

He said, "I do not! Get out!"

And he started screaming for the nurse. In order to stop him, I ran to the door as if I were going to leave. Then I quickly came back and put my head down alongside his face on the pillow and I said, "Just one thing, William. Promise me before you die tonight you will say, 'My Jesus, mercy.'"

He said, "I will not! Get out!"

I had to leave. I told the nurse that if he wanted me during the night I would come back. About four o'clock in the morning the nurse called and she said, "He just died."

And I said, "How did he die?"

"Well," she said, "about a minute after you left he began saying, 'My Jesus, mercy,' and he never stopped saying it until he died."

You see there was nothing in me that influenced him. Here was a divine invasion upon someone who had the faith once and lost it. It makes no difference whether one has the faith or not. There is this constant intrusion from the outside. It comes to everyone so subtly that many reject it. It came to St. Augustine in the voice of a child when he was leading a wild and furious life. Then Augustine wrote those famous lines, "Our hearts were made for thee, O Lord, and they are restless until they rest in thee" (CONFESSIONS, I.I). There was that famous playboy Charles Foucauld, who in the midst of his wild life slept under the stars in the Sahara and endured what Francis Thompson called "the abashless inquisition of each star." He found grace and entered his life as a priest among the Moslems in the Sahara and died a martyr there. This was practically in our times.

I might go on to mention many such cases of the divine invasion. Suppose we turn from just the stories to what form this divine invasion takes. It's a grace, but up to this point we do not know exactly the meaning of the word "grace." I may anticipate a bit and say there are two kinds of graces: white grace, which makes us pleasing to God, and black grace, in which we feel His absence. Most people in the world today feel His absence, even the atheists. You see it is not man who is on the quest of God; it is God that's on the quest of man! He leaves us restless. The first question we have from the Scripture is *Man, where art thou?* (GN 3:9).

No poet has ever expressed this divine invasion better

than Francis Thompson in his magnificent poem "The Hound of Heaven." Thompson was a student of medicine at one time. About the only thing he learned was how to take dope. He became a bum, slept in Covent Garden, London, under the vegetable trucks, and contemplated suicide. The Meynells befriended him, and a poem was found in his pocket which sold fifty thousand copies within a few years after his death. Within thirty years it was studied at the University of Tokyo in Japanese. This poem suits the modern mood, since men are beginning to feel this stirring of God's finger. Thompson narrates the various escapes he used. God is the Hound of Heaven, and first is the subconscious, or unconscious mind. He feels if he sank down into the subconscious, he would be less conscious of this Hound who was pursuing him. He says he fled God:

> *I fled Him, down the nights and down the days;*
> *I fled Him, down the arches of the years;*
> *I fled Him, down the labyrinthine ways*
> *Of my own mind; and in the mist of tears*
> *I hid from Him, and under running laughter.*
> *Up vistaed hopes I sped;*
> *And shot, precipitated,*
> *Adown Titanic glooms of chasmèd fears,*
> *From those strong Feet that followed, followed after*
> *But with unhurrying chase,*
> *And unperturbèd pace,*
> *Deliberate speed, majestic instancy,*
> *They beat—and a Voice beat*
> *More instant than the Feet—*
> *"All things betray thee, who betrayest Me."*

He tries nature and has a very rare and unique way of expressing the secrets of science. He says, "I . . . drew the bolt of Nature's secrecies." You can almost imagine somebody pulling a giant bolt on the door and all the secrets of science and nature pouring out:

> *I in their delicate fellowship was one—*
> *Drew the bolt of Nature's secrecies.*
> *I knew all the swift importings*
> *On the willful face of skies;*
> *I knew how the clouds arise*
> *Spumèd of the wild sea-snortings;*
> *All that's born or dies*

He tries another escape from the Hound, and that is illegitimate love. And herein is hidden the story of one that he calls "a bud that fell from the coronal crown of spring." He uses the example of a hearted casement in a window in the northern part of England, where there was a girl that he used to know. He says, "By many a hearted casement, curtained red, trellised by intertwining charities." He goes on to speak of how he sought love with all of these little ivy growths of affection that never quite satisfied. Then he adds his fear, "For, though I knew His love Who followed, yet was I sore adread lest, having Him, I must have naught beside." How many think God is a kind of competitor? Then, "If I have Him, I must reject everything else." He goes on to say, "But, if one little casement parted wide, the gust of His approach would clash it to: Fear whist not to evade, as Love whist to pursue." In other words, I did not know how to run away as fast as love knew how to catch me. He's fearful at the end. Who is the one pursuing him? Maybe He's going to bring some amount of detachment, and Thompson asks, "Ah! is Thy love indeed a weed, albeit an amaranthine weed, suffering no flowers except its own to mount?"

Resorting to another example, he asks, "Ah! must Thou char the wood ere Thou canst limn with it?" In other words, you must put wood into a fire and burn, purge, or sacrifice it before it becomes charcoal and you can trace with it. Another question, "Must Thy harvest-fields be dunged with rotten death?" Is there sacrifice everywhere? Finally, before giving you his answer, unless this just be the poetic exploration of Thompson, let's find out about divine invasion in our own hearts.

Suppose you could take out your own heart and put it into your hand as a kind of crucible to distill your inmost cravings, yearnings, and aspirations. What would you find them to be? What do you want most? First we seek life. What good are honor, ambition, and power without life? At night we put out our hand instinctively in the dark ready to lose that member rather than lose what we treasure most, our life.

As we continue, we find there's something else we want in life, and that is truth. One of the first questions we ask coming into the world is "Why?" We tear apart our toys to find out what makes the wheels go round. Later on, we tear apart the very wheels of the universe to find out what makes them go round. We are bent on knowing causes, which is why we hate to have secrets kept from us. We were made to know.

There's still something else we want besides life and truth, we want love. Every child instinctively presses himself to his mother's breast in token of affection. He goes to his mother to have play wounds bound, and then later on seeks a young companion to whom he can unpack his heart with words, one who measures up to the beautiful definition of a friend, one in whose presence you can keep silence.

The quest for love continues from the cradle to the grave; yet, though we want these things, do we find them here? Do we find life here in its fullness? Certainly not. Each tick of the clock brings us closer to the grave. Our hearts are but muffled drums beating a funeral march. As Shakespeare wrote in *As You Like It,* "From hour to hour we ripe and ripe, and from hour to hour we rot and rot" (2.7). Life is not here, nor truth, in all of its fullness. The more we study, the less we know because we see new avenues of knowledge down which we might travel for a lifetime. I wish I knew now just one ten-millionth as much as I thought I knew the night I graduated from high school!

Truth and love are not here. When love does remain fine and noble, a day must come when the last embrace is passed from friend to friend and the last cake is crumbled at life's great feast. Are we destined to live an absurd life? Would we ever have eyes unless there was something to see? We ask ourselves, "What's the source of light in a room?" Certainly not under a microscope, where light is mingled with shadow, or under chairs, where light is mingled with darkness. If we wish to find the source of life, truth, and love that is pure light in this world, we must go out to a life that is not mingled with its shadow, death; out to a truth that is not mingled with its shadow, error; out to a love that is not mingled with its shadow, hate or satiety. We must go out to pure life, pure truth, pure love, and that is the definition of God! That's what we want and were made for.

After all of these evasions from the divine invasion of the soul, Thompson concludes his poem with God saying:

> *"Strange, piteous, futile thing!*
> *Wherefore should any set thee love apart?*
> *Seeing none but I makes much of naught" (He said),*
> *"And human love needs human meriting:*
> *How hast thou merited—*
> *Of all man's clotted clay the dingiest clot?*
> *Alack, thou knowest not*
> *How little worthy of any love thou art!*
> *Whom wilt thou find to love ignoble thee,*
> *Save Me, save only Me?*
> *All which I took from thee I did but take,*
> *Not for thy harms,*
> *But just that thou might'st seek it in My arms.*
> *All which thy child's mistake*
> *Fancies as lost, I have stored for thee at home:*
> *Rise, clasp My hand, and come!"*

5

LINE UP THE CLAIMANTS

Throughout the course of history there have been many who have appeared upon its stage and declared they were messengers of God. Each and every one of them had a right to be heard. There's no reason why we should pick out Christ more than anyone else, but we do have a right to suggest certain tests or standards by which each of these claimants can be judged. We simply cannot allow anyone to appear upon the stage of history and say, "Here I am. Believe me," or "This is a book from God which an angel gave me. I want you to read it."

When we start a discussion of revealed religion, we are never to abdicate human reason nor lose sight of the fact we are in history. Therefore, one of the arguments we will use is what might be called the argument of prophecy or prediction: Has any one of the claimants ever been preannounced or foretold? Certainly the least God could do if He sends a messenger to this earth is say, "I preannounce him. I am going to let you know he is coming." Our friends call before they come to visit us; appointments are made in business; certainly God should let us know His divine Son is coming to this earth.

It might be argued there are many other great world religions, such as Buddhism and Confucianism, and we should investigate them. There are many myths in history, and many great men, like Buddha, Confucius, and Socrates. Each one of them is something like a bird that prepares a nest before laying eggs. A bird is governed solely by instinct, so providence has prepared for the coming of a perfect revelation. Divine truth might be looked upon as a circle. There is not a religion in the world without some segment of the circle of truth.

It may only be two percent, but it is part of the circle. Some have more than others do of this complete circle of truth. We recognize what is good in every single religion. Some of them yearn for a redeemer. It may be argued there are similarities in all religions; therefore, they are very much the same. It is true there are natural truths which are the same. This is because every human being in the world has reason; thus, he is bound to arrive at certain conclusions in the ethical order which will guide both himself and society. We are not surprised that many ethical principles are the same. To argue that all religions have similarities and, therefore, have the same cause, namely, the dreams of mankind, is quite untrue. When you go into a picture gallery, you notice that every one of the paintings has certain basic colors. Because they have the same colors you do not conclude they were painted by the same artist. Though there are similarities in religions, we are not to argue God made them all.

God chose to make an historical revelation. There are truths above human reason called revealed truths. Christ came preannounced as the founder of Christianity. The founder of no other religion is absolutely essential for that religion in the same way Christ is essential for Christianity.

True, the founder was necessary for the founding, but the believer in a particular religion does not enter into the same kind of an encounter as a Christian does with Christ. The personal relationship with Him is decisive.

Christ occupies a different place in Christianity than Buddha does in Buddhism, than Confucius in Confucianism, Mohammed in Islam and even Moses in Judaism. Buddhism does not demand you believe in Buddha, but that you become an enlightened one and follow his teachings concerning the suppression of desires. Confucianism does not demand an intimate relation with Confucius. What are important are the ethical precepts, and anyone who follows those precepts is presumed to enter into peace with his ancestors. Moses did not command people to believe in him, but to put their trust in the Lord, God. He was not pointing to himself. Islam demands faith in God and the other four tenets, but not necessarily in Mohammed. But when you come to Christ, here Christianity demands a personal, intimate bond. We have to be one with Him. We cannot in any way claim to be Christian unless we reflect the person, mind, will, heart, and humanity of Christ.

The argument from prophecy is really very simple. Just ask yourself if any founder of a world religion, or any innovator of a modern religion, was ever preannounced. His own mother could not have preannounced five years before his exact birth. No one knew Buddha, Confucius, or Mohammed was coming. But all through the centuries there was some dim expectation that Christ was coming.

The argument of prophecy involves history and a person. Christianity is an historical religion. Notice that in the Creed, whenever we speak of our blessed Lord, we always say, "He suffered under Pontius Pilate." He's fixed at a very definite point in world history. No other founder of a world religion was ever so bound up with history. We're concerned not just with the fact He was born and suffered under Pontius Pilate, but rather with the whole background of history.

In the Old Testament, we find that God seems to be making a covenant, a treaty, with a small group within humanity. We find this in the very beginning, that God enters into a pact with Adam involving all humanity. Adam was the head. Whatever he did, we did. Later on, God enters into a testament and a covenant with Noah providing promises and agreements on both sides. If one party remained moral, on the human side, God, on the divine side, would give them blessings.

From the moment of the very initial covenant and its breaking, God said the seed of a woman would come who would undo the work of evil. This tradition is caught up among the Jews and particularly the prophets. After the treaty with Noah, God enters into a new treaty with Abraham, whom He calls from the land of Ur. He promises Abraham:

> And the Lord said to Abram: Go forth out of thy country, and from thy kindred, and out of thy father's house, and come into the land which I shall shew thee. And I will make of thee a great nation, and I will bless thee, and magnify thy name, and thou shalt be blessed. I will bless them that bless thee, and curse them that curse thee, and in thee shall all the kindreds of the earth be blessed. (GN 12:1–3)

Abraham was told the people of God that would come from him would be as numerous as the sands of the sea.

Later on these people are led into bondage in Egypt. A new covenant is made with Moses; they break it and it is renewed again. New prophets come saying that into this people of God there will one day come a Savior and a Redeemer.

We are not speaking just about a people continuing a tradition and having an expectation of a Savior. We are speaking of many details given concerning that particular person. Many prophecies were made concerning our blessed Lord; for example, He would be a member of the tribe of Judah and would be born of a virgin. One of the astounding prophecies of Micah was that He would be born in the city of Bethlehem. If you were predicting the birth of someone who would be a great world politician, you would certainly choose a big city. But lo and behold the prophet Micah, under divine inspiration, chooses the tiny village of Bethlehem, called the least of cities. He says out of that city will come forth the One that is to be the ruler of Israel (MI 5:2).

Many centuries before His coming, it was foretold He would be meek and humble of heart, the suffering Servant, God as well as man. Sometime pick up the Old Testament, turn to chapter 53, and read the prophecy of Isaiah concerning the death and the sufferings of Christ. He would be refuted with the wicked in His death because He was crucified between two thieves, and He would be laid in a stranger's grave. It almost seems as if the prophecy of Isaiah were written at the foot of the Cross.

Many prophecies stated He would come from the royal line of David. For about a thousand years there had to be a male descendant in every single generation from David to have fulfillment of the prophecy. Now that's very difficult. A great character like Abraham Lincoln had four children. Even in the short span of history since his death there is not a single male descendant of his alive today. No other prophecy was ever made about the founders of world religions, only about Christ.

A Jewish scholar, who became a Christian and knew the Old Testament and all of the traditions of the Jews very well, said that at the time of Christ the Rabbis had gathered together 456 prophecies concerning the Messiah, who would be born of Israel and enter into a new covenant with mankind. Four hundred and fifty-six prophecies! If all of these prophecies were fulfilled in Christ, what would be the chance of them all concurring at the appointed moment, not only in place, but also in time, as was foretold by the prophet Daniel? If you take a pencil and write on a sheet of paper "1" and then draw a line beneath it, then under the line write "84," and after "84," if you have time, write 126 zeros. That is the chance of all of the prophecies of Christ being fulfilled. You see it runs into the trillions.

Many prophecies from other religions foretold the coming of Christ. Confucius said he was expecting some great wise man from the East. Buddha said he was not the wise man, someone else was to come. The great Plato said a just man was to come who would tell us how we are to conduct ourselves before God and men. The Greek dramatists always felt there was some God to come. As Aeschylus stated in his work *Prometheus*, "Look not for any end moreover to this curse until some God appears to accept upon His head the pangs of our own sins." In other words, He would bear our sins. Socrates expected someone whom he called a just man. Remember the Fourth Eclogue of Virgil? Sometimes it has been called the messianic eclogue because he told a virgin, "Smile on thy infant boy with whom the Iron Age will pass away and the Golden Age when all the earth will be born."

When Christ appeared He said, *I am the One whom the Prophets foretold* (LK 22:37). That is one of the reasons why Herod was not surprised when the Messiah was born. The Rabbis told him; they knew the prophecies. He knew Christ was to be a king, the new King of mankind; therefore, he wanted to kill Him. When our blessed Lord had reached the age of about thirty, He walked into His synagogue at Nazareth. The clerk handed Him a scroll of the prophet Isaiah, and He began to read off a passage of Isaiah about what the Messiah would be like: His gentleness, how He would bind up wounds, how He would forgive, how He would release captives. The audience listened with rapt attention. He said, *This day sacred Scripture is fulfilled in your ears* (LK 4:21). No one else can claim this background. We study Christ and no other. From now on my heart and soul will be absorbed in Him who was preannounced.

6

REVEALED TRUTH

Ours is a free universe of character and soul making. Almighty God has placed into our hands the power to make us saints or devils. It is up to us. There are some laws we cannot disobey, for example, the law of gravitation and certain biological laws like circulation of blood. But in a moral universe we are free either to obey the laws of God or to disobey them, just as we are perfectly free to obey the laws of health or to disobey them.

What makes a thing good? A thing is good when it attains the purpose for which it was made. I have a stopwatch. How will I know whether it is good? By asking, "What is the purpose of a watch?"

"The purpose of a watch is to keep time."

"Does it keep time?"

"Yes."

"Then it is a good watch."

Let us apply this to our ultimate end.

"Why were we made? What is the purpose of living?"

"The purpose of living is to be supremely happy."

"How do we become supremely happy?"

"By attaining the life, truth, and love which is God. Anything I do that helps me to achieve this goal or purpose is good."

Suppose I were to look at the musical notes on an organ. Which note is right and which note is wrong? One cannot say any particular note is right or wrong. What makes it right or wrong is its correspondence to a standard. Once I have a piece of music before me, I know what I ought to do, what note I should or should not play.

We have a moral standard within our conscience. What is good and bad is in relationship to a standard which is not of our own making. We do not draw our own maps and decide the distance from Chicago to New York. We do not arbitrarily set our own watches; we set them by a standard outside of us. We do not decide that a yard would be twenty-four inches instead of thirty-six. Good helps us reach the attainment of purpose, goals, and destinies in accordance with right reason.

What makes a thing bad? I have a pencil.

"Is it a good pencil?"

"Yes, it writes, that is why it was made."

"Is it a good can opener?"

"It certainly is not."

Suppose I use it as a can opener. What happens? First of all, I do not open the can. I do not attain the purpose for which I use the pencil, and secondly, I destroy the pencil. If I decide to do certain things which I ought not to do, I do not attain the purpose that I hope to attain. Becoming an alcoholic does not make me happy, and furthermore, I destroy myself just as I destroy the pencil in using it to open a can.

When I disobey God, I do not make myself happy on the inside and I certainly destroy any peace of soul I ought to have. Evil, you see, is not positive. Evil is either an excess or a defect of what is good. Food and drink are good. Too little or too much are bad. Sleep is good. When sleep interferes with duty it is not good. Evil is like darkness; it is the absence of light with no substance of its own. All badness is spoiled goodness. A bad apple is a good apple that became rotten. Evil is a parasite on goodness because it has no capital of its own.

This universe is a veil of soul making utilizing our reason and will. We were made to be good and to attain the truth, but how weak we are! Look at the limitations of our reason and then look at the limitations of our will. Even those who had very good reason admitted in the end they had captured just a little of what was true. Isaac Newton, the great scientist, said he felt as if he were standing on the seashore of infinite truth and the vast waters of knowledge stretched endlessly before him. Socrates, one of the wisest of the Greeks, said, "There is only one thing I know, and that is that I know nothing." Thomas Aquinas, who had the greatest mind that ever lived, said at the end of his life all he had written seemed to him as so much straw in comparison to a dim vision he received of heaven.

Quite apart from these learned men, look at the weak reason of people today, their confusion of mind, their failure to recognize any such thing as truth or goodness. They will read one book on Monday and say, "Oh, I am a materialist." Then they'll read another book on Tuesday and they're a communist. They read another book later on in the week and reject both of those systems. They are laying down tracks one day, tearing them up the next. They're never working toward one goal. It's no wonder there are so many psychotics and neurotics in our world; they're just rehashing a lot of old errors and giving them new labels.

Our reason and will are weak. Even when we know what is right, how hard it is sometimes to do it. We are besieged by temptations. We often feel like Goethe, who said he was one man yet felt there was enough evil and goodness in him to make both a rogue and a gentleman. St. Augustine said, "Whatever I am, I am not what I ought to be."

Looking back, we have to admit our reason is weak, our will is feeble, our mind is dark, and our will is lame. We need help! We need more truth for our mind; we need more love and goodness for our will. Where are we going to get it? Could God give it to us? Oh, certainly. God could, not because we are worthy, but because it would be in keeping with His goodness to tell us something and give us added power. We are teachable; we have minds. God could certainly give us new truths. Our nature is constantly receiving invisible forces. We would not have flowers and trees if there were no sun communicating light we do not see. God might send either a visible or an invisible force to illumine us. He could strengthen our will, which we need. We cannot lift ourselves by the lobes of our ears! Our aspirations are too weak. Look at the resolutions we make on New Year's and break. We need power from the outside! An electric lightbulb requires a power source from without. We have a stomach, but we need food from the outside. We have ears, but we need sound from the outside.

God might indeed illumine our reason, but how would we know it? Certainly there are many who claim to be messengers from God. Reason has to set up certain standards even before there is any revelation. We cannot allow some man to come upon the stage of history and say, "Listen to me, I am from God" or "I had a revelation."

I once received a telegram from someone with the request

"Report to Port 53, New York Harbor, to receive illumination from the Holy Spirit." I'm very sure the author, whoever he was, believed he had a revelation. However, we cannot accept the revelation of any individual who claims merely to have one. We cannot accept someone who says, "I've got a book an angel wrote for me." If anyone is coming from God with a revelation for our reason and strength for our will, reason is going to impose certain tests. They can be verified by reason and by history. First, whoever comes should be preannounced. Second, he should work miracles showing he is a messenger. Third, nothing he teaches or reveals should be contrary to human reason, though it may be above it. Those standards are a measuring rod.

Anyone who comes should be preannounced. Brides preannounce their weddings and automobile manufacturers tell us when a new model will appear. If God is going to send someone to this earth, certainly the least that He can do is to let us know. This requirement will do away with the idea of any individual suddenly appearing upon the stage of history and saying, "I am God" or "I have a message from God." He who comes ought to be able to do marvels, signs, to authenticate his message. Not to do things that would excite our wonder and make us say, "Oh!" Rather, miracles that would prove God was with him. Anyone who comes to this earth must never contradict human reason in his teaching. We may have mysteries revealed to us that are above our reason, but they can never be contrary. We would know a person could not come from God who teaches immorality or that the soul is not immortal because statements of this kind are contrary to reason.

We have three measuring rods or tests, designed by reason, applicable to history. Line up all the claimants that come from God according to their words. Let us say to them, "We are going to judge you. Buddha, Confucius, Lao-tzu, Mohammed, Marx, Brahmans, witch doctors, Hindu philosophers, university professors, Eddy, Heidegger, anyone you please and the founder of the latest cult in New York or Los Angeles! Stand there, we want to ask you questions."

"We're just going to use one test in this lesson: 'Were you ever preannounced, any one of you?' Answer!"

"Buddha, did anyone ever know you were coming to this earth?"

"Confucius, was the place of your birth prophesied?"

"Socrates, did anyone foretell you would die of hemlock juice?"

"Mohammed, was there ever an ancient tradition you would be born among a certain people? Was there ever a description as to how you would die?"

"Did any one of your mothers know you were coming?"

"Is there a single one of you who can point to an historical record in which it was foretold where you would live, where and how you would die, what your character would be, the manner of your teaching, the kinds of enemies you would provoke and evoke by the dignity of teaching?"

Up to this moment, you see, we have not regarded Christ as different from any other messenger from God. Now, one steps out of the ranks.

"What is your name?"

"My name is Jesus Christ."

"Were you ever preannounced? Are there any historical records long before your coming describing the details of your existence? Are there documents attesting to the work you would do and the purpose of your coming?"

He is the only one who can answer "Yes." We say to the

others, "Step back; you may be interesting, but you do not satisfy my first test. You were not preannounced, and that's the least that God could do. You have only your own word." But we are interested in the person of Christ. He says He was preannounced.

7

MIRACLES

We said there were three motives of credibility, three reasons why one might believe in anyone, or in the person of Christ. First, that he be preannounced, which we have already discussed; and second, if He came from God, there should be certain signs, wonders, or miracles to attest His truthfulness. Now, a word about miracles.

Let us recall miracles are not violations of the laws of nature. God and the universe are not on opposite sides. Let us take this example. Nearly all the great railroad stations, where there are junctions of tracks and lines running side by side, meeting and intersecting, have a control tower in their midst. From that little building all lines are directed and signals sent in various ways. A pull of a great lever and a mighty train passes on its appointed way. The working of another lever sends a freight train into a siding until the express train is past. All railway traffic would be disorganized if the important work were not carried on in that control tower; in fact, there would be disorder and collisions.

This is a feeble illustration of the laws of nature, for the whole universe works upon fixed lines. We cannot see God's signals or understand how He conveys His power to the forces of nature. We do not see Him work His levers. We only know that His laws obey Him with an exactness and a promptness unknown in any railway system of the world. When there is a miracle that seems to be in variance with the universal law of gravitation, there is merely a higher power introduced. The law of gravitation can be actually overcome by the right arm of a little child. The ball, according to the natural laws, ought to fall to the ground. When bounced, it bounds up to the ceiling. The hand of a little child can stop the operation of the law of gravity by catching the ball. When God puts forth the strength of His arm, He can suspend the action of some laws He has made in order to manifest His goodness and His justice. He is Lord of creation, witnessing the truth of the messenger and the message.

Our Lord worked many miracles, and here are some of the characteristics of them. He worked them as signs to convince men of the fact that He who came to work these miracles was the One who was promised. He never worked a miracle to amaze a multitude. He never worked a miracle to satisfy His hunger or thirst. He never worked a miracle to obtain a living. He never received money for the things which He accomplished. He refused to convert the stones of the wilderness into bread to satisfy His own hunger or to cause water to gush out of a rock to slake His thirst; instead, He asked a woman to let down her bucket to give Him a drink.

Our Lord explained why He worked miracles. He said, *If I act like the Son of My Father, then let My actions convince you where I cannot so you will recognize and learn to believe that the Father is in Me and I in Him* (JN 10:38). And on another occasion He said, *The actions which My Father has enabled Me to achieve, those very actions which I perform, bear Me witness that it is the Father Who has sent Me* (JN 5:36). If it were God's will to give a revelation, miracles would be well fitted to certify and guarantee the message as true. If a miracle occurs in connection with a word or act of a person who professes to deliver a revelation from God, the coincidence proclaims the divine approval of both the teacher and the message. The miracles were seals which God set upon His revelation of Christ as His divine Son. If Jesus shows it is by His own power He works a miracle, He proves Himself to be Lord of the universe and to be God.

Another characteristic of the recorded miracles of our blessed Lord is that there is nothing unreasonable in any of them. They were subject to the tests of everyone. The vast majority of the miracles never took place in the secret places of people's lives but in what might be called the physical world, where they could be verified scientifically. Our Lord never performed a miracle unless there were witnesses present. When He healed the leper there was a great multitude following Him (MT 8:1-4). In the healing of the centurion's servant, He did not even go where the servant was dying (MT 8:8). When He raised Peter's mother-in-law from her sickbed, the Apostles and others were present (MT 8:14-15). Our Lord never went up into a mountain to perform some miracle alone with no person being present, and then came out saying He had done it. His works were accomplished before the eyes of multitudes of people, and that is why none of the miracles of our blessed Lord were ever actually denied, not even His Resurrection. The Apostles were forbidden to teach it, but the miracles were never denied.

His miracles are inseparable from His person. They differed from those of prophets and others, since theirs were answers to prayers granted by a higher power. His flowed from the majestic life resident in Him. In his gospel, St. John calls them signs or works, meaning they were the sorts of things that might be expected from Jesus, being what He was. They were evidences of His divine revelation; they were even more, for they testified to His redemptive action as the Savior of the world. By healing the palsied, lame, and blind, Christ clothed His power with visible form to cure spiritual diseases. Physical diseases were symbols of that which was spiritual. He often passed from the physical fact of a miracle to its symbolic and spiritual meaning; for example, blindness was a symbol of blindness to the light of faith. By casting devils from those who were possessed, He pointed out His victory over the powers of evil whereby men would be freed from slavery to evil and restored to moral liberty.

If you expel miracles from the life of Christ, you destroy the identity of Christ and the Gospels. Even a neutral attitude toward the miraculous element in the Gospels is impossible. The claim to work miracles is not the least important element of our Lord's teachings, nor are the miracles which were wrought by Him merely ornaments to His life. The miraculous is interwoven with His entire life. The moral integrity of our Lord's character is dependent upon the reality of His miracles. If He were a deceiver, He was not what He claimed to be. We cannot put asunder two things God has joined together; namely, the beauty of Christ's character and the reality of the miracles He worked.

How many miracles did He work? The specific number of miracles mentioned in the Gospels is thirty-five. Three of these miracles tell of raising the dead: a child, a young man, and an adult; nine relate to nature; and twenty-three to healing. In addition to these there are miracles related to the life of Christ Himself, like the virgin birth, the Resurrection, and the Ascension. Though there are only thirty-five specific miracles mentioned, it must not be thought these are the only miracles our blessed Lord ever worked. Listen to the way St. John concludes his gospel: *There is much else besides that Jesus did. If all of it were put in writing, I do not think the world itself would contain the books which would have to be written* (JN 21:25). There must have been miracles beyond counting. When the multitude had witnessed one miracle they said, *Can the Christ be expected to do more miracles at His coming than this man has done?* (JN 7:31). It was preannounced that the Messiah would work miracles. Since He performed miracles in abundance, He must be the Christ.

We are going to take the most important miracle in particular to study; namely, the Resurrection. There are five distinct accounts of the Resurrection in the New Testament, and all of them are independent: four are of the Gospels, one of St. Paul. St. Paul had conversed with Peter and James about three years after his conversion and was in personal relationship with the Apostles. These five distinct records give at least eleven accounts of the Resurrection of our blessed Lord and of His various appearances, one to five hundred people. The fact is our blessed Lord died on the Cross, was buried in a hundred pounds of spices as was the custom, and a watch, or a guard, was set. In the history of the world only one tomb has ever had a rock rolled before it and a soldier set as guard to prevent a dead man from rising; and that was the tomb of Christ on the evening of Good Friday.

What spectacle could be more ridiculous than armed soldiers keeping their eyes on a corpse? But sentinels were set in case the dead walk, the silent speak, and the pierced heart quicken to the throb of life. They knew He was dead.

They said He would never rise again, yet they watched. They remembered He called His body the Temple and said that three days after they had destroyed it, He would rebuild it (JN 2:19). They recalled He had compared Himself to Jonah, and said that as Jonah was in the belly of the whale for three days (JON 1:17) so He would be in the belly of the earth for three days and then rise again (MT 12:40). After three days Abraham received back his son Isaac, who was offered in sacrifice (GN 22:4-19). They were familiar with that idea. For three days Egypt was in darkness that was not of nature (EX 10:22). On the third day God came down on Mount Sinai (EX 19:11) and, once again, there was worry about the third day. Early Saturday morning, the Chief Priest and the Pharisees broke the Sabbath and presented themselves to Pilate saying:

> Sir, we have recalled it to memory that this deceiver, while He yet lived, said: "I am to rise again after three days." Give orders then that His tomb shall be securely guarded until the third day, or perhaps His disciples will come and steal Him away. If they should then say to the people "He has risen from the dead," this last deceit would be more dangerous than the old. (MT 27:62-64)

Their request for a guard until the third day had more reference to Christ's words about His Resurrection than it did to the fear of the Apostles stealing a corpse and propping it up in simulation of a resurrection. Pilate was in no mood to see this group; they were the reason why he had condemned innocent blood. He made his own official investigation; Christ was dead. He would not submit to the absurdity of using Caesar's armies to guard a dead Jew. Pilate said to them, *You have guards, away with you! Make it secure as best you know how* (MT 27:65).

The watch was to prevent violence; the seal was to prevent fraud. There must be a seal, and the enemies would seal it. There must be a watch, and the enemies must keep it. The enemies themselves must sign the certificates of the death and resurrection. The Gentiles were satisfied through nature that Christ was dead, and the Jews were satisfied through the law that He was dead. Then as the Gospel of Matthew puts it, *And they went and made the tomb secure, putting a seal on the stone and setting a guard over it* (66). A King lay in state with His guard about Him, and the most astounding fact about this spectacle of vigilance over the dead was that the enemies of Christ expected the Resurrection, but His friends did not. It was the believers who were the skeptics; it was the unbelievers who were credulous. His followers needed and demanded proofs before they would be convinced.

Suppose we do not accept the witnesses of the Resurrection and other proofs of miracles attesting the trustworthiness of Christ. How can we explain the empty tomb? How do we account for the fact that the Apostles went about preaching the Resurrection, which no one denied? The two popular explanations that are given by those who deny the Resurrection are the following. First, the lie theory. This theory says that the Apostles, as well as every other witness who claimed that he had seen the risen Christ, lied about the Resurrection. This theory is manifestly false. For what chance was there of persuading the world He had risen from the dead if He had not done so? There was nothing less than the conviction of the Lord's Resurrection that could have induced men to have ventured their lives on it. Furthermore, their conduct proved they believed overwhelmingly. They preached the Crucifixion in the very place where He was crucified and in the very place where they had to suffer for preaching. Persons do not suffer for what they believe to be false. The Resurrection was not a lie.

But there is another theory to explain away the Resurrection in popular psychological language. This theory holds that the Apostles were very anxious to see the risen Savior. They had heard Him say He would rise from the dead, and all of these words about the Resurrection had seeped down into their subconscious. The ideas rested there as a kind of a desire. The terrible defeat and crucifixion came on Good Friday. They knew their cause was lost. Having been defeated in their messianic hopes by seeing their Savior killed and crucified, they now began to imagine His Resurrection. They believed they had seen Him. They were convinced He said He would rise.

This theory is false for many reasons. The Apostles knew the difference between a trance and a reality. There are many passages in the Scriptures concerning this difference. The appearances did not take place when the disciples were at prayer, worship, or when they might have been subject to religious fantasies. The appearances of the Risen Christ took place in the ordinary, everyday occupations, when they were going for a walk, seated at supper, or out fishing. They took place in the most trivial of circumstances, quite different from what enthusiasts would have imagined or where visions were likely to occur; namely, in sleep.

The most astounding thing about the Resurrection is that no one believed He would rise from the dead. None of His followers believed it. That is why the women brought spices on Easter Sunday morn, to anoint and embalm a dead body, not to greet a Risen one. Furthermore, the appearances of Christ were not while people were looking for them. No one was anticipating Him, even hoping for a Resurrection. When Mary Magdalene found the tomb empty, it never occurred to her that He had come to life. She said somebody had moved Him from one burial place to another. When the news of the empty tomb was first brought to Peter and John, their explanation was "Oh, it's a woman's story! You know how women are, always imagining things." There was one Apostle who remained doubtful for a whole week, and that was Thomas.

Another argument against psychological theory is that visions do not occur to different persons simultaneously. People's private illusions, like their dreams, are their own. We do not dream the same dream at exactly the same time. Was there any evidence that when Christ appeared to the five hundred any one of them doubted the reality of it? As regards this subjective theory, a vision could never roll away the stone from the door of the tomb. There were the Jewish guard and soldiers, too. People could not have honestly visited the tomb and found it empty. If the body were there all the time, they would never have had that kind of a vision. If the Resurrection were merely an illusion, the touching of the body of Christ, the putting of the finger into the hand, and the hand into the side, as Thomas did, would certainly have cured any such illusion. When our Lord appeared, He ate food; they saw the food vanish. He took bread; they saw the bread break. On another occasion He gave them bread and fish and they were satisfied of their hunger. This certainly does not happen when there is only a dream or an illusion.

The fact is none of the Apostles expected a Resurrection.

They had to be convinced the hard way, as Thomas had to be convinced. Believe me, the skeptics of today cannot compare with the skeptics of those days; namely, the Apostles. They were the doubted. When they were convinced, they proved they believed in it by having their throats cut for that cause. Our blessed Lord went before the world with miracles as signs of His divinity. When He had risen from the dead, He asked men to be prepared to die for what was low in them so they might rise again.

8

NEW TESTAMENT REVELATION

We have studied the Old Testament prophecies showing Jesus Christ alone was preannounced. Now we must study the New Testament documents concerning His life from the historical point of view.

We do not know as yet that the Scriptures are inspired. It may be asked, "If there were so many prophecies in the Old Testament, why didn't the Jews accept them? Why didn't they recognize Christ as the Son of God and the Messiah?" One reason is that they made no objection to the fulfillment of individual prophecies in our Lord. The general conception which the Rabbis had formed of the Messiah differed totally from that in which He revealed Himself. Remember the Babylonians, Chaldeans, Greeks, and Romans had subjected the Jews for centuries to all forms of political slavery. Wasn't it natural for them to begin to lose the spiritual aspects of the promises and to begin to expect a Savior who would save them from political bondage rather than from the spiritual bondage of sin? That was what happened in many instances. The Romans were walking their streets. Roman judges were in their courtrooms. They thought "Savior" meant a political liberator. Why should we blame them?

Remember we have exactly the same prophecies today in the Old Testament and they are just as valid for us as they were for the Jews. Why don't more believe them today than actually do?

Just as there is evolution in the material universe, there is a gradual unfolding of the divine plan in the spiritual universe. In the cosmos, man has a unique position. All evolution tends toward him! Everything beneath him ministers to his purposes. Chemicals, plants, and animals would never have come into being if there had not been a higher creature which they were destined to serve; namely, man. Evolution has God for its cause, man for its goal. As the material universe is a vestibule for man, so all human history, Jew and Gentile, is a vestibule for Christ. As the universe would be chaos without our organization, so history would be meaningless if it were not a highway which provided the way for people to realize their capacities for love and truth in Christ. This centrality of Christ in history is revealed in the New Testament. But here we must make certain ideas very clear.

Though it is too early to speak of the Church, we must anticipate just a bit and tell you the Church did not come out of the Bible. The Church did not begin as a religion of a book. It was first preached as a living voice, fallen not from a pen but from the lips of the Master. The doctrine of the Church in the beginning was not a collection of writings. It was called the Word of God, the word of salvation, and the first Apostles and ministers of the Church were called Ministers of the Word.

Our Lord did not write, nor were the Gospels written immediately after His death. When the Church emerged from Her cradle and carried Her zeal across Asia Minor,

Greece, as far as Caesar's Rome, then the New Testament was written. The only time our blessed Lord ever wrote was in the sand when a woman was taken in adultery (JN 8:6). Nor did our Lord tell His Apostles to write. Our Lord did not write because He was not an author, but an authority. When a man leaves a literary work behind him, there is a tendency to forget the man and to concentrate on his writings. Socrates never wrote. He was known through his disciples; therefore, his personality remains a living one. Plato, on the other hand, wrote, and he is known mostly through his writings, only secondarily in his person. Not that there is any comparison between Socrates and Christ, but the fact is Christ did not want to give grounds to the temptation to look upon the words written about Him. He wanted us to take hold of His Person! He would set His doctrine in the members of His new covenant, or New Testament. The very first task of the Apostles after the death of the divine Master, in obedience to His command, was to preach.

Our Lord had many firsthand witnesses of His Resurrection all around Him. The Apostles began preaching the Gospel orally. The earliest converts were gathered around the Apostles to receive the revelations from their lips. Men who had seen, heard, and touched Christ taught them. They learned about Christ and His Gospel from those who had lived intimately with Him for three years, as written in the Acts, *had eaten and also taken drink with Him* (AC 2:42).

About thirty years after His death, the first Canonical Gospels were written and, far from replacing oral teaching, the written text was a help, not an obstacle, to the leaders of the Church. The Church existed before the Gospels. It was the Church that composed the Gospels. It was in the Church where the New Testament was written. During the first thirty years the Church knew Christ's message chiefly through the preaching of the Apostles and others. This is the meaning of the word "evangel," or gospel. It means good tidings, not a good book, but good tidings of salvation brought by servants of the Word.

It must be kept in mind that the teaching of our Christ was not put into writing until the first witnesses were beginning to disappear. Actually, it was the sudden and unforeseen acceptance of Christianity by the pagans that called forth the Christian writings. Many of the writings were written to answer very specific needs of the moment. For example, Paul had to carry on a tremendous correspondence with missions he had started. He had no intention of producing literature in the Greek sense of the word. Furthermore, the rapid growth of the Church brought new problems. By the year 50 it was becoming imperative that the Apostles' oral method of teaching should be communicated through writing so the content of the oral teaching would be preserved. St. Luke tells us in the beginning of his gospel of several attempts made in this direction (LK 1:1–4), and his statement has been verified from recently discovered fragments of hitherto unknown, though not inspired gospels.

The New Testament documents reveal the Bible has two acts, as do many dramas in the theater. These acts are vitally related one to the other. The second act is an advance upon the first and carries the plot to its full realization. Both acts are covenants, agreements, or testaments. These covenants were given in the old and in the new time. One of the principal covenants of the Old Testament was given on Mount Sinai, and the New is very much related to Calvary. Under the Old Testament or covenant, God dealt with one nation only and indirectly with others. Under the New Testament,

God is dealing with all nations. Under the Old Testament or old covenant, justification was by the law. In the New Testament, justification is by grace. The emphasis in the Old Testament was on doing certain things God commanded; and the emphasis in the New Testament is on being something. The Old Testament created expectations; the New, realizations. The Old stirs a longing in the heart; the New, satisfaction. In the Old, man seeks God; in the New, God seeks man. In the Old, man is condemned as a sinner; in the New, he is delivered from sin. If we had only the Old Testament, we would have a lock without a key, a story without a plot, a promise without fulfillment, a seed without fruit. If we had the New Testament without the Old, it would be an end without a beginning, a fulfillment without a promise, a superstructure without a foundation. As it was said long ago:

> The New is in the Old, concealed,
> The Old is in the New, revealed;
> The New is in the Old, contained,
> The Old is in the New, explained.

We've already told you the Old Testament had a collection of books. The number is forty-five. Protestant churches give the number as thirty-eight. Thus, there are seven books in the Old Testament of the Catholic Bible which are not found in Protestant Bibles. What these books are you can discover by further reading on the subject. The New Testament is composed of twenty-seven books, four of which are historical narratives of the life of our Lord called the Gospels. There is an account of the early years of the Church; this is known as the Acts of the Apostles. There are fourteen epistles of St. Paul. In addition, there are seven other epistles: two of St. Peter, one of James, one of Jude, and three of John. At the end, there is the book called the Apocalypse, written by St. John, who is also the author of the fourth Gospel.

Now we come to each of the four documents known as the Gospels. It may be asked why there are four. Why should there be different accounts of our blessed Lord? The answer is because they are addressed to different audiences, which is something you must always keep in mind when reading each of the four Gospels.

St. Paul's conversion is told three times in the Acts of the Apostles. There was a different intention each time it was told. The first time explained how he became an Apostle; the second was Paul's defense before the Jews in the Temple; and the third was Paul's defense before the Romans; namely, Agrippa and Festus. So it is with the life of our Lord. Each of the evangelists—Matthew, Mark, Luke, and John—wrote for a different audience. Each wanted to bring out a different phase of the life of our Lord. Light is the same by nature and is governed by fixed laws. Note how reflection is infinitely varied, turning to purple, blue, gold, according to the nature upon which it shines. Light plays in different keys, just as each of the four Gospels is addressed to a different audience to bring out one phase of the multiple variety of the person of Christ. Matthew wrote principally for the Jews; Mark, for the Romans; Luke, for the Greeks, and John, for the Christian world.

We begin with Matthew, who wrote his gospel for the Jews to show Jesus of Nazareth is the promised Messiah. His audience was a shut-in group whose gaze did not go beyond the horizons of Judea. It was wholly Palestinian in character. We are steeped everywhere in Matthew in the Old Testament. It is obvious that the very best way to convince the Jews our Lord was the promised Messiah of the Old Testament is to quote the Old Testament, and to show our blessed Lord is preannounced. Therefore, Matthew directs his gospel to the Jews and is very careful to unite the Old and the New Testaments, often quoting Christ to say, *I am come not to destroy the law but to fulfill it* (MT 5:17).

There are 1,068 verses in the Gospel of Matthew, and about three-fifths of those relate the words of our Lord. The point to be emphasized is that he was addressing the Jews: *You must believe that Christ is the Son of God because He was prefigured in our Scriptures* (MT 2:5–6). In Matthew there are 129 Old Testament references; 53 of them are citations, or text, and 76 are allusions. These references are taken from twenty-five books of the Old Testament, and from the major parts of the Law, the Prophets, and Psalms.

We have been showing Christ is the expected Messiah and saying Matthew used that as his argument. Ten times Matthew uses the expression after or before a text in the Old Testament, "That it might be fulfilled." For example, "That it might be fulfilled what was spoken by the prophet Micah" or "What was spoken by the prophet Isaiah." He also uses the expression "which was spoken of," by Jeremiah, David, and so forth. He uses that expression fourteen times. The law of the Old Testament demanded a priest, a prophet, and a king; and therefore, in the first part of the Gospel of Matthew, we find Christ presented as a King, then we find Him presented as a Teacher, and finally, as a Priest.

Matthew was a tax collector. He was a dishonest and disloyal Jew because he sold himself out to the Romans. He was known as a publican, one who had bargained with the Romans, the captors and masters of the country, for the collection of taxes. He might promise, in our money, say $200,000 for a certain area in Capernaum. Then he would collect $400,000 and pocket $200,000. Hence, he was much despised by his own people. The Lord said to him, *Come follow me* (MT 9:9). Matthew leaves everything, including his counting table and his money, but he takes his pen with him to write a gospel and becomes the most patriotic of all the evangelists.

No one loves Israel more than Matthew. He loves the Old Testament simply because he discovered its fulfillment. His vocation as a tax collector is reflected in what he writes. Matthew uses three words for money which occur nowhere else: "tribute" (MT 17:24), "piece of money" (17:27), and "talent" (25:15). Then he uses words like "gold" (23:16) and "silver" (26:15), which do not occur in the other Gospels. Two parables of the talent are only recorded by Matthew. He is the one evangelist who handled that much money. A talent was worth about three hundred times as much as a dollar and about eight thousand times as much as a penny, of which Mark speaks. Matthew, the tax collector, also uses the word "moneychangers" (21:12), which does not occur elsewhere except as a debt, and to which a publican, such as Matthew, would naturally make reference. Such, in brief, is the Gospel of Matthew.

Mark wrote for Gentile and Roman readers in particular. The Gentile destination of the gospel is rather evident from the fact that there are few Old Testament quotations. Furthermore, there are a number of Latin words found in Mark which are not found in the other Gospels because he is addressing the Roman mind. He omits certain parables which had Jewish significance: like the laborers in the vineyard (MT 20:1-16), the parable of the two sons (MT 21:28-32), and the marriage of the King's son (MT 22: 1-14). Old Testament Scripture and prophecy, which meant so much to the Jew, did not mean quite so much to the Roman.

Another fact about Mark is that he was a follower of Peter. They are often mentioned in Scripture together. In tradition, Peter calls Mark his spiritual son and implies Mark was in Rome once with him. The Gospel of Mark indicates he was very close to Peter. There is much about Galilee, and particularly Capernaum, which was Peter's place of residence. The gospel points to an eyewitness as its author who was obviously Peter. We are told about Peter's home and his mother-in-law (MT 8:14). Mark says it was Peter who called our Lord's attention to the withered tree (MK 11:21). It is also worth noting details favorable to Peter are omitted in the gospel while others, not at all favorable to Peter, are recorded. The hand that transcribed the story was Mark's, but the voice speaking is unquestionably that of Peter, who was there.

What Mark brings out with swift and vivid touches is the personal action and work of the Son of God as Lord of the world and Conqueror of the hearts of men. This was something the Roman mind could understand, and so he represented Christ as establishing an increasing dominion over evil and over nature by overcoming the powers that opposed Him until, at last, He rose from the dead.

Luke wrote his gospel sometime before the year 67, and Mark's, of course, was written before that time. Luke was born in Antioch, and by education and birth he belonged to the Greek world. His gospel is addressed principally to the Greeks and is composed in Greek surroundings without precluding the hypothesis of it being completed in Rome. Perhaps Luke had the evangelist Mark at his side, or certainly his gospel, when he was writing.

Luke was a medical doctor, which is evident from medical terms he uses. Paul speaks of Luke as the "beloved physician." Luke's narrative shows a preference for stories of healing. His language is covered by technical medical terms, traces of diagnosis occur, also medical phraseology. You can prove Luke was a doctor by examining certain words he uses. Mark and Matthew have occasion to use the Greek word for "needle" as in "sewing needle." When Luke uses the word "needle," he does not use the Greek word for "sewing needle," but rather the word for a surgical needle, a word used by a Greek physician who lived after him by only seventy or eighty years. Luke records that our Lord sent forth His missionaries to preach and to heal. He also preserves our Lord's word *Physician, heal thyself* (LK 4:23). Most important, Luke narrates the virgin birth (2:1–20).

John wrote toward the end of the first century and for the Christian world. By this time a generation had lived that had seen God in the flesh. The burning words of the Master had circulated from home to home and from city to city. Men were eating the Bread of Life. Paul's epistles were circulated and spread like prairie fire over the Roman Empire. Matthew had written for the Jews; Mark, especially for the Romans; and Luke, for the Greeks. These were three representative peoples of the world, but John wished to put on record those spiritual aspects of our Lord's ministry that had not been recorded by the other three and for which the Jews, Romans, and Greeks were not ready.

John directs his gospel to the Christians. The fourth Gospel, before its writing and publishing, had been spoken to an immediate circle of disciples by its author. He presumes his readers already know about the life of Christ. St. John proposes to perfect this knowledge and make his readers penetrate into the intimacy of the Master and to understand His most profound thoughts. St. John also says at the end of his gospel that the world would not be large enough to contain the books if he had written down all the miracles our Lord had worked (JN 21:25).

The Church was finally established throughout the Roman Empire when John wrote. After John had seen the persecution under Nero, after he had suffered his own banishment under Domitian, and after he had heard of the trials of Paul, the time came for him to write his Gospel. The Gospel of John would echo a harp whose perturbed strings were smitten by bloodstained hands and swept by the mighty wind of inspiration of the Spirit into the greatest Gospel ever written.

PART II

CHRIST AND HIS CHURCH

I see that our gravity is too earthly—

We are weighted with prayerless days.

Oh! To trust our weight on the Weightless Spirit,

And step out like astronauts on the shelf of Grace,

And not fall,

As Christ holds our hand.

—FULTON J. SHEEN

9

DIVINITY OF CHRIST

Our blessed Lord called Himself Son of God and Son of man. He was both God and man. This is indeed a great mystery and is called the mystery of the Incarnation. Incarnation means incarnate, in the flesh. God assumed a human nature; He was enfleshed. St. John has a very beautiful description; he says, *The Word became flesh* (JN 1:14). The Word means God, or the Second Person of the blessed Trinity.

This is a difficult mystery, and we are going to explain it with a number of examples. When we say God became man, we do not mean to say heaven was empty like a room that was twenty by thirty feet. When God came to this world, He did not leave heaven empty, and when He came to this world, He was not whittled down to human proportions. Christ was the life of God dwelling in human flesh. St. Thomas Aquinas has a very beautiful description of this in one of his own hymns. He said, "The heavenly Word proceeding forth, yet leaving not the Father's side."

Let us begin by answering the question "Why did God become man?" We limit ourselves to the historical order in which we live. The answer is: He became man in order to redeem us from sin; therefore, we have to describe why it was necessary for God to become man to completely atone for our sins. Whenever we sin we contract an infinite debt, but we cannot pay an infinite debt, because we are finite and limited. We will state the reason in the form of a principle and then we will give examples. Honor is in the one honoring. Suppose a citizen of the United States, the mayor of a city, the governor of a state, and the President of the United States pay a visit to the Holy Father. Who pays the Holy Father the greater honor, the citizen or the president? Is it not the president? Honor is in the one honoring.

The other side of the proposition is this: guilt or sin is always measured by the one sinned against. If a citizen and a mayor commit a crime, which is the greater sin? Guilt or sin is always measured by the one sinned against. If the sin or the guilt was against the President of the United States, obviously, the mayor would be guilty of the greater sin, would he not? Let us apply this to humanity.

We have sinned.

Against whom have we sinned?

Against God.

Sin is measured by the one sinned against.

We sinned against God,

He is infinite; therefore, our guilt and sin are infinite.

Let us take the other proposition: Honor is in the one honoring. We are going to try to pay the debt. Man is finite and limited; thus, he cannot pay an infinite debt in strict justice. That should not surprise us. It's very easy for all of us to run up greater debts than we can pay.

Imagine, we have an infinite debt against God, which we cannot pay. Could God forgive us? Could He say, "Oh, forget it! It's nothing." He might say, "Forget it," but He could not say it is nothing. Suppose He did forgive us. He would be merciful, but He would not satisfy justice. If we owe somebody twenty dollars, the debt can be forgiven, but justice is not satisfied unless we completely pay the debt. I can remember when I was a boy I often used to break the next-door neighbor's window. The next-door neighbor sometimes would say, "Forget it," but somehow or other I never just wanted to be let off. I would go to my piggy bank and take out my savings to pay for the broken window. Man does not want to be let off by God; he has a sense of his own dignity. He wants to pay the debt in some way that he owes to God.

We have yet to answer how it is to be paid. If justice and mercy were to be satisfied, then God had to become man. Unless He became man, He could not be our representative. He could not stand for us, and man would not be paying the debt. Just suppose I were arrested for speeding. Could you walk into the courtroom the moment I was on trial and say, "Judge, let him go. I will take it over." The judge would say to you, "Stay out of this! You're not involved; he is." Inasmuch as man is involved, in some way, God has to share our nature. Furthermore, sin demands some kind of suffering and expiation. If He ever became man, He could suffer as man and suffer in our name.

Not only would He have to be man, but He would also have to be God. He would have to be man in order to act in our name; He would have to be God so the infinite debt could be paid by someone Who was infinite. Every action of God would have an infinite value. The outrage against God could be atoned for, and He would have to be God to be sinless. If He were full of sin, He would need redemption. No man can atone for his own sins. If both justice and mercy

are to be satisfied, God would have to become man to pay
the infinite debt. We can explain this in the terms of the old
nursery rhyme

> *Humpty Dumpty sat on a wall,*
> *Humpty Dumpty had a great fall,*
> *And all the King's horses and all the King's men,*
> *Could not put Humpty Dumpty together again.*

That rhyme pretty well expresses the condition of man as
a result of sin. Since the fall of man, he is much like a broken
egg and can't put himself together. There is some kind of a
disorder inside of him, and the mere arrangement of wealth
in the social order outside of him is not going to change
man himself. He needs God to put him together again.

Take the example of a clock whose mainspring is broken. We have the works, but somehow they just do not go.
What two conditions have to be fulfilled to make the clock
work? First, the mainspring must be supplied from the
outside. Two, the mainspring must be placed inside of the
clock. Man cannot redeem himself any more than the clock
can fix itself. If man is ever to be redeemed, the redemption
must come from without and must be done from within. We
can never restore our vision if we are blind. If we have broken communion with God by sin, we cannot restore it. Have
you ever taken a rose petal into your fingers and pressed and
squeezed the rose petal? Did you notice if you could ever
restore its tint? You could not. Lift a dewdrop from a leaf;
you can never replace it. Evil is just a little too deep-seated
to be righted by a little bit of kindness, reason, and toler-
ance. You might just as well tell a man who is suffering from
consumption all he needs to do is play six sets of tennis.

The clock whose mainspring is broken cannot repair itself. Salvation has to come from without. Our human will is too weak to conquer its own evil. Just as the sick need medicine outside of themselves, we need a teacher for our minds, we need a physician for our bodies, and we need a redeemer for our souls, a redeemer outside of humanity with all its weakness, sin, and rebellion.

Let's take the other side. We said if the mainspring is broken, a new mainspring has to be supplied from without and inside of the clock. Salvation must come from without humanity, but it has to be done, in some way, within humanity. God had to become man to be redeemed from within. If God did not become man, He would have no relation to us. Man does not want just to have his sins forgiven; he wants to atone for them. So God became man. You put these two conditions together and you have the reason why the redeemer should be both God and man: God, from without; man to be within humanity. That is the Incarnation, God becoming man in the person of Christ so He might save us from our sins.

Here we come to something just a little more difficult, and we are going to use a word you may not hear often. We have to spend about six months when we are studying for the priesthood studying the meaning of these words: "hypostatic union." "Hypostatic union" means there are two natures and one person in Christ. That is something you must always remember. Embed it in your memory, in your mind. Christ has two natures: one human; one divine. They are both united in the person of God. Was God, therefore, a human person? No, He was a divine person. Did He have a human nature? Yes. Did He have a divine nature? Yes. They were united in the divine Person of God. Obviously, I am not using the words "nature" and "person" in the same sense, am I?

Perhaps we can make this clear if you will take a pencil in your hand. The pencil has a nature. A nature is a thing, something that operates. For example, a cow has a nature; a pig has a nature; a carpet has a nature; a pigeon has a nature; your finger has a nature. Is a cow a person? If your cow comes over into my pasture and eats all of my grass, I cannot sue the cow. I can sue you. There must be some difference between a nature and a person. A person is a source of responsibility. A dog is not responsible for its actions, but man is.

Using the pencil in your hand, do you notice there are before you two natures: one, the nature of the pencil; the other, the nature of your hand? Is your hand a person? No, because you could lose your hand and still be yourself. We have in the hand now, combined with the pencil, two natures. How are they united? In your one person. It is possible to have a union of two natures in one person. You have a body, you have a soul. They are very different in nature; one is material, and the other is spiritual, yet you're only one person. That is a very incomplete and imperfect analogy of what happens.

The pencil of and by itself cannot write. Put it down on a chair or table. That pencil cannot write. When you bring your hand down to that pencil, you have a union of two natures in one person. Now the pencil can write. It could do something it could not do before. When it writes do you say, "The pencil writes" or "I write"?

You do not say, "My eye sees you."

You say, "I see you."

You do not say, "My ear hears you."

You say, "I hear you."

You do not say, "My stomach digests."

You say, "I digest food."

Notice we are always attributing the actions of a nature to a person. If you sign a check, there is a responsibility involved, and neither the hand nor the pencil is the source of that responsibility.

Let us apply the analogy. Put the pencil down again on the table. The pencil is like man; he cannot pay the debt he owes to God. Pick up the pencil. Here you have a union of the nature of the hand, which is united with your person, and the nature of a pencil. The hand, with your personality coming down to the pencil, represents the person of God and the divine nature coming down to human nature. When God comes down and takes upon Himself a human nature, unites it with His divine nature and divine Person, you have the union of two natures; namely, the nature of God, and the nature of man in the unity of the person of God. Just as that pencil in your hand could do something which of and by itself it could not do, so human nature, united with the person of God, can begin to do something which of and by itself it could not do before. The pencil is the instrument of my personality. When God, with His divine nature, came down to this world and took upon Himself a human nature from the womb of His blessed Mother, He took upon Himself an instrument. Once God took upon Himself our human nature, He could act in our name. Every one of the actions of that human nature would have an infinite value. Not a sigh, a word, a tear, a step of that human nature was inseparable from the person of God. One breath of God would have been enough to have redeemed the world. Why? Because it was the breath of God and had an infinite value.

Why did God suffer so much when He took upon Himself our human nature? There are more grains of sand in this world than are necessary, and so love knows no limits. The only way to prove perfect love is by a surrender of all one has. God took upon Himself our human nature, and He said He loved us unto the end, even unto death. Now you see the beauty and the majesty of Christ. He became man at Bethlehem and took upon Himself the form of a babe. He was born without a mother in heaven and without a father on earth. He who made the world was born in it. The maker of the sun, born under the sun; molder of the earth, born on the earth; ineffably wise, born a little infant; filling the world, lying in a manger; ruling the stars, nursed by His mother. The mirth of heaven weeps, God becomes man. Divinity, incarnate; Eternity, time; Lord, scourged; Power, bound with ropes; King, crowned with thorns. If you were the only person in the world who ever lived and sinned, He would have come down to earth, died and suffered just for you alone. That is how much He loves you.

10

HUMANITY OF CHRIST

We have emphasized the divinity of Christ, but it often happens we forget the humanity of Christ. There are two verses in the Scripture, one from Isaiah and the other from the epistle to the Hebrews, that seem to be contradictory. Isaiah says our blessed Lord was reckoned with the transgressors (IS 53:12), or sinners, but the epistle to the Hebrews says He was separated from sinners (HEB 7:26), one with them and at the same time not with them. He took upon Himself all of the penalties of sin. He was separated simply because He was God, and because in His human nature, He was like to us in all things save sin.

Now we will penetrate rather deeply into the meaning of this human nature Christ assumed. Remember it had no human personality. In a certain sense, the human nature of our blessed Lord was unlimited. It was almost as if we had a playground in which there were no fences or walls; then all children could come into this playground. The human nature of Christ, because it was not capped, was not limited or confined by a human personality. The human nature of Christ represented, to a great extent, the human nature of every single person who has ever lived.

When we read His genealogy in the Gospel of Matthew and the genealogy of Luke, we will find saints, but we will also find sinners. We find Gentile women like Ruth; we find a public sinner like Rahab, and these were typical of the humanity Christ assumed into Himself when He became incarnate. Every single human being that would ever be born until the end of time was incorporated into this humanity. Hence, there is not a Buddhist, Confucianist, communist, sinner, or saint who is not in this human nature of Christ. We're in it. Our neighbor next door is in it. Every persecutor of the Church is, too.

When we are puzzled about how other people are saved, we need only realize that implicitly all salvation, all men, are in Christ. They may not recognize their incorporation to Christ, but in a certain sense every person in the world is implicitly a Christian in his human nature.

Just go back and think of all the repercussions of Adam's sin. There isn't an Arab, American, European, or Asiatic in the world who does not feel within himself something of the complexes, contradictions, civil wars, or rebellions inside his human nature, which he has inherited from Adam. We all struggle against temptation, and why? Simply because our human nature was disordered in the beginning. Let me tell you, there is a terrific monotony about human nature. You must not think you are the only one in the world who has a tortured soul.

If the sin of Adam had so many repercussions in every human being who has lived, shall we deny the Incarnation of our blessed Lord has had a greater repercussion? Can the sin of one man have greater effects and disorder in human nature than the Incarnation of the Son of God has in ordering all humanity? Thus, I say everybody in the world is

implicitly Christian. They may not make themselves explicitly Christian, but that is not the fault of Christ. He took
their humanity upon Himself.

Suppose there were a great plague which affected a wide
area of the world, and then some doctor in his laboratory
found a remedy and made it available to everyone. Not everyone would seek the remedy. They might say, "How do I
know he has the remedy? I will cure myself." Can they all be
potentially saved? It is certainly not the fault of the scientist
if they are not cured. It is the fault of the people themselves.
The person of Christ brought salvation to all men, and it is
up to us to find salvation in Him.

Our blessed Lord was hopeful about humanity. He always saw men the way He originally designed them. He saw
through the surface, grime, and dirt to the real man under-
neath. He never identified a person with sin. He saw sin as
something alien and foreign which did not belong to man.
Sin had mastered man, but he could be freed from it to be
his real self. Just as every mother sees her own image and
likeness on her child's face, so God always saw the divine
image and likeness beneath us.

He looked on us very much the same way a bride looks on
a bridegroom the day of the marriage, and as a bridegroom
looks on a bride. They are at their best. Later on in life they
may fall away from this ideal, or they will forget the ideal.
One day a woman came to me and told me she could never
love her husband again. I told her to try and think back to
how much she loved him the day of the marriage when they
stood side by side at the altar. What the woman had to do
was to see the real person to whom she committed her life
beneath the distorted image. This is precisely what our Lord
does in coming to earth. Even when men raged and stormed

beneath His Cross, He saw them as homeless and unhappy children of the Father in heaven; for them He grieved and died. This is the vision our Lord has of humanity.

We want to bring this home in a little more intimate way, and here we're going to use a term called transference and try to make clear what the humanity of our blessed Lord did in relationship to our sins and our sufferings. There are three kinds of transferences in the life of Christ: there is physical transference; there is psychic transference; and there is moral transference. If our blessed Lord did not come to this earth to undergo every single kind of agony, torture, and pain that we ourselves suffer, then we could say, "Does God know what it is to suffer?" "Did He ever go without food?" "Was He ever betrayed?" "Was He ever blind?" Let me tell you, the best way to describe our blessed Lord's humanity is that He is a God who took His own medicine. He made man free. Man abused freedom and brought upon himself all of the ills to which he is heir. God came down and took upon Himself a human nature so He might feel every kind of torture of the human soul and every twisting pain of a human body. That is what I mean by transference.

First of all, physical transference. We read about this in the Gospels; namely, our blessed Lord took upon Himself our sicknesses and our illnesses (MT 8:17). I was always very much disturbed about this particular passage because there seems to be no record our Lord was ever sick. He must have had a perfect human nature. He was conceived by the divine Spirit of Love and also born of a woman who was immaculately conceived. His physical organism must have been a perfect specimen of man. I suppose every woman wants to be the mother of a great son, and one day when our Lord was preaching some woman shouted out in the crowd, *Blessed is the womb that bore Thee and the breasts that nursed Thee* (LK 11:27). She would have loved to have been the mother of that Man.

When we find the soldiers and the enemies crowning Him with thorns, beating, scourging, buffeting Him, spitting in His face, ridiculing Him, what did all this mean but an attempt to drag the lovely human nature of Christ down to their level? They could not bear the majesty of His being; as they would rob a man of his reputation, so they would rob Him of the nobility of His character.

Our Lord must have had a perfect human nature. What does sacred Scripture mean by *He took upon Himself our sicknesses and illnesses*? I think for about two years I pondered that passage over in my mind, and the answer came in reading the work of a famous Swiss psychiatrist. He tells the story of two doctors, both of whom had healing hands. One of the doctors stated whenever he healed anyone, something of the sickness of the other person passed to himself. The other doctor stated he often cured patients of angina, and he had to give up healing because he suffered so many attacks of angina. Is this the key?

Let us go into some of the cures of our Lord. We often read in the Gospel He sighed when He cured the deaf and the blind. We read He groaned when He raised Lazarus from the dead (JN 11:38). I believe at that moment, our blessed Lord took upon Himself the ills and the sicknesses of others. When He cured the blind man (MK 8:22–26), I think He felt inside of Himself not just the blindness of one man, but the blindness of all men who have ever lived. There's not a blind man in the world, in the deep cavern of senses where there is no light, who could ever say, "Did Christ know what it was to be blind?" Yes, He did. When He raised the dead and brought them back to newness of life, I think He felt the agony of death. He went into fear in the Garden of Gethsemane (MT 26:36–46).

St. Paul tells us He died for all men (2 CO 5:15). He knows what death is, knows what fear of death is. This is the Christ who comes to us. We say He is the only one understanding our illness, and why? Simply because He has that illness inside of Himself. He bore it for us, and with us, so we might have strength and patience as He did.

There was not only physical transference; He also suffered psychic transference. By "psychic transference" I mean He took upon Himself all the loneliness of people; their mental ills; the tragic effects of their psychoses and neuroses. He felt all of the darkness of the atheist. He knew what it was to be a skeptic and a doubter. He knew what went on in the heart of any man who raises a clenched fist, of all those hating so much their mouths are craters of hate and volcanoes of blasphemy. After all, if our blessed Lord was to redeem the atheists and communists, He had to know how it felt to be an atheist and how it felt to be a communist. He had to feel their God forsakenness as His own. On the Cross the darkness crept into His soul. He confessed to His Father and in His human nature, His utter abandonment uttering, *My God, My God, why hast Thou abandoned Me?* (MT 27:46).

Here He traversed the darkest valleys and deserts of mystery with all human brothers. We might almost say this is a moment when God was almost an atheist! It was a moment when He almost went into hell, but with this difference: Within this terrible torment of loneliness, He cried to God. When anyone says he is forsaken by God, or denies God, he must realize he has a brother who endured the bitterness of separation to the very last extremity of Golgotha. If He showed the way, then we can find the way out, too. This was the loneliness of Christ in the garden and the loneliness on the Cross.

The silence of our Lord soaked up all the evil like a sponge, and evil lost all of its strength. When an atheist complains about the ugliness and evil of the world, does he not know in his inmost heart this is not the way this world was intended to be? He is affirming the very existence of God by the intensity of his complaint. Without God there would be no one to complain to, and in his complaint, he has Christ to whom he can go.

Finally, there was moral transference of sin. Sacred Scripture says our blessed Lord was made sin (IS 53:12). He took upon Himself all of the sins of the world as if they were His own. Every blasphemy was put upon His lips as if He Himself had spoken the blasphemy. Every theft was in His hand as if He Himself had committed the theft. His flesh hanging from Him was in token of all the rebellion of all the flesh in the world. He knew what sin is.

Perhaps I can make this clearer. Some years ago a girl wrote to me from a large city of this country. At the age of eighteen, she went to her first dance. She went in company with her cousin. Her house was some distance from the gate. The cousin dropped her at the gate, and in that distance between the gate and the front porch a stranger attacked her. In due time, she found herself with child. The only ones who would believe her were her mother and the pastor. Neighbor women said, "Oh, isn't it terrible the poor woman has one bad daughter." Some girls in the choir would not allow her to sing because she was wicked. She told me of all of the torture she endured.

She asked, "What's the answer?"

I wrote back to her:

My dear girl, all of this suffering has come upon you simply because you bore the sin of one man. I assume if you ever bore the sins of ten men, you probably would have suffered ten times more. If you ever took upon yourself the sins of a hundred men, your sufferings would have been a hundred times worse. If you ever took upon yourself the sins of the world, you might have had a bloody sweat. Your sin and mine was in the bloody sweat on Calvary [LK 22:44], in this human nature, the soul of dust we call the Sacred Heart.

11

THE BLESSED TRINITY

Now we come to a point where we propose to discuss the Trinity.

As I was preparing for the Trinity, two possible objections came to mind which you might have had concerning original sin, and may we treat those briefly. One objection might be this: "Why is it I have to suffer on account of Adam? I had nothing to do with him. I was not involved with his sin." The answer is: Yes, you were involved. So was I. We were all involved simply because Adam was the head of the human race. A river polluted at its source affects the entire current. Parents are infected; the infection passes on to their children. When the president declares war, we are at war without any individual declaration on our part because the president is the head of our country. Adam was the head of the human race. What he did, we did. Just as one man's evil can affect a whole nation, the good and honor of a father can affect the family. The disobedience of one man, Adam, affected us all. God, in His mercy, has repaired that harm through the obedience of the new Adam, who is our blessed Lord.

The second objection urged against original sin is "Why

should I lose the blessings Adam had on account of his sins? Is there an injustice on God's part to deprive me of the many favors he had simply because he sinned?" It must be recalled there is no injustice done, because injustice is depriving people of something that is theirs. When Adam sinned, he lost only gifts God gave him, not things to which he was entitled because of his nature. On Christmas Day you might give gifts to all your friends. If you did not give them anything, you would not be depriving them of that which was their due. Furthermore, though we lost gifts, we get them all back. We get back communion with God through grace. The other gifts Adam lost, we do not get back until the general resurrection and we get back more than we lost! As the priest says when he puts water into the wine at the Offertory of the Mass, *Mirabiliter condidisti et mirabilius reformasti.* "What Thou did so wonderfully make, Thou did so more wonderfully reform."

Leaving those objections behind, we come to the Trinity. You know how to bless yourself *In the name of the Father, and of the Son, and of the Holy Spirit, Amen.* When you say, "In the name of the Father," you put your hand to your forehead. When you say, "of the Son," you put your hand below to the breast. And when you say, "of the Holy Spirit," you place your hand, first on your left shoulder, then on your right. In the name of the Father and of the Son and of the Holy Spirit, Amen. Notice that as you do that you also make the sign of a cross, the sign of our redemption. You were baptized in the name of the Trinity, and our blessed Lord often spoke of it when He said, *Go ye and teach all nations, baptizing them in the name of the Father and of the Son and of the Holy Spirit* (MT 28:19). Our blessed Lord did not say "in the names of." He said "in the name of" because there is only one nature, the nature of God. The Trinity means there are three persons in God and only one nature.

Without going into very profound explanations of nature and person, a nature answers the question "what?" and a person answers the question "who?" I repeat, there are three persons in God and only one nature. A person in the Trinity does not mean the same as a person in this world. Thus, a person in the Trinity is not someone with hands and feet and a beard. A person in the Trinity means a relation, or a relationship. For example, there is a road that runs between Chicago and New York. There is a road that runs between New York and Chicago. It's the same road, but it is a different road under a different relationship. You see how out of one thing you get the multiple?

Remember your chemistry? The chemical symbol for water is H_2O. That is its nature. It has only one nature. But is it possible to have various relationships within that one nature? Most certainly, H_2O can be liquid; it can be ice, and it can be steam. Is the liquid a different nature from H_2O? No. The ice? No. The steam? No. Somehow the three are in one, just as in the sun there is substance, light, and heat, yet only one sun.

I remember once having spent an hour describing the Trinity with analogies to someone who was taking instructions, and I insisted it was a mystery. When I finished, the good lady said, "At the beginning you said that this was a mystery. It's no longer a mystery to me. You made it perfectly clear!"

"Well," I said, "Madam, if I made it perfectly clear to you, I did not explain it right. It should be a mystery."

There are various ways of approaching this subject. I'm going to start with the complexity of life; then, I'm gradually going to take life right up to the Trinity by analogy. It will seem as if I'm a million miles away from it, but bear with me. I hope the explanation will not be like that of a confusing lawyer who, arguing before a judge, went into a long history of cases, legal decisions, and precedents. He had a dim suspicion that he was not perfectly clear and he said to the judge, "Your Honor, do you follow me?"

The judge said, "Yes, I do, but if I knew the way back I would leave you now!"

So I beg you, bear with me.

Life is mysteriously bound up with all of our pleasures and destiny, both thrilling and saddening. Sometimes it seems the greatest of all gifts and at other times the most burdensome. Life, which I know best and which I know least, what is it? The first obvious answer is given to us by the commonplace things round about us. We always associate life with some kind of movement or activity. If we see an animal lying motionless in a field, it gives rise to the suspicion that possibly the animal is dead because there seems to be no movement. When a child is full of exuberance and joy, we say it is full of life. Notice that we associate life with movement. When you come to a more scientific definition, you find out that the movement or the activity has to be what is called immanent; it has to be inside of the thing.

There is another kind of movement, which is called transitive: for example, the light that seems to come from phosphorus. Heat that comes from a radiator has no power of generating heat within itself; it just passes from the outside. Coal has purely transitive activity; so does radium. A stone rolling down a hill has transitive activity. Life, on the other side, has this different kind of activity, which is called immanent, from the inside.

Let us try and find a law concerning life. Note it carefully: The greater the immanent activity, the higher the life. In other words, the more the activity is inside of the living thing, the higher it is. All creation, as you know, is a pyramid. At the base of the pyramid is the material chemical order; then there are plants, animals, man, angels, and God.

We are going to apply this law. It is so universal it can be verified in every one of the orders. A stone, as we know, has no immanent activity, although when Michelangelo finished the statue of Moses, he struck it with his chisel and said, "Speak!" It seemed so lifelike that it ought to speak, but it had no inner activity. But there is inner activity in a plant. It always has its mouth to the breast of Mother Nature and takes all the vital elements it needs. When we come to an animal, it has higher life than the plant. The plant has the power of vegetation; it has the power of generation, of begetting seeds. But the animal has two immanent powers and the plant does not. One is the ability to move, and the other is the ability to see, taste, touch, and smell, what is called sense activity. A plant cannot decide during the winter to move from New York down to Florida or California. An animal can move from light to shade. Thanks to its sense knowledge, it gets the outside world inside of itself. Animals possess an inner world; a dog can know its master's voice.

When you come to man, is there a higher activity? Yes, thinking and willing. Man has all of the immanent activity of plants and animals, but something else that the plants and animals have not: knowledge and love. First of all, he thinks thoughts like faith, justice, hope, relationship, and fortitude. Where do these thoughts come from? They're not in the outside world. You never saw faith out for a walk. You never saw fortitude eating a dessert. You never saw relationship climbing a hill. Where did you get these ideas? Your mind generated them. Your mind is fecund. Do not think the only kind of generation in the world is the generation that the animal and human being has to beget his kind. There's the chaste generation of the mind, the ability to beget ideas or words.

When the mind begets an idea, what it generates does not fall from it like an apple falls from a tree, like an animal falls from its kind when born. The fruit of our mind stays inside of the mind. All we've got to do is look into the mind and there it is. It is distinct from the mind, but it is never separate. When I want to find a thought, I just go back into my mind. I do not look for it on a shelf.

We have a will and we can choose. We can love, and we have the power, thanks to our will, of loving what we think about. We can love the truth in our own mind. We do not always need to love things outside of us. The amazing thing about our will is that our loves, just like our thoughts, can be immanent on the inside of us.

Let us go to God. God is perfect Life; therefore, He will have perfect immanent activity. I say "perfect immanent activity." Since He is a spirit, we will have to understand that perfect immanent activity after the analogy of our own; namely, after the intellect and our will. We look inside of ourselves to find some faint resemblance to this divine life. What we do in our mind is to think and to love. God thinks a thought or a word distinct from Him, but it is not separate from Him, as my thought is not separate from my mind though distinct from my mind. I have many thoughts, so do you, but God has only one thought. In that one thought is contained all knowledge that is possible. God does not need any word but that one, which is the image and the splendor of His substance.

Recall the words of the Gospel of John, *The Word became flesh and dwelled amongst us* (JN 1:14). Who is the Word that became flesh? The Son of God, the Second Person of the Trinity, the thought of God. Why do we call Him the Son of God? That's not difficult to answer. Did we not say you generate the thought in your mind or the word in your mind? Did we not say there is a higher generation than carnal generation? God generates an eternal Word.

Now applying it to the human order. What do we call the principle of generation? The father, do we not? What is the term of generation in the earthly order? A son. Instead of calling God, who thinks, the Thinker, and instead of calling the thought or the word of God just the thought, why not call God, who thinks, the Father? And why not call God, or the Person who is Thought, the Son? Then the Word that became flesh is called the Son. The Psalmist said, *Thou art My Son, this day have I begotten Thee* (PS 2:7). The Son of God who became the Son of man is Jesus Christ our Lord.

Let us take another analogy. We have the Third Person of the blessed Trinity. We said we not only think but we also love. Love is a relationship; it is a movement toward that which is loved to unite it to one's self. I love you simply because I am communicating truth to you. Love is not something in me; love is not something in you. Love is a mysterious bond uniting both of us. Though love is distinct from the thought, it proceeds from the thought and also from the thinker. God loves His perfection; every being loves its perfection. The perfection of the eye is color; it loves color. The perfection of the ear is harmony; it loves harmony. The perfection of the stomach is food; it loves food. The perfection of God the Father is God the Son. The perfection of God the Thinker is the Word of God. And the Father loves the Son. Love is not something in the Father alone. Love is not something in the Son alone.

Love is a mysterious bond uniting the two, and here we are not dealing with the personal and the biological, but with something infinite. Love cannot express itself by canticles, words, or embraces. It cannot express itself likened to anything that we have on this earth. It can only express itself by that which signifies the very fullness of all giving; namely, a sigh, something that lies too deep for words. All deep love is speechless, and love uniting Father and Son is called the Holy Breath, the Holy Spirit, and the Holy Love. Just as the color, perfume, and beauty of the rose do not make three roses, but one; just as I am, I think, and I love; yet I have only one nature. In a far more mysterious way there are three persons in God, and only one God.

A tremendous encircling love is in God. God is Life, Truth, and Love. Now we know the Life is the Father; the Truth is the Son; and Love is the Holy Spirit. And with John Donne we say:

> Batter my heart, three person'd God; for you
> As yet but knock, breathe, shine, and seek to mend;
> That I may rise and stand, o'erthrow me, and bend
> Your force to break, blow, burn, and make me new.
> I, like an usurpt towne, to another due,
> Labor to admit you, but O, to no end;
> Reason, your viceroy in me, me should defend,
> But is captived, and proves weak or untrue.
> Yet dearly I love you, and would be loved fain,

But am betroth'd unto your enemy.
Divorce me, untie or break that knot again;
Take me to you, imprison me, for I,
Except you enthrall me, never shall be free,
Nor ever chaste, except you ravish me.

(HOLY SONNET 14, *Divine Poems*)

12

THE MOTHER OF JESUS

At this point in the divine mysteries of Christian doctrine we come to some very important words in the Creed; namely, our blessed Lord "was born of the Virgin Mary" (LK 1:34). We will try to give some evidence for this and show how it was necessary in the present plan of the world for redemption.

In order to understand proofs we must realize the Gospels were not first, they were tradition. Every member in the early Church, after Pentecost and until the Gospels were written, already knew about the miracle of the loaves and fishes (MT 15:32–39), about the Resurrection (MK 16:9–20), and about the virgin birth (MT 1:18–25). It is something like the knowledge we have that World War I began in 1914. The fact that we read it in the book does not create belief in us. Does it? It merely confirms what we already know. So the Gospels set down in a more systematic way what was already believed.

Just suppose you lived during the first twenty-five years of the Church after Pentecost. How would you have answered the question "How can I know what I am to believe?" You could not say, "I will look in the Bible." There was no New

Testament Bible then. You would have to believe what the Church was teaching in those days. Never once did our Lord tell the witnesses of His life to write. He wrote only once in His life, and that was in the sand (JN 8:6, 8). But He did tell His Apostles to preach in His name and to be witnesses to Him to the ends of the earth (AC 13:47). Hence, those who take text out of the Gospels to prove a point are very often isolating it from the historical atmosphere in which it arose and from the word of mouth which passed on Christ's truth.

When the Gospels were written, they recorded a tradition that was already there. They did not create it. After a while men had decided to put the tradition in writing, which explains the beginning of the Gospel of St. Luke. He begins, *That thou mayest know the verity of these words in which thou hast been instructed* (LK 1:1–4). He assumes people already had been instructed. The Gospels did not start the Church; the Church started the Gospels. The Church did not come out of the Gospels; it was the Gospels that came out of the Church. The Church preceded the New Testament, not the New Testament, the Church. Men did not believe in the Resurrection because the Gospels said there was a Resurrection. The Gospel writers recorded the story of the Crucifixion and the Resurrection because they believed it.

In like manner, the Church did not come to believe in the virgin birth because the Gospels tell us there was a virgin birth; it was because the Living Word of God, in His Mystical Body, the Church, already believed it and the sacred writers set it down in the Gospels. If the Apostles, who lived with our Lord, who heard Him speak in the open hills and in the Temple, if the Apostles did not teach the virgin birth, no one else would have taught it; no one else would have written it. It was too unusual an idea for men to make up. It would have been ordinarily too difficult for acceptance if it had not come from Christ, Himself.

The one man who might be inclined to doubt the virgin birth on natural grounds was the man who writes it in his gospel, namely, St. Luke. I say "on natural grounds" because Luke was a physician, and yet it is the medical doctor who sets down the virgin birth and tells us most about it (LK 1:26–38). Heretics denied many of the teachings of our Lord because there were protests against Christ and His Church from the very beginning. These heretics denied some of His doctrines, but there was one teaching no early heretic denied, and that is that our Lord was born of a virgin. One would think that would be the very first doctrine to be attacked, but the virgin birth was accepted both by heretics and by believers alike. It would have been rather silly to try to convince anyone of the virgin birth if he did not already believe in the divinity of Christ. And that is why, probably, Mary did not speak of it herself until after the Resurrection.

Now we come to an objection often heard: "Does the Gospel say our blessed Lord had brothers? If He had brothers, then Mary had other children and was not always a virgin." We will try to give some answers.

I stand in the pulpit very often and begin my sermon by saying, "My dear brothers and sisters." Does that mean everyone in the congregation had exactly the same mother, or is it just a form of speech? This wide meaning of the words "brothers and sisters" in modern language was used by the authors of sacred Scripture. In the Scriptures the word "brother" means a relative, sometimes a friend; for example, Abraham calls Lot his brother. As we read in the book of Genesis, *Pray, let us have no strife between us two; between my shepherds and thine, for we are brethren* (GN 13:8). Lot was not a brother of Abraham, he was a nephew; but that's the way Scripture speaks of friends and relatives.

There are several that are mentioned as brothers of Christ, such as James, but they are indicated as the sons of another Mary elsewhere in Scripture. They mean Mary, the sister of the mother of our Lord, and the wife of Cleophas (JN 19:25). James is described as the brother of our Lord by St. Paul, who said, *But I did not see any of the other Apostles except James, the Lord's brother* (GA 1:19). But this James is regularly named in the enumeration of the Apostles as the son of another father, namely, Alphaeus (MT 10:3). You'll find that recorded in Matthew, Mark, and Luke. Furthermore, the so-called brethren of our Lord are not mentioned in the Scripture as the sons and the daughters of Joseph and Mary. Nowhere in Scripture is it said that Joseph had begotten brothers and sisters of Jesus, as nowhere does it say that Mary had other children besides her divine Son.

Now we come to some rather unusual proofs of the virgin birth from sacred Scripture independent from the obvious references there are in St. Luke. Two of these proofs we're going to draw from the Gospel of St. John and from the writings of St. Paul.

St. John assumes the virgin birth; throughout his gospel there is the assumption of a double birth. We are born of our parents and then we are born of God by the waters of the Holy Spirit in baptism. Remember, our Lord meant this when He told Nicodemus he must be born again; the first birth, he took from his mother in the flesh, and the second is the birth of water and the Spirit (JN 3:1–21). What makes us Christian is not being born of our parents, but being born of God through baptism.

Notice when St. John speaks of the birth of God, he practically assumes the virgin birth. He says in the beginning of his gospel that our Lord gave us the power to become the sons of God (JN 1:12). He tells us this happens by a birth, but he immediately says this is not a human birth. Then he goes on to enumerate the reasons why it's not a human birth. He says, *It is neither of blood, sex, nor of the human will, but solely by the power of God* (JN 1:13).

This statement of John assumed a Christian and common understanding of the virgin birth. What is blood, what is sex, what is the human will, but a human birth. All of these elements are eliminated in the story of the birth of our Lord. The blessed Mother says she is a virgin, that she knows not man, and the angel says the power of God will overshadow her (LK 1:26–38). You get the same elements you see in the Gospel of St. John in the Gospel of St. Luke. How could any Christians in those days have understood the spiritual kind of birth unless they understood the virgin birth? At the end of the first century, no one read the beginning of the Gospel of St. John and was amazed that he should have spoken of a new generation without sex. They were not amazed because at this time the whole Christian world knew that this was how Christianity came into being. The virgin birth is God's idea, not man's. No one would ever have thought of it if it had not happened.

Now we come to another proof, from the epistles of St. Paul. St. Paul also assumes the virgin birth. As you know, the epistles were originally written in Greek. When St. Paul speaks of the birth of our Lord, he uses a very peculiar expression in Greek. St. Paul's message to the Galatians was, Then God sent out His Son on a mission to us. He took birth (GA 4:4–5). Notice that "He took birth from a woman," took birth as a subject of the law to make us sons by adoption. Whenever St. Paul describes the birth of our Lord, he never uses the ordinary word to describe birth. In other words, he never uses the word to describe a human birth which is the result of a conjunction of a man and a woman, the word that is used in every other New Testament passage.

The common word in Greek is some form of the Greek word *gennao,* a birth such as you had and I had. But St. Paul, in four instances, speaks of the temporal beginnings of our Lord. Remember the person of our Lord was eternal; it was only His human nature that had a beginning. Now in the four instances where St. Paul touches on the temporal beginnings of our Lord, as a man, in those four instances St. Paul uses an entirely different Greek word because it was not the ordinary kind of birth. He uses some form of the word *ginomai.* Never once does he employ that other word which means a common ordinary birth, such as all mortals have, to describe the birth of our Lord. He uses a word that means to come into existence, or to become.

One very interesting example of this is a passage in Galatians (4:23–29). In that epistle, St. Paul uses a word three times meaning to be born in the ordinary way. He uses it to describe the birth of Ishmael and the birth of Isaac, but when he comes to the birth of our Lord, he refuses to use that word. He uses another word, a form of the verb *ginomai,* because the birth of our Lord was a virgin birth.

In the New Testament, the birth of a child is recorded thirty-three times, and in every single instance the New Testament uses the word *gennao,* the ordinary birth like yours and mine, but that word is never used once concerning the birth of our Lord. Our Lord, as a person, had an eternal birth. Inasmuch as He assumed human nature, He had a temporal birth—a beginning, yes, but the beginning came from a virgin.

You see the reason for the difference is this: Our Lord was born *into* the human family, into the human race, He was not born of it. God formed Adam, the first man, without the seed of a man, so why should we shrink from the thought that the new Adam would also be formed without the seed of a man? As Adam was made of the earth into which God breathed a living soul, so the Holy Spirit formed the body of Christ in the flesh of Mary. So firmly rooted was the virgin birth in Christian tradition that none of the early apologists ever had to defend it. Even heretics believed because it stood on exactly the same footing as a historical fact.

Here's another interesting point. There are two birth stories in the gospel: the birth of our Lord (LK 2:1–7) and the birth of John the Baptist (LK 1:57–58), but notice the different stress. The Gospel story of John the Baptist centers on the father, Zachary. The Gospel story of the birth of Jesus centers on the mother. Why does it center on the mother? Again, because of the virgin birth. You may ask, "Well, why is there a virgin birth? Could our blessed Lord have come to this earth in any other way?" Oh, certainly! Our Lord really need not have been born at all. But given the present order of things, why is there a virgin birth?

Here we come to something that is a little difficult to understand, and we hope that we can make it clear. The reason we believe in a virgin birth, and the reason in the present order that our Lord chose that way was He wanted someone very good to bring Him into this world. No great triumphant leader makes his entrance into the city over dust-covered roads when he could come on the flower-strewn avenue. Had Infinite Purity chosen any other port of entrance into humanity but that of human purity, it would have created a tremendous difficulty for us; namely, how could He be sinless if He was born of a sin-laden humanity? If a brush dipped in black becomes black and if a cloth takes on the color of the dye, would not He, in the eyes of the world, have partaken of the guilt in which all humanity shared? If He came to this earth through the wheat field of moral weakness, He certainly would have some chaff hanging on to the garment of His human nature. In other words, our problem is this: How could God become man and yet be a sinless man?

First of all, He had to be man. He had to be like us in order that He might be involved in our humanity. He took upon Himself our sins. But at the same time, though our blessed Lord had to be a perfect man, He could not be a sinful man. He had to be a sinless man. He had to be outside of that terrible current of sin that is passed on and infected all humanity. You see the problem? He had to be a man; He had to be different from all other men in the sense that He had to be our Redeemer and sinless as the new Adam.

The problem is very much like that of a ship. Imagine a ship sailing on a sea that is very dirty and foul. It wishes to pass to another sea or lake immediately nearby where the waters are crystal clear and pure. Evidently there has to be some break between the foul waters and the clear waters; otherwise, they would merge. So what happens? Often a lock is built. A ship sails along those foul waters, then comes into the lock, where the foul waters are completely separated from it, and then the ship is finally lifted into the clear waters.

Our blessed Lord had to be related to the sinful humanity that went on before, related inasmuch as He would be a man. He had to be sinless so that He Himself would not need redemption but would be our Redeemer. Our blessed Lord was lifted out of that sinful current of humanity and made the new head of the human race through the virgin birth. Think of the beautiful application that it has for all of us. The blessed Mother is the inspiration of everyone. A mother is the protectress of the virgin and, the virgin is the inspiration of motherhood. Without mothers there would be no virgins in the next generation, and without the virgins, mothers would forget the sublime ideal that lives beyond the earth. How often when you visit someone, you hear it said, "Oh, the child looks exactly like the father." If we had looked at our blessed Lord, we would have said, "He looks exactly like His mother." He got something from His Father's side, namely, divinity. But He also got something from His mother's side, namely, a sinless humanity. That's why we love Mary. Hail Mary, full of grace!

13

CHRIST IN THE CREED: BIRTH

It is to be noted our Creed almost summarizes a life. How quickly it passes over the public life of our Lord: He was born; He suffered; He was buried; He rose; now He sits at the right hand of the Father in glory. This is destined to be the summary of every human life. Note how the life of our Lord is divided: thirty years obeying, three years teaching, and three hours redeeming.

We begin with His birth. Caesar Augustus, the master bookkeeper of the world, was seated at his desk at the Tiber in Rome, and before him was a map. It was labeled *Orbis Terrarum Imperium Romanum.* Because he was master of the world, he was going to take a census. All the civilized nations of the world were subject to the capital, Rome. Latin was the official language and Caesar was the ruler. The order went out to every outpost and governor that every Roman must be enrolled in his own city (LK 2:1–5). On the fringe of the Empire in the little village of Nazareth, soldiers tacked up on the wall the order for all citizens to register in the towns of their family origins.

Joseph, a carpenter, a very obscure descendant of the great King David, was obliged to register in Bethlehem, which was the city of David. In accordance with the edict, Mary and Joseph set out from the village of Nazareth for the village of Bethlehem, which lies about five miles on the other side of Jerusalem. They made the journey from Nazareth. Five hundred years earlier it had been prophesied by the great prophet Micah that our blessed Lord would be born in the city of Bethlehem (MI 5:2). He dies in the great city of Jerusalem. The ignominy of His Crucifixion may be known to all, but the glory of His birth is hidden in the least of the cities.

Mary was with child and awaiting birth. Joseph was full of expectancy as he entered the city of his own family. He searched for a place where He, to whom heaven and earth belonged, might be born. Could it be that the Creator would not find room in His own creation? Certainly, thought Joseph, there would be room in the village inn. There was room for the rich. There was room for those who were clothed in soft garments. There was room for everyone who had a tip to give to the innkeeper, but when the scrolls of history were completed down to the last words of time, the saddest lines of all would be:

There was no room in the inn (LK 2:7).

But there was room in the stable. The inn is the gathering place of public opinion, the focal point of the world's moods, the rendezvous of the worldly, the rallying place of the popular and the successful, but there is no room in the place where the world gathers. The stable is a place for outcasts, the ignored, and the forgotten. The world might have expected the Son of God to be born in an inn. A stable would certainly be the last place in the world where one would look for Him. The lesson is: Divinity is where you least expect to find it.

The Son of God made man was invited to enter into His own world through a back door. Exiled from the earth, He was born under the earth, for the stable was a cave. He was the first cave man of recorded history. There He shook the earth to its very foundations. Because He was born in a cave, all who wish to see Him must bend, and the stoop is the mark of humility. The proud refused to stoop; therefore, they missed divinity. Those who were willing to bend their egos and go into that cave found that they were not in a cave at all, but in a universe where a Babe sat on His mother's lap, the Babe who made the world. Shepherds and wise men came to visit Him: shepherds, who knew they knew nothing; wise men, who knew they did not know everything.

Time passed; after the flight into Egypt, His mother and foster father brought our blessed Lord to Nazareth, which was to be His hometown and where He was to spend His time until He began His public life (MT 2:19–23). It seemed like a very long preparation. One wonders why it was so long, practically thirty years for three years' ministry. One can only guess, and this is our guess.

The reason might be that He waited until the human nature which He had assumed had grown in age to full perfection; thus, He might offer a perfect sacrifice to His heavenly Father. Does not the farmer wait until the wheat is ripe before cutting it and subjecting it to the mill? He would wait until His human nature had reached the most perfect proportions, the peak of loveliness, before surrendering it to the hammer of the crucifiers and the sickle of those who would cut down the Living Bread of heaven. The Jews never offered the newborn lamb in sacrifice, nor is the first blush of the rose cut to pay tribute to a friend. Each thing has its hour of perfection. He was the Lamb setting the hour for His own sacrifice; He was the Rose choosing the moment of its own cutting. He waited patiently, humbly, obediently, while He grew in age, grace, and wisdom before God and man. Then He would say, "This is my hour." Thus, the choicest wheat and the reddest wine would become the worthiest elements of sacrifice. Perhaps that is why He waited.

We've already said something about His temptation, namely, the reversal of the temptation of Adam and Eve. Satan solicited our blessed Lord to forgo the Cross, to give people bread, to work some kinds of wonders, to do anything except treat with human guilt and Satan (MT 4:1–11). After the temptation, as our Lord began His public life, He went beyond the Jordan where John the Baptist was preaching. It was about the season of Passover, the feast which takes its name from the time when the Jews were in bondage in Egypt. In order to release the Jews, God punished the Egyptians. They were to lose their firstborn. So the destroying angel would not touch the firstborn of the Jews, they were asked to sacrifice a lamb and sprinkle the blood of the lamb above the doorposts, not on the earth, where it could be trampled. The destroying angel, seeing the blood as a promise and sign of redemption from slavery, would pass over that house. The sacrifice of the Pascal lamb became known as the "Pass over" (EX 12:27).

The Jews continue to offer the sacrifice of the Pascal lamb at the season of Passover. In the course of centuries, hundreds of thousands of lambs have been sacrificed. Remember that even before Moses, Abraham was asked to sacrifice his son, Isaac (GN 22:2). He loaded Isaac with wood and told him to carry the wood, which was preparatory and necessary for the sacrifice. This was the symbol of God, the Father, offering His Son. As Isaac was the only son of Abraham, so our

Lord was the Son of the heavenly Father. When Abraham and Isaac got to the top of the mountain, Isaac asked, *Where is the lamb? What are we going to sacrifice?* (GN 22:7). God provided a substitute for Isaac that typified the fact our blessed Lord would in some way substitute Himself for our sins. But the point is, Isaac asked, *Where is the lamb?* Abraham said, *My son, God will see to it there is a lamb to be sacrificed* (GN 22:8). *Agnum providebit:* God will provide a lamb.

With this memory of the sacrifice of Abraham and Isaac, and the memory of the Passover season and all of the lambs that had been sacrificed, the Jews were now going up to Jerusalem. Every family was to have its own Pascal lamb. Imagine the banks of the Jordan being almost white with the fleece of the lambs that were being brought up to the city for sacrifice. The Jews understood the meaning. It was a recall and a memory of how they were rescued from political slavery. The prophets told them that it was to be a symbol of being rescued from spiritual slavery. Their prophet Isaiah had told them when the true Lamb of God would come, that He would be a man. Isaiah had written, *And God laid on His shoulders our guilt, the guilt of us all* (IS 53:6). A victim? Yes, He Himself bows to the stroke. No words come from Him.

As John the Baptist was preaching, he saw all of these lambs before him, but he also saw our blessed Lord in the crowd. John the Baptist let his voice ring out and, pointing to our blessed Lord, he said, *Behold the Lamb of God who takes away the sins of the world!* (JN 1:29). All through the centuries those words of Isaac's inquiry had been repeated, "Where's the lamb, where's the lamb, where is the lamb?" John the Baptist gave the answer: "Behold the Lamb of God." The lamb was the sacrifice and Christ would be the sacrifice. John the Baptist called Him the Lamb of God. He was not the people's Lamb, or the Lamb of the Jews, or the Lamb of any human owner, but the Lamb of God. When the time came for that Lamb to be sacrificed, He would not be a victim of those who were stronger than He; rather, He would be fulfilling His own willing duty of love for sinners. It was not man who offered this sacrifice, although it was man who slew the victim. It would be God Himself. At the very beginning of the public life of our Lord, we have a foretelling of the sacrifice. The Cross is no afterthought in the life of our Lord.

John the Evangelist, in the Apocalypse, speaks of the Lamb slain in sacrifice, ever since the world was made or even before the world was made (RV 13:8). This means the Lamb was slain by divine decree from all eternity, though the temporal fulfillment of that sacrifice would only be on the hill of Calvary. If we had time to go into every single detail of the life of our blessed Lord, we would see how the Cross was dominant in everything He said and did. Yet, the Cross is not final. Our Lord never once spoke of the Cross without speaking also of the Resurrection.

In a long conversation our blessed Lord had one night with Nicodemus, when He said he did not know as much about the Mosaic laws as he thought, He told Nicodemus He was not only the Son of man but the Son of God. He said, *What will you make of it if you see the Son of man ascending to the place where He was before?* (JN 3:13). He came down from heaven to this world. Our blessed Lord used a figure that was very well known to Nicodemus and to the Jews. What our Lord said that night to Nicodemus was *This Son of man must be lifted up in the wilderness so those who believe in Him will not perish but have everlasting life as the serpent was lifted up by*

Moses (3:14). What did our Lord mean, "the serpent . . . lifted up by Moses"?

If you go back to the book of Numbers, you will see the people rebelling against God in the desert. They were punished with the plague of fiery serpents, and many of them lost their lives (NB 21:6). Moses was told by God to make a brazen serpent of brass, and set it up in the crotch of a tree. Then God told Moses everyone who had looked at the serpent of brass in the crotch of that tree would be healed of the poisonous serpent's bite (NB 21:8).

Certainly there was nothing in a serpent of brass that could cure any of those who were suffering from the bite of a serpent. No intrinsic relationship between the two, and everyone who looked upon it was healed and those who refused to look upon that serpent of brass were not healed. After hundreds of years have passed, our blessed Lord comes to this earth, goes back to that symbol, and gives it real meaning. Our Lord now said He is the serpent of brass. Just as Moses lifted up that serpent of brass on the tree, so He, our blessed Lord, will be lifted up on the tree of the Cross, and all who look upon Him will be saved. The connection is this: That brass serpent in the desert looked exactly like the fiery serpent that had stung the Jews, but it did not have venom inside of it. It looked as if it were poisonous, but it was not poisonous. Our blessed Lord now implied that He, too, would be lifted up on a tree. He would look as if he were a sinner. He would look as if He were full of the venom of guilt. Would not judges condemn Him? If He were condemned, would it not seem as if He were a sinner Himself? Yet, He would be without sin, and all that would look upon Him would be healed.

Once more our Lord was saying He was not just a teacher, but a redeemer. He was coming to redeem man in the likeness of human flesh. Teachers change men by their lives; our blessed Lord would change men by His death. And the poison of hate, sensuality, and envy which is in the hearts of men could not be healed simply by wild exhortations of social reform. The wages of sin is death; therefore, it was to be by death that sin would be atoned. As in the ancient sacrifices, the fire symbolically burned up the imputed sin along with the victim, so on the Cross the world's sin would be put away in Christ's suffering; He would be upright as a Priest and prostrate as a Victim. If there is anything that every good teacher wants, it is a long life which will make his teaching known. Death is always a great tragedy to a teacher. When Socrates was given the hemlock juice, his message was cut off once and for all. Death to Buddha was a stumbling block that stood in the way of all the teachings of the Eastern mystics. Our blessed Lord was always proclaiming His death, by which He takes upon Himself the sins of the world and appears as if He were a sinner.

Our blessed Lord talks with Nicodemus and proclaims Himself the Light of the world. The most astounding part of it was that He said no one would understand His teaching until after His death and Resurrection. No other teacher in the world ever said that it would take a violent death to clarify his teaching. Here was a teacher who made His teaching secondary. He would draw men to Himself, not by His doctrine, not by what He said, but by His Crucifixion. Our blessed Lord put it, *When you have lifted up the Son of man, you will recognize that it is Myself you look for* (JN 8:28). He did not say that it would be by His teaching they would understand; rather, it would be by His personality that they would grasp the meaning of His coming. Only then would they know, after they had put Him to death that he spoke the truth.

Instead of being the last in a series of failures, his death would be a glorious success and the climax of His mission on earth. The great difference in the statues and pictures of Buddha and Christ is that Buddha is always seated, eyes closed, hands folded across his fat, sleek body, intently looking inward; Christ is not seated on this earth, He's lifted up, He's enthroned. His person and His death are the heart and soul of His teaching. The Cross is the very center of His life. What remains? Only to tell you about His Cross, His death, and His burial.

14

SUFFERINGS, DEATH, AND RESURRECTION

In this lesson we continue the Creed, which links together the birth of our Lord, His Cross, and His Resurrection. We consider particularly His sufferings and Resurrection, and we begin with the agony of our Lord. Here we are dealing with a great mystery. Our blessed Lord suffered mentally and physically.

We touch upon His mental sufferings in the Garden of Gethsemane. The time was immediately after the Last Supper. There is only one recorded time in the life of our blessed Lord when he sang (MT 26:30), and that was after the Last Supper, when He went out to His death. He told His Apostles that they would all be shaken during this hour. Remember, our Lord always spoke of His Crucifixion and His sufferings in terms of hour, His glory in terms of day. Evil has its hour, God has His day.

As He entered the garden into which He had often gone to pray, He told His Apostles they would be scandalized in Him that night because the Shepherd would be struck (MT 26:31). They were scandalized for a short time after the agony. They fled. But He told them when He went in, *I will go before you into Galilee when I have risen from the dead* (26:32).

Such a promise was never made before, that a dead man would keep an appointment with His friends after three days in a tomb.

Though the sheep would forsake the Shepherd, the Shepherd would not forsake the sheep. As Adam lost the heritage of union with God in a garden, so now our blessed Lord ushers in our restoration in a garden. Eden and Gethsemane are two gardens around which revolve the fate of humanity. In Eden, Adam sinned; in Gethsemane, Christ took humanity's sin upon Himself. In Eden, Adam hid from God; in Gethsemane, Christ interceded with His Father. In Eden, God sought out Adam in his sin of rebellion; in Gethsemane, the new Adam, Christ, sought out the Father in submission and resignation. In Eden, a sword was drawn to prevent entrance into the Garden of Eden to immortalize evil. In Gethsemane, our Lord told Peter to sheath the sword he had carried.

There are two elements bound up together in this agony: sin bearing, and sinless obedience. He goes afar from His Apostles, about as far, the Scriptures say, as a man could throw a stone (LK 22:41). What a curious way to measure distance. And our Lord threw Himself upon His face, saying, *My Father, if it be possible, let this chalice pass Me by. Only as Thy will is, not as Mine is* (MK 14:36). Notice how the two natures of our Lord are involved here. He and the Father were one, so He did not pray, "Our Father, if it be possible, let this chalice pass," but "My Father." The consciousness of His Father's love was unbroken. On the other hand, remember that He's man as well as God. His human nature recoiled from death as a penalty for sin. It was very natural for a human nature to shrink from the punishment which sin deserves. The prayer to have the cup of passion pass was human. In other words, the "no" was human; the "yes" to the divine will was the overcoming of human reluctance to suffering for the sake of redemption.

Our blessed Lord takes upon Himself the sins of the world as if He, Himself, were guilty. This is very difficult for us to understand because we always think of physical suffering as something beyond moral evil. Furthermore, we become so used to sin we do not realize its horror. The innocent understands sin much better than the sinful. The one thing from which man never learns anything by experience is sinning. A sinner becomes infected with sin; it becomes so much a part of him that he may even think himself virtuous, as the feverish think themselves well at times. It is only the virtuous, who stand outside of the current of sin, who can look upon evil as a doctor looks upon disease and understand the full horror of evil.

It is impossible for us to realize how God felt the opposition of human will to the divine will. I wonder what example we could find to illustrate that. Perhaps the closest is when a parent feels the strange power of an obstinate will of one of his children. That child can resist and spurn persuasion, love, hope, and fear of punishment. What a strong power abides in a body so slight and a mind so childish. This is a faint picture of men when they have sinned willfully. What is sin for the soul but a separate principle of wisdom working out its own ends as if there were no God? Anti-Christ is nothing but the full, unhindered growth of self-will. That's what our Lord had to face in the garden, the opposition of all human wills to the divine will.

In obedience to the Father's will, our Lord takes upon Himself the iniquities of the entire world to become a sin bearer. There never was a sin committed in the world for which He did not suffer. The sin of Adam was there when, as the head of all humanity, he lost for all men the heritage of God's grace. Cain was there, purple in the sheet of his brother's blood. The abominations of Sodom and Gomorrah were there. The forgetfulness of His chosen people, who fell down before false gods, was there. The coarseness of pagans, who had revolted against the natural law, these pagans were there, too. All sins were there: sins committed in the country that made all nature blush; sins of the young, for whom the tender heart of Christ was pierced; sins of the old, who should have passed the age of sinning; sins committed in the darkness, where it was thought the eyes of God could not pierce; sins committed in the light that made even the wicked shudder. Blasphemies seemed to be on His lips as if He had spoken them.

From the north and the south, the east and the west, the foul miasma of the world's sin washes upon Him like a flood. Samson-like, He reaches up and pulls down the whole guilt of the world upon Himself as if He were guilty, paying for the debt in our name so we might once more have access to the Father. He was mentally preparing Himself for the great sacrifice, laying upon His sinless soul the sins of a guilty world. I say every sin was there; your sin was there and so was mine. Is it any wonder blood began to pour from His body (LK 22:44), drops of blood, that fell upon the ground like beads forming a rosary of redemption? Sin is in the blood, and for the remission of sin, blood had to be poured forth. He was guiltless, but He prayed and suffered in our name.

Then came Judas. Our Lord had to understand even false brethren. Judas threw his arms around the neck of our blessed Lord and blistered his lips with a kiss (MT 26:49). Our

Lord is made a buffoon during the night as He is tried before
two religious judges: Annas and Caiaphas (MT 26:57–68). In
all, our Lord was tried before four judges. Two of them were
religious judges; they belonged to the Jews. Two were civil
judges, Pilate and Herod (LK 23:1–25). Pilate was a Roman
and a Gentile, and Herod an Edomite. The judges could not
agree on why He should be condemned. Different charges
were made in different courts. In the religious court our
blessed Lord was condemned for blasphemy. In the civil
court our blessed Lord was condemned for treason. Before
the religious judges, He was found to be too religious, too
divine, too unworldly. Before the civil judges, He was found
to be too political, too human, too worldly. They cannot
agree on why He should be condemned; they can only agree
that He should be. He is to be condemned on contradictory
charges; one, because He's too divine, and the other because
He's too human; the fitting punishment was the sign of contradiction, which is the Cross.

Let us take a brief scene from each of these trials. In the
trial before the religious judges, Caiaphas was unable to find
any reason why he could condemn our Lord. He introduced
false witnesses, but the witnesses could not agree among
themselves. Caiaphas finally resorted to an oath. He put our
blessed Lord under it and with all of the sternness he could
muster, and annoyed by all the contradictions of the witnesses he had heard, said to our blessed Lord, *I adjure Thee
by the Living God to tell us whether Thou art the Christ, the Son of
God* (MT 26:63). Now, when Caiaphas asked the question, if
He was the Christ, the Son of God, remember his mind was
not like ours. When you and I hear the word Christ, we go
back to His earthly life. Not Caiaphas. Caiaphas was going
back through all of the prophecies. He was going back to

the book of Genesis. He knew how the Messiah had been foretold. So the question was, Was He the Messiah? Was He the Son of God? Was He clad with divine power? Was He the Word made flesh? Was it true that God, who at sundry times and in diverse manners spoke to us through the prophets, in these last days was speaking through Him, the Son? He asked, "Art Thou the Son of God?" Our Lord answered, "I am" (MT 26:64). With sublime consciousness and majestic dignity, He announced He was the Messiah and the Son of the living God. When He said, "I am," I'm sure Caiaphas remembered when God spoke to Moses on Mount Sinai, those were the words God used of Himself, *I am Who am* (EX 3:14).

Our Lord now speaks to Caiaphas again and says, *Moreover, I tell you this; you will see the Son of man again when He is seated at the right hand of God's power and comes on the clouds of heaven* (MT 26:64). Notice our blessed Lord affirmed His divinity, then His humanity, and both under the personal pronoun "I." He is telling Caiaphas someday he will be judged.

Caiaphas finds our blessed Lord guilty. He rends his garments as a token of the fact he heard blasphemy because Christ was making Himself God. But Caiaphas, the Sanhedrin, and the people could not put our blessed Lord to death. The power belonged to the Romans, so they hustle our blessed Lord, the prisoner, off to Pilate. He had several trials before Pilate sent Him off to Herod (MT 27:11–26). It is interesting to note the charge that was brought before Pilate against our blessed Lord. In the trial of any ordinary human being there is a continuity of charges. Our blessed Lord was found guilty of blasphemy. When the prisoner was brought to a higher court, you would think He would still be condemned of blasphemy, but He was not. Why not? Because if Caiaphas and his friends told Pilate our blessed

Lord had made Himself God, Pilate would laugh at them. Pilate was a pagan; he would say, "I have my gods, you have yours! I sprinkle incense before mine every morning." They had to find some other charge. The charge they would bring against our blessed Lord would be treason. He would be too political, too human, too worldly!

It must be remembered Caiaphas and the Sanhedrin hated the Romans. The Romans had conquered their country. Roman judges were seated in judgment, Roman coinage was in their pockets, and Caesar's ensigns were all over the city of Jerusalem and all through the Holy Land. They hated the invader; they hated Rome. When they brought our blessed Lord before Pilate and he asked what charges they brought against the man, they said they had found Him guilty of perverting the nation, refusing to give tribute to Caesar. Imagine, refusing to give tribute to Caesar, Caesar whom they hated! Pilate knew they did not love Caesar, but in order to win their release, after many incidents in the trial, they finally said to him, "Thou art no friend of Caesar if thou dost release Him. The man who pretends to be a King is Caesar's rival" (JN 19:12). Pilate was afraid of being reported to Rome. What would Tiberius do to him? Would he unseat him? Though Pilate tried to save our Lord—he had called our Lord innocent seven times—now he scourges our blessed Lord, brings Him out before the people, and says, "Behold, your King!" Up against the marble balustrade there comes a wave of voices saying, "We have no King but Caesar!" Then Pilate gives up Jesus into their hands to be crucified.

Our Lord is now led to Calvary. Once on those heights, He offers His hands to His executioners, the hands from which the world's graces flow. The first dull knock of the hammer is heard in silence. Mary and John hold their ears; the sound is unendurable. The echo sounds as another stroke. Then the Cross is lifted slowly off the ground. Then with a thud that seems to shake even hell itself, it sinks into the pit prepared for it. Our Lord has mounted His pulpit for the last time.

He speaks seven times. The first word of our blessed Lord is for all who had crucified and all who had brought Him to death: *Father, forgive them, they know not what they do* (LK 23:34). It is not wisdom that saves; it is ignorance. Then after hanging three hours on the Cross, our blessed Lord prepares to surrender His life. Remember He had often said, No man takes My life away from Me. I lay it down of Myself (JN 10:18). It is to be noted when our blessed Lord came to the seventh word, the Scriptures say He spoke those words in a loud voice to show He was the Master of His own life. Just as planets, after a long period of time, complete their orbits and then come back to their starting points as if to salute Him who sent them on their way, so He who was the Prodigal Son, who left the Father's house, wasted His life and His blood for our sake, was preparing to go back home. He lets fall from His lips the perfect prayer: *Father, into Thy hands I commend My Spirit* (LK 23:46). There was a rupture of a heart through a rapture of love, He bowed His head and died.

Nicodemus and Joseph of Arimathea came to take Him down from the Cross. They embalmed Him in a hundred pounds of spices, and Scripture says, *In the same quarter where He was crucified, there was a garden* (JN 19:41). The word "garden" hints at Eden and the fall of man; it also suggests through its flowers in the springtime the resurrection from the dead. In that garden there was a tomb in which, in the language of Scripture, no man had ever been buried. Born of a virgin womb, He was buried in a virgin tomb.

Nothing seems more repellent than to have a crucifixion in a garden, and yet there would be compensation, for the garden would have its resurrection. He is born in a stranger's cave, and so He is buried in a stranger's grave, because human birth and human death are equally foreign to Him. Dying for others, He is placed in another's grave. His grave was borrowed, borrowed for He would give it back on Easter as He gave back the beast which He rode on Palm Sunday, when He said, *The Lord hath need of it* (MT 21:3).

When He rose from the dead, He made many appearances, and one of the appearances of the Resurrection was a week after. All of the other Apostles had seen our blessed Lord. They had become convinced, but only after much evidence and after much doubting. Our blessed Lord came into the Upper Room and said, *Peace be to you* (LK 24:36). Thomas, one of the Apostles, had refused to believe. He said, *I will not believe until I have seen the mark of nails on His hands. Until I have put my finger into the mark of the nails and put my hands into His side, you will never make me believe!* (JN 20:25). Our blessed Lord appeared and spoke to Thomas: *Let Me have thy finger. See, here are my hands. Let Me have thy hand. Put it into My side! Cease thy doubting and believe!* (20:27). Throwing himself on his knees, Thomas said to the Risen Savior, *Thou art my Lord and my God!* (JN 20:28).

There are some that will never believe, even when they see. Thomas thought that he was doing the right thing in demanding the full evidence of sensible proof, but what would become of future generations if the same evidence were to be demanded by them? Suppose you would not believe the Resurrection until you could put finger into His hand and hand into His side. The future believers, our Lord implied, must accept the fact of the Resurrection from those who had been with Him. Our Lord thus pictured the faith of believers after the apostolic age, when there would be none who would have seen it, but their faith would have a foundation because the Apostles had seen the Risen Christ.

How do we know there was a Resurrection? Simply because the Church was there, the Church was there in the Apostles; they saw the Resurrection. Thomas was there, the doubter. Thomas believed! And he believed in the name of all who could not see sensibly but who could accept the testimony of those whom Christ sent out to preach the Gospel of the Resurrection to all nations. The story is not over. In the next lesson we will touch on His Ascension to the right hand of the Father.

15

ASCENSION

In this lesson we consider the Creed, particularly those words that refer to the Ascension of our blessed Lord and the fact that He is seated at the right hand of God the Father Almighty.

After the Resurrection our blessed Lord remained forty days on the earth. During that time He instructed the Apostles about the Kingdom of God and laid the structure for His Mystical Body, the Church. Moses had fasted forty days before giving the law, Elias had fasted forty days before the restoration of the law, and now for forty days the Risen Savior set the pillars of the Church and the new law of the Gospel. The "forties" were about to end, and the Apostles were bidden to awaken the fiftieth day, which was the day of jubilee.

When the Thursday came for the Ascension of our divine Savior, He led His Apostles out to Mount Olivet. Not from Galilee but from Jerusalem, where He had suffered, would He leave earth for His heavenly Father. The sacrifice was now completed. He gathered His Apostles about Him as He prepared to ascend to the heavenly Throne; He raised His hands in benediction over them, and the Hands pulled down from heaven to earth to give them blessing bore the imprint of nails. Pierced hands best distribute blessings. If you ever want good counsel, go to someone who has suffered.

Scripture, now speaking of the Ascension says that even as He blessed them He parted from them and was carried up into heaven and is seated now at the right hand of God (LK 24:50–53). There are several words here which need explanations, such as the fact our blessed Lord "ascended," He is "seated," and is "at the right hand of the Father." The Ascension we are not to think of as a locomotion. We are not to think of our blessed Lord as going beyond the farthest star, or to think of Him as being so many millions of light-years away, nor are we to think of Him as going up from one point to another, and certainly not are we to envisage Him in the Ascension as a form of space travel. Our blessed Lord once had a descent; he came down from heaven. This did not mean a physical descent; it was rather a drawing aside of the veil in which divinity was revealed to humanity. So the Ascension is not like a rocket. Our blessed Lord is no closer to heaven when He passes the star Arcturus. Rather, the ascent and the descent mentioned in the Creed and in Christian doctrine refer to humiliation and exaltation. When our blessed Lord came to this earth, He humbled Himself. When He ascended into heaven, He was exalted, which is the way Scripture always speaks of Him. He ascended into heaven because He had humbled Himself and was made obedient to the death of the Cross.

What does the word "seated" mean: *He sitteth at the right hand of God the Father Almighty* (COL 3:1)? The word "seated" here means repose after conflict. The Cross is left behind with all of its dust, thirst, struggle, and pain. Being seated does not mean our Lord is passive. You remember in the book of Genesis, God was said to have rested after creation

(GN 2:2). Did that mean He was tired? Certainly it did not imply His creative arm was weary. Our blessed Lord seeks to recuperate because His work is done. On the Cross our blessed Lord said, *It is finished* (JN 19:30). All the types and figures and symbols of the Old Testament has now been completed. Every word of Scripture has been fulfilled. There is no other mediator. The Cross is the perpetual atonement and satisfaction for the sins of men. Our Lord, praying to His heavenly Father, said, *I have finished the work that Thou hast given Me to do* (JN 19:28). That is the meaning of our Lord being seated.

What does it mean: "He is at the right hand of the Father." Well, the right hand implies power, and it means that He has the power of God and has power throughout the universe. The right hand does not mean a physical nearness; it means a sharing of glory. Our Lord is acting as a mediator between God and man; that is His power.

The Ascension of our blessed Lord is described in sacred Scripture, too, as a high priest entering the sanctuary beyond the veil (HEB 6:19). "Beyond the veil" is a rather unusual expression. What does it mean? It refers to something in the Old Testament. In the Temple of Jerusalem, and in the Tabernacle in the desert before, was hanging before the Holy of Holies a very heavy, gorgeous, and mysterious veil. It was hung and suspended according to the pattern that was given on the Mount. It was highly embroidered in purple, blue, scarlet, and finely twisted linen. Then the golden cherubim were woven into it as described in the book of Exodus (37:7–8).

Behind the veil lay enshrined the gorgeous symbols of Jewish history and Jewish faith. Behind it was the Holy of Holies. The priest was allowed to enter the Holy of Holies once a year and then only after he had purified himself with blood and sprinkled the veil with blood. When this happened the people had, for one brief moment, some communication, thanks to their priest, with this Holy of Holies, but for the rest of the year it was hidden. From behind that veil the sound of bells and the rustle of the beautiful vestments of the priest and the movement of feet were heard. There was some dim adumbration of a mystery. What must the Jews have said to themselves as they looked at the veil? They knew they could not enter. They must have said, "Separated, separated, cut off we are from God." This sentiment must have continued in the heart of every true man of the Old Testament.

This veil in the New Testament is called the flesh of our Lord. When our blessed Lord died on the Cross, the Temple veil was rent asunder (MK 15:38). It was rent from top to bottom as if to indicate it was not done in any way by the hand of man. In other words, this barrier between heaven and earth, between God and man, was now destroyed. Thanks to the death of Christ there was access to heaven, access to the heavenly Father. There might have been some symbolism in the fact the centurion pierced the side of our blessed Lord (JN 19:34). Sacred Scripture calls His flesh the "Veil," and when His side was pierced, there was revealed the Holy of Holies, which was the heart of the living God. In any case, sin for humanity before the redemption could never enter behind the veil. Now Christ took upon Himself our human nature; He bore it; He lived it; He died in it; and He resumed it after He laid it down. He broke down the middle wall of partition between God and man; thus, He made peace. I look down to my nature laden with sin, and I despair. I look up to Christ's nature; it is now risen and ascended, and I'm full of joy. I look to my own nature, and I see my helplessness. I look up to Christ's nature, I see my hope. I look down to my nature, I see my sin. I look up to His, and I see His Holiness, and it is that Holiness of the human nature of Christ that is risen to heaven.

What does it mean to us? It means many things, but we will just mention two. It means a human nature like ours is in heaven. Think of it, the marvel of what our bodies will be if we live in them the very life of Christ. Secondly, it means we have a high priest in heaven that can sympathize with our weaknesses because He once bore our human lot.

We say there is a human nature in heaven. When God came to this earth He took upon Himself a human nature. Human nature was thrown into the fires of Calvary in reparation for the sins of man. Risen, it now ascends so there is continuity between the Incarnation and the Ascension. In the Incarnation, our Lord took a body, but not just a body to suffer; otherwise He would have taken it for a time. If He took that human nature to suffer for our sakes, why did He not divest Himself of that human nature? After all, His garments had been soiled and stained; they had borne the heat and burdens of the day. Why not throw them off? Well, because human nature was taken not just to atone for our sins. The end and purpose of God coming to this earth was to bring us to perfect union with the Father. How could He do this? By showing our flesh is not a barrier to divine intimacy, by taking it up to heaven itself, by showing those who pass through trials, sufferings, misunderstandings, whatever they be in this life, that they will have their bodies glorified. By sharing in Christ's Cross we share in His glory. The goal of all humanity is in some way reached in the Ascension.

The full beauty of our Lord is returning again to the Father. He brought back with Him something He did not have when He came to this earth. He brought His divinity, yes; He took His divinity back with Him. He also took something else back. He took back the human nature. The most blessed and wonderful truth is taught in that fact. Remember our Lord reiterated it when He was talking to Caiaphas, and He told him that one day he would see the Son of man seated at the right hand of power (MT 26:64). Human nature, which was so humiliated, was no longer a humiliated human nature, became glorified. His Ascension is the true carrying of that ring of humanity, complete in all its parts, body, and soul, up to the very throne of God. The purpose of the Incarnation is to be our marvel, to be our pattern. In a certain sense, because He is the new Adam in heaven, you and I are there. We are there potentially so long as we remain in the state of grace on this earth.

But that's not the only reason He took a human nature with Him. He also took a human nature in order that He might be able to sympathize with our own weaknesses. The epistle to the Hebrews has a beautiful text on this point; it reads, *It is not as if our High Priest was incapable of feeling for us in our humiliations. He has been brought through every trial, fashioned as we are, only sinless* (HEB 4:15). Our blessed Lord in heaven is our High Priest. He is our mediator. He is one who can understand us. He's not apart from us because He had our human nature. His human nature, when it was on this earth, was so sensitive that it was thrilled by the beauty of a lily, was moved by the fall of a wounded sparrow. It was keenly touched by anything that could touch a human heart, whether high or low, good or bad, friend or enemy.

No man can be beyond the reach of that all-comprehending sympathy because no man can ever be beyond the embrace of that love. He can sympathize with the poor because He was poor, with the weary and heavy laden because He has been tired and worn, with the lonely and misrepresented and persecuted, simply because He has been in that position. Because He was tried, tried in mind as well as in heart, tried by fear, by sad surprise, by mental perplexity, with a hard conflict with evil and great spiritual depression, He's able to feel to the uttermost for the keenest sorrows of our earthly lot. And the beauty of it all is that this tried One is without sin. And that is what enabled Him to drink in sympathy, and nothing but sympathy and all of sorrow, simply because He was without sin. Thus, we have a human nature in heaven that knows all of our weaknesses and all of our trials. What a beautiful hope this is to all of us, a high priest who can understand our infirmities.

Now that He has taken this human nature and is in glory at the right hand of the Father, what does He do there? Has He no work? Certainly! He's a mediator; we might almost say He is constantly showing His scars to His heavenly Father and saying, "See these, I was wounded in the house of those who love Me. I love men. I suffered for them! Forgive them, heavenly Father." He is our sacrifice; He is ever present before the Father. As Scripture puts it, *ever making intercession for us* (HEB 7:25).

You see we often get a wrong understanding of the life of our blessed Lord. We think of Him as living on this earth preaching the Beatitudes and suffering. Our blessed Lord did not come down just for that. He is living, making intercession for us, the representative of all who invoke Him. He has finished the work of justice on earth because He paid the debt of sin, but the work of mercy in heaven is unfinished. That goes on and on because we need His intercession.

I would like to continue speaking of the mystery of the Ascension, but we ought to treat one other point in the Creed. Our Lord said He would come to judge the world (MT 24:30). No other teacher ever said that. He said He would return as the Judge seated at the Throne of Glory, attended by angels to judge all men according to their works. Imagination recoiled at the thought of any human being able to penetrate into the depths of consciences, to fetter out the hidden motives and pass judgment on them for all eternity.

This final judgment is not hidden from the eyes of God nor from man. As our Lord put it:

> And then the sign of the Son of man will be seen in heaven. Then it is that all the tribes of the land will mourn and they will see the Son of man coming upon the clouds of heaven with great power and glory and He will send out His angels with a loud blast of the trumpet to gather His elect from the four winds, from one end of heaven to the other. (MT 24:30–31)

When He comes, it will not be just to judge a mere circumscribed area of the earth in which He labored and revealed Himself. It will be to reveal Himself and to judge all nations and all empires. He refuses to tell us when. He only says it will be sudden, like a flash of lightning (MT 24:27).

The Savior is the Judge. What a beautiful way to have a judgment. Can you imagine any earthly judge saying to a criminal before him, "You are guilty. I am going to take all of your sins and crimes upon myself. I will suffer for you." Our blessed Lord took upon Himself all of our sins as we stood before the bar of divine justice, and He who suffered for us will come to judge us. What a judgment it will be when we see the One who loved us so much, and as the Gospel of Matthew puts it:

And when the Son of man shall come in his majesty, and all the angels with him, then shall he sit upon the seat of his majesty. And all nations shall be gathered together before him: and he shall separate them one from another, as the shepherd separateth the sheep from the goats: And he shall set the sheep on his right hand, but the goats on his left.

Then shall the king say to them that shall be on his right hand: Come, ye blessed of my Father, possess you the kingdom prepared for you from the foundation of the world. For I was hungry, and you gave me to eat: I was thirsty, and you gave me to drink: I was a stranger, and you took me in: naked, and you covered me: sick, and you visited me: I was in prison, and you came to me.

Then shall the just answer him, saying: Lord, when did we see thee hungry and fed thee: thirsty and gave thee drink? Or when did we see thee a stranger and took thee in? Or naked and covered thee? Or when did we see thee sick or in prison and came to thee?

And the king answering shall say to them: Amen I say to you, as long as you did it to one of these my least brethren, you did it to me. Then he shall say to them also that shall be on his left hand: Depart from me, you cursed, into everlasting fire, which was prepared for the devil and his angels.

For I was hungry and you gave me not to eat: I was thirsty and you gave me not to drink. I was a stranger and you took me not in: naked and you covered me not: sick and in prison and you did not visit me.

Then they also shall answer him, saying: Lord, when did we see thee hungry or thirsty or a stranger or naked or sick or in prison and did not minister to thee?

Then he shall answer them, saying: Amen: I say to you, as long as you did it not to one of these least, neither did you do it to me.

And these shall go into everlasting punishment: but the just, into life everlasting. (MT 25:31–46)

Such is the Gospel of Matthew and the story of the return of our Lord. The point is our blessed Lord took upon Himself a pattern of human nature. Human nature was something like a die a government makes when it wishes to mint coins. When the die is fashioned, millions of coins can be fashioned like unto it. Christ, our pattern man, was born; He suffered, He overcame temptations, and He rose from the dead and was glorified at the right hand of the Father. We are the coins. Because He was born, we are to be born, not physically, but spiritually. Because He denied Himself and suffered, we are to deny ourselves. The Cross becomes the condition of the empty tomb, and once our life is patterned upon His Crucifixion, then our life shall be patterned upon His glorious Resurrection and His glorious Ascension. Are we His coins? He will ask for coins and He will say, "Whose inscription is there on it, is it Caesar's?" Do we belong to the world, or do we belong to God? May it be so.

16

HOLY SPIRIT

In this lesson we come to a detail of the Creed which states, "I believe in the Holy Ghost." "Holy Ghost" and "Holy Spirit" may be used interchangeably. It might be well to introduce this particular subject by pondering on some questions which you have probably asked yourself many times.

"Would it have been better for me to have lived in the days of our blessed Lord?"

"Have I missed much by not being a contemporary of the incarnate life of God who walked this earth?"

"Did we lose something?"

"Is the twentieth century at a disadvantage being so far removed from Him?"

In answer to those questions it must be admitted that there would have been some advantages living at the time of our blessed Lord. We could have heard His voice and been tremendously impressed by the ring of its authority. Parents could have brought their children to Him to be blessed. Sinners would have been charmed by the majesty of His bearing. All of us would have been stirred by the eloquence of His words, as were the police when they set out to arrest our blessed Lord. They were arrested by His eloquence. When they went back to the Temple authorities, they said to the police, *Why did you not arrest Him?* And they said, *No man ever spoke as that Man spoke* (JN 7:45–46).

These would have been some advantages, but we must remember the words of our blessed Lord, who said it was better for us that He go. This is what He said the night of the Last Supper. It was only a few hours before His agony in the garden and just the night before His death on the Cross; He said to His Apostles:

> Now I am going back to Him who sent Me. I can say
> truly, it is better for you that I should go away. He who
> is to befriend you will not come to you unless I do go,
> but if only I make my way there I will send Him to you.
> (JN 16:7)

Our Lord was saying it was expedient that He go, for if He goes not, the Holy Spirit would not come to us. If our Lord had remained on earth, we could have gotten no closer than to have seen Him with our eyes and to have heard Him with our ears or possibly, even an embrace. It would have been a sensible outer love. But if He left, then He could send us His Spirit; then He would not be an example to copy; then He would be a veritable life to be lived. Certainly, we have lost His corporal presence, but the spiritual presence has taken its place. Christ is no longer localized, external, but He's indwelling, vivifying, not in one place but in His Church and in the souls that belong to It.

Are we at a disadvantage? No, we are at a great advantage. Do not think that if you had lived in the time of our blessed Lord it would have been any easier to have believed in His divinity than it would be to believe in the divinity of

His Church now. Those who missed Him, miss the Church now. Look at the Apostles; they did not understand the meaning of His death until the Holy Spirit came upon them at Pentecost. It is vanity for us to say we would have understood our Lord better than the Apostles.

Now that brings us to some lessons of the Holy Spirit, and we are going to enumerate about four of them. The Holy Spirit, first of all, reveals the Son, that is to say the Son of God, Christ. The Holy Spirit reveals the Son as the Son reveals the Father. When our blessed Lord was on this earth, He revealed the heavenly Father. It was only thanks to Him that we knew how much love the Father had for us. The Father so loved the world that He sent His only begotten Son into this world. The night of the Last Supper, Philip said to Him, *Show us the Father,* and our Lord said to him, *Philip, have I been with you all this time and still you do not understand the Father and I are one?* (JN 14:8–11). It was the Father's love that sent the Son, so our blessed Lord was a kind of a prism. When the sun shines through a prism, it splits up into the seven rays of the spectrum. Thanks to our blessed Lord, we understand the full love and goodness of the heavenly Father.

Just as the Son revealed the Father, our Lord said He would send the Holy Spirit to reveal the Son. These are the words of our Lord, *And He will bring honor to Me because it is from Me that He will derive what He makes plain to you because all that belongs to the Father belongs to Me* (JN 16:13–15). In these words our blessed Lord is saying once He ascends to the Father, then all of the spiritual blessings won by Him on Calvary would be conveyed to us by the Holy Spirit. For our blessed Lord had said during His earthly life we would not understand His life. We would not receive all the merits of His life until the Spirit came to this earth, and the great role of the Holy Spirit is to stand behind the scenes to make Christ more real. Hence, the Apostles did not understand the Crucifixion until after Pentecost.

St. Paul goes so far as to say no one can call Jesus "Lord," except by the Spirit. Yes, you can pronounce the word "Jesus," but you do not know Jesus is the Christ, the Son of God, the Savior of the world, the Lord of the universe, except by the Holy Spirit. If you believe in the divinity of Christ by this time, it is through the Holy Spirit you believe, not through any words of mine. I am giving you only certain motives of credibility, but the full assurance of it comes from the Spirit. As the telescope reveals not itself, but the stars beyond, so the Holy Spirit reveals not Himself, but Christ. Just think how we are able in this age of ours to communicate with distant parts of the earth thanks to electric or light waves. Why can't our Lord, who dwells in heaven, be within whispering distance of us through His Holy Spirit?

Our blessed Lord said to His Apostles, *It is only for a short time I am with you, my children. I will not leave you orphans* (JN 14:18). Then He promised His Spirit would abide with them forever as another comforter.

He was their comfort on earth, and now His Spirit would be their comfort, their Paraclete, their advocate. Listen to the words of our Lord: *I will ask the Father and He will give you another comforter, one who would dwell with you forever. It is the Truth-giving Spirit, whom the world cannot receive, because it cannot see Him, cannot recognize Him* (JN 14:16–17). Our Lord is here saying that the world cannot understand the Holy Spirit because the world goes only by the evidence of the eyes and the ears. It cannot see the Holy Spirit.

In these words our Lord speaks to us from without, but the Holy Spirit speaks to us from within. Does this mean the Holy Spirit is to be a substitute for Christ? No! The Holy Spirit will make Christ more real than ever. Hear the words of our Lord: *And that day you shall know that I am in the Father, and you in Me, and I in you* (JN 17:21). How would He be in us? By revealing His hidden excellence in our hearts. St. Paul said, *If we have known Christ according to the flesh, we know him so no longer* (2 CO 5:16). Now we know Him in another way, we know Him through the Holy Spirit; therefore, the Holy Spirit, as our Lord said, will bear witness to Him, not to Himself. One almost gets the impression the different persons of the Trinity were hiding. It is almost as if the Father hid Himself for the sake of the Son, who revealed Him, and it almost seems the Son was now hiding Himself for the sake of the Holy Spirit. The Holy Spirit seems to hide Himself, too, for He does not manifest Himself.

The word "hiding" is not a proper word to use. We can make our idea clear by quoting the words of our blessed Lord, *He will not utter a message of His own; He will utter the message that has been given to Him, and He will make plain to you what is to come* (JN 16:13). The Holy Spirit witnesses not to Himself, but to the Son. Those who have the Spirit understand Christ. We often hear people say, "Oh, Jesus was a great teacher. Really He, Lincoln, and Plato have done a great deal for the world. If we wanted to solve our economic and social problems, all we would have to do is read the Beatitudes of Jesus." Some people do not understand Jesus is the Christ, the Son of God, and the Redeemer of the world. For them, Jesus is just another man. Why do they not know Him? Because they do not have the Spirit. Why do they not have the Spirit? Because they have not obeyed the law of God. Our Lord said, *If you love Me, keep My Commandments* (JN 14:15). Then the Holy Spirit will manifest Himself to us.

The purpose of the Holy Spirit then is as an artist. He draws a picture of our Lord on the canvas. He makes Him real to us so we understand Him. Just as the artist stays outside of the canvas, so the Holy Spirit is staying outside the Christ, whom He reveals. To be filled with the Spirit is to be filled with Christ. When we put on the mind of Christ, we put on the will of Christ. There is nothing in the Gospel that gives us an answer to many of the problems of life and the difficulties of the day. If we were just simply to imitate the life of our blessed Lord as found in the Gospel, we would all have to be carpenters. How do we know what to do? The spirit of Christ manifests what we are to do in each and every circumstance: the proper word to say, the right action to do, the kind of charity to perform.

The spirit of Christ in our souls manifests Christ to us. St. Paul uses the example of the human mind to make clear the Holy Spirit. He asks, *How do we know the thoughts of another person?* (I COR 2:11). It is because we have a soul and a spirit, just as he has. Engineers understand engineers; brokers understand brokers; and students of the same college understand each other. They all have the same spirit. They have both the natural and supernatural spirit of Christ. How do we understand Christ? We must have the spirit of Christ. Those who share His spirit understand one another. The natural spirit, the purely human spirit, the spirit not yet holy, cannot grasp the deep meaning of Christ. It's almost like expecting a canary in a cage to learn Shakespeare. He cannot do so. You would have to put your own brain inside of the canary's brain. As St. Paul said, *The natural man receiveth not the things of the spirit of God, for they are foolishness unto him. Neither can he know them because they are spiritually discerned* (I CO 2:14).

Teaching people about Christ and the mysteries of our holy Faith is almost like trying to teach a blind man color unless those people are ready to receive the spirit of Christ Himself. Converts who take instruction come to know that Jesus is our Lord. Where do they learn it? From the Spirit. The first lesson we gave in this course, we said one becomes interested in the Church simply because one has received a grace that illumined the mind and strengthened the will. The Holy Spirit woos the soul, draws it to closer fellowship, to more intimate union, becomes our sanctifier just as the Father is our Creator and the Son is our Redeemer. This is one of the fruits of the Spirit in our daily lives.

We come to another point, namely, the Holy Spirit in relationship to our understanding of sin. The night of the Last Supper, our blessed Lord said the Holy Spirit would convict us of sin: *The Spirit will come and it will be for Him to prove the world wrong about sin. They have not found belief in Me* (JN 15:25–26). When do we come to a real understanding of sin? Our Lord says here, through the Holy Spirit.

No one really grasps the evil of sin if he thinks it is just the breaking of a law. When we have the Spirit of Christ, we understand sin is doing harm to one we love. The Crucifixion is the manifestation of sin, unbelief in its essence, the absolute refusal to have the love and the blessings of God. The Holy Spirit reveals to us that sin is the refusal to accept that deliverance purchased by Christ. Nothing but the Spirit can convince us of sin. How often our conscience can be smothered by repeated evil actions and rationalize our evil deeds. Public opinion sometimes even approves of sin. The Holy Spirit is in us and reveals to us that all unbelief is sin tied up with the Crucifixion, with the Cross. Then we begin to understand the Cross is a kind of an autobiography. We can see our own lives there: our pride in the crown of thorns, our avarice in the nailing of hands, our flight from grace in the pinioned feet, our rebellious loves in the pierced side, and our disrespect to the body and the flesh hanging from Him like purple rags. The blood is the ink and His skin is the parchment and our sins constitute the writing. Every sinner who has the spirit of Christ always thinks of sin in relationship to the Crucifixion. Then our blessed Lord becomes our hope.

There is nothing like the enlightened conscience when we are not under a law. Those who really loved Christ were beyond it. The Holy Spirit gives us a sense of holiness, and holiness is separation from the world. St. Paul says his conscience was enlightened by the Holy Spirit. Whenever we do wrong, it is not the law; it is not the Commandments; it is the Spirit that tells us we are breaking off a relationship with love. St. Paul tells us as we sin we crucify Christ anew in our hearts (HEB 6:6). The life of a true Christian is not so much concerned with the avoidance of sin; rather, it is an attempt to reproduce in ourselves the life of Christ. As our Lord said of His heavenly Father, *All things that are pleasing to Him, that I do* (JN 8:29). We say to the Trinity, "All things that are pleasing to God, that we do." Our attitude toward sin is done through the inspiration of the Holy Spirit.

I proposed to mention many other effects of the Holy Spirit in our lives. We will talk about the Holy Spirit in relationship to the body because hardly anyone ever thinks of that. St. Paul asks, *Know ye not that your body is the temple of God, and the Holy Spirit dwelleth in you?* (I CO 6:19). How does our body become the temple of God? It is made holy by the indwelling of the Father, Son, and Holy Spirit in our soul. Remember when our blessed Lord went into the Temple in Jerusalem and drove out the buyers and the sellers? The Pharisees asked Him for a sign if He had such authority, and our blessed Lord said, *Destroy this Temple and in three days I will rebuild it* (JN 2:19). He was not referring to the earthly, material temple in construction under Herod. He was referring to the temple of His body. What is a temple? A temple is a place where God dwells, and since He was the Son of God in the flesh, His body was the supreme Temple.

Our bodies, when we are in the state of grace and possess the life of Christ in our souls, also become temples. Thus, the Holy Spirit gives medicine its dignity. A truly spiritual man cannot treat a sick person as a guinea pig. Our Lord has a double glory: one, with the Father, for He is glorified at the right hand, and He is glorified in us. He said, *The Holy Spirit shall glorify Me* (JN 16:14). The Holy Spirit glorifies Him in us by making us witnesses to Christ, declaring Him in our minds and in our actions.

Let the practical result of this lesson be to pray to the Holy Spirit that you may know Christ in the fullness of His Gospel and the love of the Father, that you may understand He is the source of power, the Holy Spirit. Our Lord said, *I will send you power from on high* (LK 24:49). Every day of my priestly life I pray for the power of the Holy Spirit. The power that is not human, not physical, not intellectual; rather, a power coming solely from living the Christ life, the power to influence people, the power to impress you with the divinity of the Holy Spirit.

If I have given you any deeper comprehension and closer understanding of the beautiful love of the Trinity, I trust you will, in gratitude, sometime say a little prayer to the Holy Spirit for me that I may more in mind, heart, and body show forth the Spirit of Christ.

17

CHURCH: BODY OF CHRIST

After having reviewed the life of our blessed Lord and His revelation of Himself as the Son of God, His bond to the Father and to the Holy Spirit, we come to the subject of the Church. What do you think of when you first hear the word "Church," an institution, an organization, a kind of an administrative body? It is the way we have too often presented the Church. We will talk about the Church in terms of the people of God and as the Mystical Body of Christ.

We look at the Bible as an historical record, and we find it is God always in search of man; it is not man in search of God. Man does seek God, but not with the same intensity with which God seeks man. Just think how much the thought and love of man is in the mind and heart of God. What is the first reflex thought that we find in sacred Scripture of God, not the first description of Him creating the world, but the first thought He has about Himself and within Himself? You would almost guess His first thought would be about His life, His truth, and His love; yet that is not the first thought in Scripture. Open Genesis and you will find God's first thought about Himself is *Let us make man* (GN 1:26). Think of it, as if God could not exist without man. God does not need man to complete Himself, to fulfill a need, but He needs man as a kind of gift; He must have someone to whom He can show His love.

Therefore, the first monologue we touch in sacred Scripture is the monologue of God thinking about man. What are the first dialogues in Scripture? The first question in Scripture is God saying to man, *Adam, where art thou? Man, why are you hiding? Why do you run from Me?* (GN 3:9). And the next dialogue is about the neighbor. God says to Cain, *Where is thy brother, Abel?* (GN 4:9). God is immersed in the thought of man. Here we find the first two laws of God, love of God and love of neighbor, in the two questions "Man, where art thou?" and "Where is thy brother?"

At the beginning, we find humanity receives a call from God to intimate communion with Him. God will not let man go. How does He deal with humanity when humanity begins to multiply? In this way, out of all the peoples of the world He chose one people who were to be called His people. This group or this special people were to be the means of bringing salvation to everyone else in the world. Who were His people? His people were the people of Israel, and He called them, first, through Abraham. He governed them through Moses; He ruled them through the judges and the kings; He threatened; He pleaded; He coaxed; He warned; He loved through the prophets. Over and over in the Old Testament we find that God, who loves humanity, deals with them through this particular group. God says in the book of Exodus, *You shall be My peculiar possession above all people, for all the earth is Mine, and you shall be to Me a priestly Kingdom, a holy nation* (19:5–6). God speaks and says, *You shall be My people and I shall be your God* (19:6). And through the centuries these facts stand out.

God has a special name for His people; He calls them a *qahal* in Hebrew. We will often use that word; it means God's elect, His chosen ones, Israel. The word is used about two hundred times in the Old Testament. Later on, when the Hebrew Old Testament was translated into Greek, that word *qahal* was translated to *ecclesia*. *Ecclesia* in Greek means church. We get the word "ecclesiastical" from it. Hence, whenever we hear the word *qahal,* or people of God, we may think of it in Greek as *ecclesia,* or in English as "church." That's the first point. Secondly, God always dealt with His people through one man whom He appointed as head and as representative: Abraham at one time, Isaac another, Jacob, Moses, kings, and prophets.

And thirdly, because Israel was His people, He made a treaty with them, a pact, a covenant, an agreement that involved mutual obligations. The Hebrew word for covenant is *berith;* you've often heard the word. It appears 275 times in the Scripture, and *berith* means they owed something to God, and God, in His turn, would bless them. As He said, *Above all the nations of the earth they would be blessed* (DT 7:14). Israel was to be His witness, for the salvation of all mankind would be effected through them. Finally, you have heard this when we spoke about all of the prophecies concerning our blessed Lord, that the fulfillment would come the day that Christ Himself would appear. This would be the perfection of all of the prophets. This is why the people of God were chosen to be the seed out of which redemption would come to the world. Finally, one day, when the fullness of time came, Christ did appear, and there was fulfilled the prophecy of Ezekiel, who said, *I Myself will seek My sheep, and I will visit them* (EZK 34:11).

God appears in the form of human nature, takes upon

Himself the form of a man. One day a beautiful woman, a virgin, brought a child to an old man; it was in the Temple of Jerusalem (LK 2:25–35). The old man's name was Simeon. He had often said a prayer many Jews were saying in those days because they knew the time was near for the coming of the Messiah. We mentioned that Herod, who was not a Jew but an Edomite, was not surprised when the wise men came. He said he would bring gifts, but the gift he promised to bring was the sword.

There are some flowers that open only in the evening; Simeon, the old man, was one of those flowers. Imagine the ecstasy of this old man when he embraced this child, and his first words were *Now I am ready to die. This is the end. This is all I've lived for* (LK 2:29–32). He speaks to the mother, and notice how he speaks of Israel and the Gentiles. Remember we said that the people of God were to be a light to all nations of the world. Simeon looks backward and forward; he looks backward to the people of God of which he was a priest and says, *This is the glory of Thy people, Israel, this Babe* (2:34). Then he looks forward: *This is the Light which shall give revelation to the Gentiles* (2:32). In other words, he saw in this Babe the maker of a new covenant, the founder of a new *qahal,* but he also saw in Him a sign to be contradicted by the very people to whom He came to bring salvation. Christ who was born was not someone who came by surprise; He's related to all of the people of God through the centuries. If you pick up the Gospels and read the two genealogies of our blessed Lord, you will find that in one instance the genealogy of our blessed Lord goes back to Abraham (MT 1:1–16), and the other genealogy goes back to Adam (JN 1:1–18). What does this mean? It means that this new head of the *qahal,* this expected of the nations and God made man, is related to the people of God, who are to be the instrument of the world's salvation.

When you hear of our blessed Lord founding a Church, a *qahal,* or a people of God, you must not think this is an innovation. Everything our Lord is saying is related to this people of God in the Old Testament. See how He sustains the relationship? First, He chooses the twelve Apostles. It is likely they were even related to the twelve tribes in some way. He chose one Apostle as His representative. We will find out his name later. Looking back on the Old Law, He said, *I came not to destroy it, but to fulfill it* (MT 5:17). He gathers these new people around Himself in order to renovate and revivify Israel, to make a new Israel. If the old Israel would reject Him, He would not eventually reject Israel. The prophet Hosea, in the Old Testament, and Paul, in the New Testament, says, *We, the new people of God, are only a branch that is grafted onto the tree; we are not the root, Israel is the root* (RM 11:17). St. Paul foretells a day when the root will be glorified and will surpass the Gentiles in glory as Israel returns (RM 15:12).

When our Lord does come to use the word *qahal,* He calls it "My *qahal.* I will found My Church, My people." The bond that Christ establishes with this new *qahal* is not a bond of law; it's a bond of love. The best moment for establishing this bond was a banquet, where His Twelve sat about Him in love. Just as Moses often sprinkled blood upon the people as a sign of covenant, so He said He will make a new covenant, a new pact, a new testament. And there will not be sprinkling of the blood of goats, bullocks, and sheep, but He will give His own blood and say, *This is the blood of the new covenant, the new testament, the new pact. This is the bond that will unite all of My people together* (MT 26:28).

Do you see the Church is not an institution? Maybe

you've said, "I do not want an institution standing between God and me." After all, you have a right to communication with God, but the Church is not an institution standing between you and God. Israel was not between the world and God. Think of the Church in somewhat the fashion of the body. Do you ever say, "I do not want your lips, eyes, and hands and so forth, standing between me and you"? After all, how can I communicate anything to you except by something visible, tangible, and carnal? Anything visible that you see about me or will ever see about me, is nothing but a sign of an invisible soul; the carnal is token of the spiritual. When our blessed Lord came to this earth and took upon Himself a human body, you would not say, "I do not want this body of Christ standing between me and my love of Christ." The only way of the Incarnation is to communicate the divine through the human.

This human nature of our blessed Lord, this body of His, was the instrument of His divinity. When our blessed Lord came as Priest, Prophet, and King, everything He did was done through the power and means of His human nature. If you heard our blessed Lord speak on the shores of Galilee, you would not say, "Oh, it is only a human tongue that is speaking." When He said to you, *I am the Truth* (JN 14:6), would you say, "How do I know God is speaking to me?" That is why He became man. If He said to you, "I forgive your sins," would you say, "All I see is a lifted hand and the movement of lips"? No, His body was the means by which He made Himself applicable to us.

Therefore, the best way to understand that the Church is not just an institution is to understand it somewhat in the fashion of the body of Christ, and that's the way St. Paul understood the Church and the way we have it in sacred Scrip-

ture. Our blessed Lord all through the Gospels is saying He
is going to establish a new body, a new *qahal*, a new people of
God. After all, when people are united for a given purpose,
they are a body. Our Lord did not use the word "body" precisely because His own physical body was before everyone.
He used the word "Kingdom" as the Jews could understand,
but when St. Paul was talking to the pagans, he had to use
a word which was more understandable by them, namely,
"body." But our Lord communicated exactly the same idea.
He said the new people He would communicate and unite
with Himself would be related to Him as branches and vine:
You are the branches, I am the Vine (JN 15:5). He said He would
give the truth to them: *My truth I give to you, My power I give
you* (JN 14:27). Then He communicated the power to forgive
sins.

Our blessed Lord said He would develop and form a new
body, which would be very small at first, like a mustard seed,
and then grow and spread throughout the entire world. But
what was the nucleus of this body? Well, we've already hinted
at that. The nucleus, the raw material of this new body, was
the Apostles. My own human body is made up of millions
and millions of cells. Yet it is one because it is vivified by one
soul, governed by an invisible mind, presided over by a visible head. All who later on will be incorporated into the new
Body of Christ will be vivified by one soul, the Holy Spirit,
governed by an invisible mind, Christ in heaven, and presided over by a visible head, the one whom Christ chose from
the beginning to bear the keys of His Kingdom.

Therefore, this Body of Christ was to be the prolongation
of His Incarnation. Our Lord was to grow and expand much
like a cell. We sometimes think a Church is formed by all of
us coming together, just like we form a tennis club. That's

not the way the Body of Christ was formed! God's power was in the midst of His people. Even your human body when it began to be was not formed that particular way. It was formed from cells of life, and those cells expanded outward. So the Body of Christ does not grow like a house grows, by the addition of brick to brick and door to door and wall to wall. It grows like a cell. First, there is this divine life, which came to this earth; namely, God in man. It starts with the humanity of Christ, this body of His. Now He says He's going to form this new body. It will not be a moral body or a political body, so He has to give it a new name, and the name given to it through the centuries is "Mystical," to indicate the unity binding it together does not come from men; it comes from His spirit, from Himself. That is why there had to be a Pentecost, to put a soul into this body, as we will see a little later on.

These twelve Apostles our Lord gathered to Himself were very much like the chemicals in a laboratory. They were very individualistic; they were like the hydrogen, phosphates, and sulfur in a laboratory. In fact, we have in a laboratory one hundred percent of all the chemicals that enter into the constitution of a baby. Why can't we make a baby? Because we lack the vivifying, unifying power which is the soul. The Apostles, disconnected and disjointed, they could not form this Body of Christ. They could be formed only by Christ sending His Spirit into them through the physical body of our Lord. It was God who talked; it was God who governed it; it was God who sanctified. Through this new Body of Christ, His Church, His new *qahal,* His new people of God, the new Israel, He will teach; He will govern; He will sanctify. This is the Church. You see, it's a long way from an institution.

Sometime pick up the Acts of the Apostles and read the story of the conversion of St. Paul (AC 9:1–22). St. Paul was a member of the old *qahal,* old Israel. He would not accept the revelation of the new *qahal,* and he started to persecute the Church. The time is well within ten years after the Ascension of our blessed Lord into heaven. That's very important to remember. The Church was beginning to spread through the entire Roman Empire, and Paul decided to go into Syria and persecute the Church in Damascus. By this time, the early members of the Church were much disturbed by this learned Saul, for that was his Jewish name. I'm sure many members of the Church must have prayed to the good Lord to send a coronary thrombosis to Saul! They must have said, "Dear Lord, send us someone to answer Saul!" He heard their prayers. He sent Paul, that was his Roman name.

On his way to Damascus, a light shone on him, and he was thrown from his beast and he heard a voice saying, *Saul, Saul, why persecutest thou Me?* (AC 9:4). Me? Why did our Lord say that? He was in heaven, how could anybody persecute Him? No wonder St. Paul asked, *Who art thou? And our Lord answered, I am Jesus, whom thou persecutest* (9:5). Saul must have thought, After all, I'm only persecuting the members of the Church in Damascus. How could I be persecuting you? How? If someone steps on your foot, do your lips complain? Someone strikes your body; does your head protest? Christ, the Son of the living God, is the head of the Mystical Body, the Church. When anyone strikes the Body, they strike Him! And that is why our Lord protested. What then is the Church? It is the people of God prolonged through the centuries in us, His poor members. The Church is the mystery of God in the world for the salvation of the world.

18

PETER: VICAR OF CHRIST

Thus far we have stressed the idea that the Church is the Mystical Body of Christ. It is visible inasmuch as it has members that walk the earth; it is invisible inasmuch as Christ is the invisible Head, and the life of it is the Holy Spirit. We also said that this Church is a society, an assembly, a *qahal*, related in some way to the assembly and *qahal* of the Old Testament, and through this Church God is diffusing the merits of Calvary.

We wish to show Peter holds the primacy not only of honor but also of jurisdiction over the Church. Peter is the vicar of Christ, the first Pontiff, the first Pope. It is very strange for those who believe it is in Scripture that the Church is the Mystical Body of Christ, who will not also admit a head. After all, how are we to know that the Body exists on this earth? It is very easy to know Christ was walking this earth simply because men saw Him. After His Ascension, how would men know His Mystical Body and where His Life was to be found? Our blessed Lord did not leave these questions unanswered until He gave a sign we would know His body. The sign was the sign of all living things. How does any life manifest itself? Does the unity of life manifest itself through the head, which is the source of the movements of the body? The head is a symbol of the unity of life. Legs and arms can be amputated without destroying the unity of life, but cut off the head and it's the end of life.

In the social order, does every club, group, society, or nation have a head, a president, or a king? Even in the psychological order, it is natural for there to be a consciousness of headship. In an infant there is a great complexity and crisscrossing of activities: vegetative, emotional, mechanical, vital, and others. As the child develops, gradually it reaches a point where all organic activities evolve in the personal pronoun "I." It comes to a consciousness of unity and a center of reference, namely, the primacy of personality.

If our blessed Lord established a life here on earth and then didn't name a head, we would eventually, in the psychological order, have to become conscious of a head. But in that half-pagan city of Caesarea Philippi (MT 16:13-18), our blessed Lord did name a head and considered three possible forms of church government. How would His Mystical Body be governed? There might be three ways: democratic, aristocratic, or theocratic. The democratic would be one in which a majority vote decides, in which everyone has an entirely different opinion of what is to be the truth and to be the law. The aristocratic is an appeal not so much for the majority or the masses, but an appeal to an aristocracy, a house of parliament, a senate, a congress, or a house of lords. The theocratic is one in which God chooses one man, as He chose Abraham, Isaac, Jacob, and Moses; and He guides, protects, and directs this man.

Our blessed Lord did not establish His Church without considering all of these possible forms of government. For He began with the democratic, and His question was *Who do men say the Son of man is?* (MT 16:13). Notice "men." In other words, "If you took a poll, if you took a vote, what is the general opinion concerning Me?" What answer did our Lord get? The answer was *Some say you're John the Baptist, and others Elias, and others Jeremiah, and others one of the prophets* (16:14). No unity, no certitude. Leave the government of the Church to individual interpretation, and you get contrary and contradictory views. Eternal Truth, who said that not a single iota of His teaching should be changed, could never accept a government in which men could not agree, and so He had nothing for it but the withering scorn of silence.

Next, He appeals to the aristocratic: *Who do you say that I am: you, My twelve Apostles; you, My aristocracy; you, My chosen group; Who am I?* (16:15). There was no answer. First of all, there had been no head appointed as their spokesman; furthermore, some of them had doubts. Thomas certainly had doubts; Judas was not very certain of His financial sagacity; Philip was troubled about relations to the heavenly Father. Our blessed Lord could not build His Church upon an aristocracy alone. At this point there was one man without the consent of the others who stepped forward and spoke in the name of all and gave a right response. His answer was *Thou art the Christ, the Son of the living God* (16:16). Here is one man with divine illumination who speaks in the name of all, who makes the confession of the divinity of Christ, who affirms faith in Him, who is to be chosen as the head of His Mystical Body. This is the theocratic form of Church government.

Before we go into the text, what objections could there be? One objection that is urged against this particular text is that our blessed Lord did not build His Church on Peter; He built it upon Peter's confession of faith in His divinity. This is not true, because our blessed Lord was addressing Peter in the second-person singular, as we shall see. Our Lord said to Peter, *Blessed art thou* (16:17); *I will give to thee* (16:19); *Whatsoever thou shalt bind* (16:19). Here there is no confession of faith. Our blessed Lord is speaking in the second-person singular to a man whose name He changed from Simon to Rock.

Coming back now to our text. Let us go through some of the words. Our blessed Lord said to Simon Peter, *Blessed art thou* (16:17). We have heard those words before. They were once spoken by an archangel at the Annunciation to Mary. When the archangel approached Mary to ask her if she would give God a human nature with which He could redeem the world, the angel saluted her, *Blessed art thou* (LK 1:42). Why "blessed"? Because she was to be given the divine privilege of motherhood of Christ. As in the Annunciation, our blessed Lord says to Simon Peter, "Blessed art thou." As Mary was blessed because she was to be the mother of Christ, the Head of the Mystical Body, so Peter is blessed because he is to be the Vicar of Christ and a visible head of the Mystical Body.

Next, our blessed Lord said, *Simon Bar-Jona, blessed art thou, Simon, son of John* (MT 16:17). Our Lord was still calling him by his personal name, his family name. Our Lord had already given him another name, the name of Cephas in Aramaic, which means rock, the name of Peter in English. Then our blessed Lord continued. Apropos of the confession of divinity, our blessed Lord said to Peter, *Flesh and blood have not revealed this to thee* (16:17). In other words, you do not know that I am Christ, the Son of God, by natural instincts or by reason. Just as you do not know by reason alone that Christ is the Son of God. Your reason gives you motives of credibility, but there had to be an illumination from above.

There was a very special illumination of Peter, because he recognized that Christ was not only the Messiah, but also the Son of the Eternal Father.

Remember all of the Apostles were there at Caesarea Philippi, yet our blessed Lord spoke only to one. Our Lord spoke to Peter; note, this is going to be personal, *Thou art the rock* (MT 16:18). Notice the parallel between Peter's confession and our blessed Lord's transfer of power. Peter says, "Thou art the Christ"; our Lord answers, "Thou art the rock." Peter confesses the grandeur of Christ; Christ confesses the grandeur of Peter. Remember, now, that Peter's name is Rock. It was a new name; it was suited to his office. This word "rock" does not appear here for the first time in Scripture. Throughout the Old Testament, God is called Rock. As we are going to see later on, God is also called Key Bearer; God is also called Shepherd. Our blessed Lord is the Son of God, the Rock of the ages, yet He makes Peter a rock. Look through the Old Testament and you'll find instances of how God is called the Rock. Remember that in the book of Exodus (EX 17:6) and in the book of Numbers (NB 20:8), there was a rock that gave forth water, and St. Paul later on says, *And the Rock that followed them was Christ* (I CO 10:4). In other words, that rock Moses struck was a prefigurement of Christ, who is the Eternal Rock.

There are forty references in the Old Testament where God is called a Rock. In the book of Daniel, the Messiah is called the Rock who smashed the statue with the feet of clay to dust (DN 2:45). Our blessed Lord Himself said those who obeyed His Commandments would be likened to a house built upon a rock (MT 7:24). The implication was the Son of God, in the Old Testament, in the book of Isaiah, is called the Rock of Israel. This Christ, as the Son of God, sustained the old *qahal,* so Peter is to sustain the new *qahal,* the new *ecclesia,* or the new Church, as a rock. In other words, there was a communication of the divine power of being a rock from God to Peter. He is the Rock, but He is the invisible Rock; and Peter is to be made the visible Rock of the Mystical Body.

If a technical reference may be permitted, in the Greek of Matthew, where we have the words *Thou art Peter and upon this rock I will build My Church* (MT 16:18), the word for Peter is *Petros* and the word for rock is *petra.* In classical literature, for example, in Homer, you find the word *petros* means a kind of small rock, part of a great and tremendous rock like Gibraltar. Our blessed Lord is really saying to Peter, "Thou art the true *petros* of Me, the divine Petra." Both are persons; Christ the Rock was a person, and Peter the Rock is a person. As the visible body, the Church had Peter as its visible rock foundation. As an invisible spiritual reality, the Mystical Body has Christ in heaven as its spiritual eternal Rock.

Our blessed Lord said, "I will build My Church, My *ecclesia,* My *qahal.*" Our Lord did not say, "I will build My Churches." The Church is His body. Christ can't have many bodies or He would be a physical monstrosity. The whole organic foundation of the Mystical Body is founded on a single man, who is to have divine assistance. Notice our Lord said, "I will build My Church." This same word "build" is used in the book of Genesis. In the Latin translation of the Scriptures, in the Vulgate, it is exactly the same word used to describe how Eve was formed out of Adam and how Christ built His Church. Adam was like an unfinished thing until Eve was formed. Scripture says Christ was to have His fullness in His Bride, the Church. As Eve was built from Adam, so the Church was built from Christ.

Our blessed Lord said, *The gates of hell shall not prevail against it* (MT 16:18), against the Church. Here our Lord is not referring to literal gates but rather to an unseen world. The word "prevail," as "evil shall not prevail," means overpower. Our blessed Lord assures Peter His Church will be indestructible, indefectible, because the gates symbolize power. It was a place where counselors, men of power, and government met. The book of Genesis says that Lot sat at the gate of Sodom (GN 19:1); the book of Ruth says that Boaz took care of legal matters at the gate of Bethlehem (RT 4:1). Hell has its gates, its seat, its council, its treasury of power. This will always be opposed to the Church, but our blessed Lord says the gates of hell shall not prevail. In other words, the Church will be indefectible through the ages. Notice this privilege is not given to the person of Simon, but it's given to Peter. Our blessed Lord said He will be with His Church even unto the consummation of the world (MT 28:20).

Then our Lord added, *I will give to thee the keys of the Kingdom of heaven* (MT 16:19). Imagine, not only is he the foundation stone, but once he is on the inside of this Church he's going to have the keys. Our blessed Lord said, *I am the Door* (JN 10:9). In the book of the Apocalypse, the glorified Christ is described as bearing keys, and the book of Apocalypse states, *So none may shut what He opens and none may open what He shuts* (RV 3:7). Just as the Eternal Rock made a visible rock, as a Good Shepherd is going to make Peter the Shepherd, so the Key Bearer, the Eternal Key Bearer, gives him the keys. In other words, he truly is the Vicar of Christ: *I give to thee the keys of the Kingdom of heaven and then whatsoever thou shalt bind on earth, is bound in heaven. Whatsoever thou shalt loose on earth, is loosed in heaven* (MT 16:19). This means whatever Peter commands, or forbids, he does in the name of Christ. What a tremendous power! Earth and heaven become a single force. For the heavens almost seem to be an echo of earth, as if God was lending His ears in order to hear what His vicar, Peter, was saying. His power is legislative because he can bind and loose. It's a power of discipline that will protect him from error. There is no limit to it, for our blessed Lord said whatsoever he binds, Christ binds.

Here our blessed Lord promised to confer this power upon Peter, but there were other instances in Scripture where He associated Peter with Himself. One particularly interesting moment is the night of the Last Supper. All of the Apostles were gathered together with our blessed Lord, and our Lord spoke to Peter and said, *Behold, Satan has claimed power over all of you so that he may sift you as wheat* (LK 22:31). Notice the plural there; our Lord is saying, "power over all of you." The words of our Lord continue: *But I prayed for thee that thy faith may not fail. When after a while thou hast come back to Me, it is for thee to be the support of thy brethren* (22:32). Notice our blessed Lord says Satan wants all of them. For whom does our Lord pray? Here He is not praying for the Twelve; He's praying for Peter alone. He addresses him in the second-person singular, and He does that because if the foundation stone crumbles, the rest of the edifice fails. Our blessed Lord is also telling Peter he is going to fail, as he will a few hours later, when he will tell the maidservants, *I know not the man!* (MT 26:72). But our Lord says He will come back at Pentecost, and then He will be the support of the Twelve. Isolated and separated from Peter as the Vicar of Christ, the Apostles are weak. We are not to assume this power was given only to Peter, because he was not called Simon then. Simon dies, but Peter lives on. Pius, Leo, and Benedict and others die, but Peter continues unto the consummation of the world.

Another instance of how our Lord associated Peter to Himself was at the payment of the Temple tax. It is the only time in Scripture where God ever associates the human being with Himself under the personal pronoun "we." Just think how proud you were when as a child perhaps your father put his arms around you and said, "We will do this." At the time of the Temple tax payment, our blessed Lord told Peter to pay it, and He said to *pay it for Me and for thee* (MT 17:27). Then He added, *That we may not be scandalized* (JN 21:15). Here He is making Himself one with Peter; Peter is associated with the Master in a way that no one else can ever be associated: "we," Christ and Peter. That is why all Papal encyclicals begin with the word "We."

This particular unity that existed between *Patros* and *Petra,* the invisible Rock and the visible Rock, is now carried after the Resurrection. Our Lord is fishing three times. He says to Peter when He comes to the shore, *Lovest thou Me?* After Peter affirms his love, because there can be no conferring of authority without love, our blessed Lord each time says to him, *Feed my lambs, tend my yearlings, feed my sheep* (JN 21:15-17). Here the power is conferred by the Good Shepherd to Peter, the shepherd. The flock is one because the Shepherd is one, and one man is at the head of the flock. In other words, the Church is to be made up of bishops, priests, and people, as on earth our blessed Lord associated with Himself apostles, disciples, and people; and Peter is to be the head. The words that our blessed Lord used in Greek were *boskine poinine;* in other words, "You have that order, you have a jurisdiction, you have the authority. In order for you to feed My lambs, to feed My sheep, I am transferring My power as Shepherd to you." Then our Lord told Peter how he would die, that he would be crucified. And Peter went to

Rome, where he was crucified. He said that he was not worthy to be crucified in the manner our blessed Lord was, so he asked to be crucified upside down.

The Eternal Rock had told him he was to be the Rock. Where is the foundation rock to be placed if not close to the ground? The Rock that was laid became the foundation stone of the Church, and from that day to this, the Church has a Shepherd, a Rock, a Key Bearer, a Pontiff, a bridge builder between earth and heaven, a Vicar of Christ, a Pope, a Holy Father. One head for the one Body so we know where the Church is. As they said in the first century, *Ubi Petrus ibi ecclesia;* wherever Peter is, there is the Church.

19

AUTHORITY AND INFALLIBILITY

When I was a boy I used to go out to a farm during the summer and I often noticed how chickens used to peck one another. At that time I did not know the meaning of it. Then, there appeared an article in *Scientific American* entitled "The Peck Order." Some scientists, much more curious than I was, marked each chicken in the barnyard a little bit differently so they could spot them, and they noticed there was a kind of chicken hierarchy, an authority, a "four hundred" among the chickens. When they lined up to eat, chicken 25, which lived on the wrong side of the tracks, would always be the last one to be fed or else stay at the end of the barnyard. Then the chickens would begin to try and get into the "four hundred." Chicken 22 would peck 21, and if 21 ran away, then 22 became 21. This is now known in scientific order as the peck order of chickens.

We know that it exists among human beings. We peck at one another in the business world to try to get ahead, trample upon one another. Monkeys do the same thing. Monkey trainers will always watch a group of monkeys to discover which one is the leader, then they train the leader and all of the others follow. I say this driving for authority is both in the animal kingdom and in the human order. When the good Lord came to this earth, He did away with the pecking order, and He introduced an entirely new principle: that the first should be last and the most important should be the servant of all (MK 9:35).

We notice this in two instances in the life of our blessed Lord. One was the night of the Last Supper. Here the twelve Apostles were gathered about our blessed Lord, and He took off His outer robe, covered Himself with a towel, and began washing the feet of the Apostles (JN 13:4–5). When He finished, He said, *You call Me Lord and Master, and you do well, I am your Lord and Master; but if I wash your feet, then you wash the feet of one another* (13:13–14). And He said among the Gentiles, *He who is greatest lords it over the others* (MT 20:25). He told His Apostles to be the least. Here was the introduction of something new in the order of authority; namely, authority is for service, particularly to those who are low and least.

Then He introduced another idea after His Resurrection. The scene was alongside the Sea of Galilee, the Sunday after the Resurrection. There were seven men out in a boat fishing, and our blessed Lord appeared on the shore (JN 21:1–14). John was the first to recognize our blessed Lord, and he said, "It's the Lord!" Impetuous Peter dove into the sea, swam a hundred yards to the shore, and then if you read the Scriptures carefully, you'll find that a few verses later, Peter was back in the boat again. I wonder why he did that. He helped the others drag in the fish. I think the reason was that when he came to the shore, he saw our blessed Lord standing near a fire, reminding him of another fire, about ten days before, the fire in the courtyard of Caiaphas (JN 18:15–18). Peter remembered he had denied our Lord, so he got away from Him.

When he came back, our Lord gave authority to Peter

over the Church. Our Lord had called Himself the Good
Shepherd. Now He made Peter a shepherd. As our Lord in
the Scripture was called the Rock in the Old Testament
many times (2 s 22:2), so He made Peter the little Rock of His
Church. But what was the condition upon which He conferred authority upon Peter? What did He say before He gave
authority? *Feed My lambs, feed My sheep* (JN 21:15-16). Three
times He said, "Do you love Me?" *Do you love Me? Do you love
Me? Do you love Me more than these?* (21:15-17). Only after these
questions does Peter reply, *Yes, Lord, I love You* (21:15). Inciden-
tally, the Greek word which St. Peter used was a very weak
word. His "I love you" was a very human, natural love. Peter
was not going to affirm greater love than he could actually
show. But the point is that authority is not only for service,
authority is to be exercised because one loves. This was the
new principle of authority introduced into the world: service
and love.

How did our blessed Lord exercise His authority, and
how did He propose to continue that authority through the
centuries? He exercised His authority through His human
nature. Because you believed in the divinity of Christ, if
you heard Him speak, you would hear human lips moving,
but you would say, "It's the Son of God who speaks." So our
blessed Lord taught, He governed, He sanctified through
this human nature, through this body of His. It was the
instrument of His authority, just as, for example, I write
through a pencil. He exercised His divine powers and communicated His truth through this human nature, which He
took from Mary.

A step higher. He now proposes to communicate this
power, this truth, this authority, and He communicates it to
His Apostles, and the Apostles became His new Body, not a

physical body. We sometimes call it a Mystical Body. He wills
to communicate His truth, His authority, His power to His
Apostles, whom He had chosen with Peter as the head. Our
blessed Lord said, *I am the Truth* (JN 14:6); every other teacher
said, "Here's the truth in this code, in this doctrine." Our
Lord said, "I am the Truth." Now to this body of the Apostles,
to His Church, He said, *My Truth I give to you. He that heareth
you, heareth Me. He that despiseth you, despiseth Me* (LK 10:16).
There was no doubt that He was communicating His truth
and His power. He said, *All power is given to Me in heaven and
on earth* (MT 28:18). He sent them out to teach all nations,
to forgive sins, and bid others to do all things that He had
commanded. Just as once He was communicating His power
through His own personal human nature, now He is doing it
through His corporate human nature, which is the Church.

What was the Church like at the beginning? It was made
up of the twelve Apostles with Peter as the head. Our Lord
did not choose Peter and then the other eleven. He chose the
twelve and then He put Peter at the top. After all, everybody
has to have a head. He made him the Rock of the Church, so
the Apostles are what might be called a college of Apostles,
and Peter, who was the head, was the first Vicar of Christ, the
first Pope. Our Lord said this truth and power He communicated to them was to continue even to the consummation of
the world. The bishops of the Church are the continuators
of the Apostles. The Pontiffs, the Vicars of Christ, the Popes
are the successors of Peter, so today the Church is governed
by the college of the Apostles, the college of bishops, in what
is called the collegiality of bishops, with Peter as their head.
They can no more do without Peter as their head than the
Apostles could have done without Peter as their head.

What are bishops? Fortunately, you do not know me well

and do not judge the bishops of the Church by me. But I will tell you what a bishop is. One of his functions is to be something like that curious list of names appearing in the genealogy of the human nature in the Gospel of Matthew (1:1–16). For example, Amminadab begot Nahshon, Nahshon begot Salmon, and so on and so forth. Remember all the begots in the gospel? What was this long list of judges, kings, and prophets? Men of the Old Testament were a kind of proof that our blessed Lord was the one who was expected through the centuries. These men mentioned are unimportant. They were not all good men; some of them were very imperfect, but they just happened to belong to a family tree. If you had ever challenged our Lord and said, "We know the One who is to come belongs to the tribe of Judah and also is a descendant of Abraham," our blessed Lord would have pointed to His family tree and He would say, "There you are. There's the proof. I can show you my line." This was the purpose of these rather insignificant men.

Who are the bishops and what function do they perform? They are witnesses in this century of the truth they teach, which goes back to our blessed Lord Himself. Suppose you ask me, "Where did you get your authority to be a bishop?" I was consecrated in Rome by Cardinal Piazza, and I know who consecrated Cardinal Piazza, and I know the one who consecrated Cardinal Piazza was in turn consecrated by Pope Pius X, and then from Pope Pius X it is easy to go all the way back to Peter. The bishops in this day and age fulfill somewhat the same function as this long genealogical line did in proving our blessed Lord belonged to the royal line of David.

Suppose a microphone cord is put within six inches of an outlet. Do you think that you would hear what I am saying? Suppose we put the cord fifteen hundred inches from the plug, or one inch—no current! Why? Too far away from the source. If you want to know where the truth and authority of the Church come from, you have to be able to follow the line of bishops. Follow them back to the dynamo, to the seat of power, to the seat of truth. Follow them back to Christ Himself.

The bishops are called to be shepherds. We bishops are supposed to be servants. You, laity, are not our servants. Police are not our servants. We are theirs! We're not just administrators. We are shepherds. We can turn into administrators in an affluent, rich country, but that's not what the Lord wants us to be. We are to be shepherds. Furthermore, we are not just each the head of a diocese, we are first consecrated for the world, then for the diocese. Then we are related one to another; but just like the arms, legs, veins, and vessels of your body would be useless unless you had a head, we have no authority except by virtue of our communion with the head, who is the Vicar of Christ, the successor of Peter. Without this, our authority is in vain.

You have heard much about the infallibility of the successor of Peter, of the Pope. Honestly, if there is anything which people do not understand, it is this notion of infallibility. What does "infallibility" mean? Infallibility is not a personal gift. If you ever visit the Holy Father and you say to the Holy Father, "I'm very interested in the stock market. Would you tell me if I should invest in General Motors?" Suppose he said, "Yes, I think General Motors is a good investment." Listen, that's no more infallible a statement than what I am making to you. He is infallible only when he functions as the Head of the Church, and I will mention some other conditions a little later on.

Furthermore, infallibility is not a positive gift; it is a

negative gift. Infallibility is taken from two Latin words, *in* and *fallor,* not to be mistaken. Our blessed Lord said to Peter that the gates of hell, that is to say, the judgments of error and sin, would not touch him or His Church (MT 16:18). It's not a positive gift. He cannot make an infallible statement on literature or science. Many people think that infallibility is like a faucet. The Holy Father goes to this great faucet of infallibility, turns it on, and the truths just pour out. No, that's not infallibility. Infallibility is a levee that prevents the river of truth from overflowing and destroying the countryside. The difference between a river and a swamp is that the swamp has no banks or limits and the river has. To be infallible, the Holy Father must fulfill three conditions: he must speak as the Head of the Church, composed of all the bishops of the Church; he must speak on the subject of faith and morals; and he must address himself to the entire Church and not to any member of it or not to any one country. Many a Pontiff goes through life without making one single infallible decision, not a one.

Now this is the authority of the Church, and many people wonder, "Why is it we obey the Church?" After all, it's hard to obey some human beings. But they are only the gloves; inside is the hand of Christ. We obey them because they are the representatives of Christ. Obeying Christ gives us a tremendous amount of consolation—to have divine truths in those things which concern the soul. For the world, the authority is "they," something anonymous. Everybody follows the styles. Or they say, "Everybody's doing it." Oh, no! Right is right if nobody is right, and wrong is wrong if everybody is wrong. Believe me, in this error-infested world we really need a Church and an authority that is right when the world is wrong!

20

COMMUNISM AND THE CHURCH

There is actually such a thing in the world as authoritarianism; it is communism. What is the essence of authoritarianism? I would say it is threefold: it subjects the mind to dogma; it makes fear the basis of obedience; and it destroys freedom of thought. The Church has none of these qualities. It could not have them because our blessed Lord lived in the midst of authoritarianism. The people among whom He lived were under the power of the Romans; furthermore, all of the Pharisees were authoritarian. When our blessed Lord founded His Church, naturally He made it a bulwark against all forms of authoritarianism. Notice how He even contrasted His Church and what it would be like under communism. He said:

> But Jesus called them to him and said: You know that the princes of the Gentiles lord it over them; and that they that are the greater, exercise power upon them. It shall not be so among you: but whosoever is the greater among you, let him be your minister. And he that will be first among you shall be your servant. (MT 20:25–27)

How did our Lord save us and His Church from authoritarianism? We're going to contrast here the three characteristics of communism with three characteristics of the Church. First, our blessed Lord established a Church where we do not obey a system, but a person; secondly, in the Church the basis of our obedience is not fear, but love; and finally, in the Church freedom of thought is saved by reverence for the truth.

Let's take these up one by one. First of all, dogma. In communism, and in any other form of authoritarianism, one has to submit to a system, a very complicated network of assumptions, codes, directives, and orders, which are very often abstract, such as the dialectical materialism of communism, the theory of class conflict, and the labor theory of value. Catholics do not subscribe to a system of dogma. We begin with a person, the person of our Lord continued in His Mystical Body, the Church. What is faith? Faith is the meeting of two personalities: you and our Lord. There is no adhesion to an abstract dogma, but rather a communion with a person who can neither deceive nor be deceived. The authoritarian starts with a party line; we start with our Lord, the Son of the living God, Who said, *I am the Truth* (JN 14:6). In other words, truth is identified with His personality.

Remember when you were a child. What did you consider your home, just a sum of commands given by either your mother or your father? It was more than that, was it not? It was the love of their personalities. Our faith then is first and foremost in Christ, who lives in His Mystical Body the Church; it is only secondarily in the explicit belief. If our blessed Lord did not reveal them, we would not believe them. If we lost Him, we would lose our belief. He comes first. Everything else is secondary. There is no doctrine, no moral, no dogma, no liturgy, no belief apart from Him. He is the object of faith, not a dogma.

There is a kind of a dogma that when a young man loves a young woman, he should give her a ring and become engaged. What is primary to that custom is a love of her person; so with us. To a Catholic there is nothing credible in the Church apart from Christ, who lives in it. If we did not believe that our Lord was God, if we said that He was only a good man, we would never believe in the Eucharist or the Trinity. If we believe our Lord was simply a human being who perished in the dust, we would not believe in forgiveness of sins. But we know our blessed Lord once taught, governed, and sanctified through a physical body, which He took from His mother, and now we know He continues to teach, to govern, and to sanctify in the Mystical Body, which He took from the womb of humanity. His first body was overshadowed by the Holy Spirit. His Mystical Body was overshadowed by the Holy Spirit on Pentecost; therefore, we accept every single word of His, not just what His secretaries wrote. What we receive is the Living Word, living through the centuries.

You have heard it said, "I don't want any church standing between me and Christ!" There is no church standing between us and Christ. The Church is Christ! Why, the Church no more stands between Him and us than my body stands between me and my invisible mind. The Church is what St. Augustine called the *totus Christus,* the whole Christ; therefore, His Truth living through the ages. Thank God for your faith, your faith in the person of Christ. It is the eternal contemporary!

Another charge is made; namely, if you belong to the Church you are subject to fear. It is true in every single system of authoritarianism that fear is the basis of obedience. Because we start with the person of Christ, the basis of our obedience is not fear; it is love. You cannot love dialectical materialism, but you can love a person. Between our Lord and us there is a bond of love, and these two are inseparable. Our Lord did not communicate to Peter the power of ruling and governing His Church until St. Peter told our Lord three times that he loved Him (JN 21:15–17). The power to command in the Church comes only from obedience to Christ. The submission Catholics make to the Church is something like the submission we make to one of our most devoted friends. It's like the obedience of a son to a loving father. We do not feel any distance between our Lord and us. As a pupil becomes more and more attached to his teacher, the more he absorbs the truths of the teacher, so we become more and more united to Christ the more we love Him and the more of His truth we absorb. The more we know our Lord, the more we obey the truth manifested through His Church, the less we fear. Scripture says, *Perfect love casteth out fear* (1 JN 4:18). The more His truth is ours, the more we love Him.

When we fall away from the faith, God forbid, it is not like falling away from the love of a book, or a song, or a trinket. It's falling from a friendship. It's falling from love. I really cannot imagine anything more cold and more enslaved, more paralyzing to human reason, more destructive of freedom than what millions of people are prostrating themselves for, namely, the terrible, anonymous authority of "they."

"They say they are wearing green this year."

"They say Catholics adore Mary."

"They say Freud is the thing."

Who are "they"? Countless slaves and puppets are bowing down daily before the invisible, tyrannical myth of "they." No wonder dictatorships arose to personalize that terrible slavery. These millions will not accept the authority of Christ, who rose from the dead, who continues to live in the Church. We know whom we obey! They do not know whom they are obeying. They cannot point to the person or to the object behind the terrible, anonymous "they." But thank God we know. We obey our Lord and the Church.

I have received thousands of letters from persons who have fallen away from the Church or who are outside of it because they entered into a second or a third invalid marriage. All express a great unhappiness on the inside, a boredom, a disgust, and an anxiety. Not because they have broken a law, but because they have broken a bond of friendship with the Sacred Heart. Their loneliness says when there is no person to love, there's no certitude; there's only subjection. When there's a love of Christ, then love begins to believe everything. No one can ever surpass the love Christ showed in redeeming us and founding His Mystical Body, the Church. There can be no greater certitude in the world. His love can save us from authoritarianism, with its fear, and make us really loving creatures bound together in the tendrils of affection to Him who loved us even to the point of death.

It is sometimes said the Church destroys freedom of thought and almost annihilates reason. Actually, the contrary is true. Authoritarianism destroys real freedom of thought. You must always make a distinction between freedom from thought and freedom of thought. The devil has pretty much convinced the world that if you accept God's truth you are not free; in fact, if you accept any truth you are destroying your reason. He has very much convinced many souls in the world that any limitation put upon reason is the destruction of reason.

In the garden he suggested to our first parents that if they did not know evil, God in some way was destroying their freedom. So he asked, *Why did God command you? For Him you are really not free until you know evil* (GN 3:5). In so many words the devil was telling our first parents the purpose of God is to prevent free inquiry; He wants to keep the human race in ignorance.

"Do not be fooled. God is an old fuddy-duddy."

"He is a reactionary!"

"He does not want you to know evil."

"Be liberal!"

Those are the words of Satan. God is made to appear as the enemy of truth in just the same way a father who refuses to let a five-year-old son have a shotgun is said, by the son, to be denying freedom. To the devil, continuing loyalty to one's wife, country, or truth is a mark of slavery and a want of freedom.

Is it true that the more you subscribe to divine truth the less free you become? Before I went to school I was free to believe Shakespeare was born in 1224. Finally I was told Shakespeare was not born in 1224, that he was born in 1564. I was given an exact date. I found education was really restricting my freedom to fall into error. Before I went to school I also thought H_2O was really the initials of a spy. Then I fell into the hands of a reactionary teacher. He stopped all of my liberalism. Do you know what he told me H_2O meant? He said it was the symbol for water! The more I studied, the less free I became to know error.

"Freedom" is a very abused word. We want to be free *from* something only for the sake *of* something. I want to be free from communism in order to perfect my soul. I want to be free from hunger in order to develop the body God gave me. I want to be free from fear in order to be free for love. You notice freedom from something is always a freedom for something. What's the use of being free from anything unless we know the purpose of freedom? Freedom is not liberation from the truth; it is the acceptance of a truth. When are you really most free? When you know the truth about anything. You are free to draw a triangle on condition that you give it three sides. You are free to draw a giraffe if you draw it with a long neck. You are free to drive your automobile in traffic on condition that you obey the traffic laws. You are free in the law; you are free in truth. You are free to pilot a plane if you respect the law of gravitation and the truths of aviation. That is what our blessed Lord meant when He said, *The truth will make you free* (JN 8:32). The truth of the Church is a truth that has come to us from Christ. When we begin to wander away from it, we lose our way. There's a map to the truth of Christ in the Church. We may get off the road by sin, or error, but as long as we've got the map, we can get back on the road. Some people get off the road and then tear up the map. That's a greater tragedy.

The Church always teaches us both sides of a question. I taught philosophy in a university for twenty-five years, and I noticed everyone who taught in the university always knew both sides of a question. Everyone in the Catholic university where I taught knew the opinions of the modern world on any given subject. In philosophy, we knew Marx, Sartre, Heidegger, Jaspers, Freud, and others. But do you think the teachers in secular universities know anything about

Christian thought? They know only one side of the question, not both. Look at the Papal encyclical on communism.

A communist once told me the finest explanation of communism he ever read was in the Holy Father's encyclical on communism; he gave both sides of the question. Look at the great work of philosophy and theology called the *Summa Theologica* of St. Thomas Aquinas. Every single question his great mind teaches begins with a doubt and a difficulty; then he answers it. We know both sides of the question. Those outside the Church know only one side, and frequently it's the wrong side. Our freedom is not an independence of truth but rather dependence on love. That's the joy of being a Catholic.

Perhaps I can make it clear with this analogy. On an island in the sea there were children. Around the island were great walls. Inside of those walls on the island children sang, danced, and played. One day some men came to the island; they were reformers. They said to the children, "Who put up those walls? Someone is restraining your freedom. Tear them down!" The children tore them down. If you go back, you will find all of the children huddled together in the center of the island, afraid to play, afraid to dance, afraid of falling into the sea. That is the Church. The wall is truth, and as Christ in the Church said, *If the Son of man makes you free, you are free indeed* (JN 8:36).

PART III

SIN

My work, please the Lord, is not finished.

Much is still to be done, while there is light.

To close the generation gap,

Each day I will say:

"I will go to the altar of God,

to God Who renews my youth."

—FULTON J. SHEEN

21

ORIGINAL SIN AND ANGELS

Our reason is capable of knowing God. By looking out upon the visible things in the world, we come to know the invisible God, His power, and His wisdom. Something of His power is shown in the mountains, and we see His beauty in the sunset, His purity in a snowflake. Though reason is able to know something about God and His nature, it cannot know everything.

We look at a painting. We can divine perhaps the era or century in which it was painted, the style of the artist. We may guess something of his technique and power with the brush and paints, but we could look innermost from now until the crack of doom and never know the thoughts of the artist. We look upon creation and we can reason to some understanding of God, but we cannot know His thoughts. God would have to reveal them to us.

How would we know He ever revealed Himself to us? There are hundreds of people in history who have come upon its stage and said, "I am from God, listen to my message. God sent me." We have to use our reason to establish certain standards by which we judge among the claimants.

Previous to the judgment of any claimant we established three tests. First, whoever comes from God must be preannounced. Secondly, God should give him certain powers to do things only God could do. Thirdly, the doctrine of this claimant must never be contrary to reason. The claimant may say something that is above reason, but he may never say anything contrary to it. His doctrine must be in keeping with right reason and the aspirations of the human heart.

Those were the tests; now we apply them. We can line up every claimant in the history of the world from the first to the last and among them we put the person of Christ. We ask, Was any one of you preannounced? Only one can answer the question, and he is the Christ. We show Christ worked miracles and particularly rose from the dead as a proof of His divinity. Nothing He ever taught was contrary to human reason, but it deeply satisfied the cravings of the heart. Then we began to study Christ, His testimony about Himself, as the Son of God and the Son of man. Then we showed how He was both God and man. He had a divine nature and a human nature, and they were both united in the unity of the divine Person. Being man, He was like unto us in all things save our guilt and our sin. Being God, He could make the reparation and pay the infinite debt we contracted because He was infinite.

We then proceeded to show that our Lord was not just a teacher but a savior from sin. There are two general kinds of sin. There is such a thing as personal sin, which we commit by an act of our own will and for which we are responsible, like stealing, lying, and bearing false witness against the neighbor. Then there is another kind of sin that is not personal at all. Our will is never explicitly involved. This sin attaches to our nature because we are human. That sin is called original sin.

There is law running throughout the universe; as sacred Scripture puts it, *No one shall be crowned unless he has struggled* (2 TM 2:5). We are offered certain gifts and blessings if we pass certain tests. It happened during our school days and it happens in courtship. A man must be deserving of the woman he loves. We are free, and freedom is the basis of all love. The right use of our freedom purchases certain privileges that would not otherwise be ours. A father intends to send his son to college. There is a condition involved; namely, the boy has to study. Suppose he does not study; he spends his time playing; thus, by an abuse of freedom he loses the privilege of a higher education. There was no change in the father's mind. One could never say to the father, "You are cruel because you do not send your son to college." The father is very willing to send his son to college, but the boy cannot get into college; he does not pass the test. God wants to crown certain gifts we have. He wants to crown the right use of our freedom. He wants to give us something as our own which is not really our own, and all we have to do to possess a great gift and privilege of God is to pass a test. It's an easy test, a test of loving Him, which is our perfection. The test is the acknowledging of our dependence upon God, which is the condition of our relative independence.

This law pervading the universe was first applied to angels. Angels are very clearly mentioned in sacred Scripture, and pagans believed in angels. Reason suggested to them that just as there is matter in the universe, the material universe is crowned with man. He is a mixture of matter and spirit. There ought to be above man certain spirits, and these were called angels. One would not say there should not be any intermediary between an oyster and a man. Between the development of the oyster in nature and the development of man, there ought to be some other kinds of life. It is equally reasonable to assume between the infinite God, who is pure spirit, and ourselves, there ought to be intermediary spirits that are not infinite but are certainly far more perfect than we are.

God created a myriad of angels who are just pure minds and bodiless spirits. They are without bodies and wings, despite all the pictures you ever see of angels. They have brilliant intellects, far greater than any human intellect. Every angel was created. They are dependent upon God and endowed with freedom. Because they are free, they also have the possibility of denying dependence on God. Perhaps this is the kind of a test God gave them. He asked them to love Him. Love would consist in their acknowledging dependence and thus perfecting themselves. Eventually, He would then confirm them in glory.

Perhaps this test could be explained to you by the spider test. One day a spider let himself down from the roof of a barn on a tender, slight, and slender web. The spider was anxious to enjoy all of the flies, gnats, and worms in the barnyard. When the spider got down to the barnyard, he spread a large web. Into that web came a great feast of flies and everything that can be served at the banquet of a spider. When the spider was full of these gifts and blessings, the spider looked up all the way to the roof of the barn and saw the slim thread reaching down, and he said, "I wonder what that's doing up there?" He cut it down, lost his web and banquet. He lost everything.

Dependence is sometimes a great independence, as it is in

the Constitution of the United States. Why are we independent? The Declaration of Independence states God endowed us with certain unalienable gifts. No state, no government, no dictator ever gave us our basic rights. They came from God. If the state gave us those rights, the state could take them away. It is by acknowledging our dependence upon God that we are independent.

The gifts the angels received were to be confirmed and made permanent only on condition that they would pass the test of love. Their sin was an abuse of freedom. It was a sin of pride. They wanted to be free and likened to God. They could not sin by sex because they had no bodies. They could not sin by avarice because they had no pockets, not even in their wings. They sinned only by an undue exaltation of their intellect, in other words, "I'm going to be independent of God, I'm going to be a god myself." The truth is they wanted to be like the uncreated, though they were the created.

The leader of them all, Lucifer, made his battle cry, *Non serviam*, "I will not serve." They were guilty because they did not love, so they lost all the blessings they received and one-third of them fell and became what are known as fallen angels, the devils. The prophet Isaiah spoke of the angels as follows, *What fallen from heaven thou Lucifer that once did herald the dawn. I will scale the heavens, such was thy thought, I will set my throne higher than God's stars, the rival, the most high* (IS 14:12–13). In the language of Isaiah, angels sinned and their sin cannot be forgiven. Our sins can.

Why can't an angel's sin be forgiven? When an angel decides anything, it sees all of the consequences of its acts with perfect clarity. The principle of contradiction is that a thing cannot be, and be, at one and the same time and under the same formal circumstances. You can never go back on the principle of contradiction. An angel sees the consequences of all its resolutions and choices just as you see that principle. You can never take the principle of contradiction back; it's part of your mental life. When an angel chose to rebel against God, to make itself God, to deny love, it made pardon forever impossible. With you and me it's a little different. We do not always see the effects of our decisions. Our mind is darkened, our intellect is weakened, and our will is poor in its resolutions; God allows pardon. In answer to Peter's question *How often should I forgive?* Our Lord said, *Seventy times seven* (MT 18:21–22). It did not mean 490, it meant no limit was to be placed upon forgiveness. In the fall of the angels we can see sin in its nakedness. There is pure sin. It is an attempt to undo the creative act, an affirmation of self-existence. There is evil in the universe by an abuse of freedom.

The world was out of joint before man arrived. Somewhere in God's universe there is a fissure; something had gone wrong because someone did not use freedom rightly. Someone used freedom as the right to do whatever he pleased instead of the right to do whatever he ought. Look back over the evolution of the universe. See all of the prehistoric animals that have come into being and passed away. Everywhere in the unfolding of the cosmos there have been blind alleys. Wouldn't you ask, "Why should the sin of the angels affect the universe?" One reason might be that lower creation was put under the supervision of some angels. When they rebelled against God, the effects were registered in the material universe. Nature became dislocated.

Look at a complicated machine and disturb one of the big wheels, break a cog, and you will disturb all of the little wheels. Throw a rock into a pond, it will affect even the most distant shore. The fall of the angels may account for the chaos that was on the earth as described in the book of Genesis. There is every indication that something went wrong before man was made. Possibly this evil influence is going to affect man.

There is evil somewhere in God's universe. Maybe those spirits lost the great blessings God gave them since they were not true to the test of love. Maybe those evil spirits are jealous of God ever giving us blessings. They might try to destroy us and take away our privileges. God will certainly put us to the test in the Garden of Paradise.

22

ORIGINAL SIN AND MANKIND

Certain privileges are given to us if we fulfill love and the right use of freedom. Anyone who gives freedom to another takes a risk, such as a parent who gives freedom to a son or daughter. When God made the angels free, He took a risk. Some of them used their freedom to declare themselves as God. They decreed their independence and forfeited the right to perpetuate themselves in glory and happiness. There is evil in the world which will get to man.

God takes another risk: He makes man. He makes him free and in a moral universe. We can be virtuous only in a universe in which it is possible to be vicious. We make ourselves free. By the right use of freedom we perfect our personality. If we abuse our freedom we become less free. One who is addicted to vices becomes the slave of vices. Anyone who becomes a communist becomes more subject to dictatorship. By the right use of freedom, we finally come to the very glorious freedom of being God's children.

The purpose of education is training in the right use of freedom. Parents encourage children to choose good rather than evil. That is what God did at the beginning. God gave to man certain blessings and privileges which would be his on condition that he used his freedom in a way that would perfect his personality. You are never happy doing things you do not want to do. Freedom implies a choice.

Our first parents were placed in the Garden of Paradise, an Eden of pleasure and joy. Adam ate a fruit, the symbolic representation of evil (GN 3:6). God gave our first parents certain gifts. Man had to decide whether he wanted those gifts for himself for all posterity. One was called supernatural. It actually was a very intimate communion with God, an inner happiness beyond description. There were other gifts, which are technically called preternatural, outside the order of nature. One of the gifts affected the mind, which was to be free from error in reasoning. Another gift was that the body would never rebel against the soul. There would never be carnal temptations. Concupiscence, vices, and sex would never completely becloud our reason. Another gift was immortality of body; the body would never die. The soul was naturally immortal.

God said our first parents would possess these gifts if they passed the test of love. How do you prove you love anyone? The only way we really prove love is by choice. Every act of love is not only an affirmation; every act of love is also a negation. In courtship, a young woman might say to a young man, who is asking for her hand and her heart, "How do I know you love me?" There may be thousands of eligible young women in the city. The young man, if he were rather skilled in philosophy, might say, "By choosing you, I negate all of the others."

In the garden there was a choice expressed in terms of trees: the Tree of life, and the Tree of the knowledge of good and evil. There were other trees in the garden which gave great pleasure, but these were the important ones because they involved alternatives. God wanted man to eat of the Tree of life, to keep in constant union with His divine life. The other tree, which God did not want man to eat of, was the Tree of the knowledge of good and evil. The choice was between a fruit and a garden, a part and a whole, something really involved in every worldly temptation.

There wasn't anything unreasonable about this trial. Life is filled with abundant instances of receiving rewards on condition of love. Imagine a wealthy man going away for the summer and telling the chauffeur and chauffeur's wife they may live in his house. They can eat his food, drink his wine, use his cars, ride his horses, but only on one condition: They must not eat the artificial fruit on the dining room table. He already knows artificial fruit is bad for digestion. They ought to trust him in light of all he is doing for them. If the wife persuades the husband to eat the artificial apple, she would not be a lady. If he ate the artificial fruit, he would not be a gentleman. By doing the one thing forbidden, they would lose all the good things provided and have indigestion besides! They would also lose the opportunity to pass on the blessings of this rich man to their children. To make light of the fruit in the story of the fall is to miss the point that it was a test of love. Eating the fruit was a sign of contempt; it was the symbol of rebellion. God was imposing a single limit to the sovereignty of man, reminding him that if he did the one thing forbidden, he would imperil all of the good things provided. Like Pandora, man opened the forbidden box and he lost all of the treasures.

Who tempted our first parents? It was the fallen angel; it was Satan. When he tempted our first parents, he began with a "why." He said, *Why has God commanded you should not eat of every tree of paradise?* (GN 3:1).

There are actually three steps in that diabolical temptation, and for a sound psychological study of the nature of temptation, there is nothing surpassing the book of Genesis story. First, he aroused a doubt.

"Why did God command you?"

"God's restrictions are unjust."

"Be free!"

"Can't you see this commandment is a restriction of liberty, of your constitutional rights to fire your conscience?"

He began to unsettle the mind. Look back on any temptation you've ever had. Has it not begun with a why? An inner voice seems to be talking to us.

"Why don't you use your sex instincts? Didn't God give them to you?"

"Why not make all the money you can? Isn't that why you're here in this world?"

"Why does the Church say you should not marry again while the first spouse is living?"

"Why?"

"Be free!"

"Throw off the shackles!"

That's what is happening every day in the world, and that's what happened in the beginning.

Satan's second step was to remove all fear of the consequences of sin. He ridiculed punishment and said, You will not die (3:4). God warned if they ate the fruit of the Tree of the knowledge of good and evil, they would die. Satan always contradicts God. He minimizes sin.

"Do you believe what God hath joined together let no man put asunder?"

"Go ahead and do it. No one will know!"

"Take that tenth cocktail, you will never be an alcoholic; it'll just make you feel good."

"Go on committing excesses of the flesh; you will never be a slave!"

"You believe in hell? Don't be silly! Hell is a punishment for sin."

That's the way the devil talks. In the book of the Apocalypse he tells us, "Oh, it's nothing" at the beginning, and then, afterward, he says, "It's everything!"

A third stage of Satan's temptation is a false promise. He said to our first parents, *You will be likened to God, knowing good and evil* (3:5). This is really what Satan was saying:

"God knows the difference between good and evil."

"The reason He does not want you to eat of the Tree of the knowledge of good and evil is because then you will know the difference."

"Once you know the difference between good and evil, you will be like God."

"You see, that's the reason He has forbidden you."

"He doesn't want you to be like Him."

"He's jealous!"

The fallacy was implying that God does not know good and evil the way we do. God knows good and evil in a very abstract fashion. When you and I know evil, we do not know it in an abstract fashion. It gets into our blood, becomes a part of us. The act becomes a habit. Satan taunts us.

"You haven't lived!"

"Innocent, aren't you?"

"You've never been drunk?"

"You have to know the difference between good and evil!"

Our first parents fell for that suggestion. The result was

their eyes were opened; they hid from God. In sin, one always hides from God. They saw themselves naked. Why did they perceive themselves to be naked now and not naked before (GN 3:7)? Because the inner glory of grace which they had in their souls suffused their bodies with a kind of light. They were filled with radiance, perhaps something like our blessed Lord on the Mount of Transfiguration. They lost their inner likeness to God and perceived themselves to be naked. The earth rebelled, thistles grew, and beasts became wild. Man had to earn his bread by the sweat of his brow. Nature became difficult to control. Woman was told she would bring forth her children in sorrow. Notice the punishment of man was in relationship to nature and the punishment of Eve was in relationship to life. All gifts were lost.

Is there anything unnatural about this story of man's fall? How often we have insisted on our own freedom in a way that hurt us. We interpreted freedom as the right to rebel. Copies, we pretended to be originals; rays, we wanted to be the sun; printed pages, we insisted we were the authors! All these things we did because we inherited that abuse of freedom from the first parents. Our parents told us not to play with matches; we disobeyed; we burned ourselves, and when Mother called, we hid. We had no fear of the mother before we burned our fingers. Adam and Eve had no fear of God before they disobeyed. After sin, God appeared to be an angry God. He was not angry. Anger is in our own disordered selves.

We know very well we are not the way God made us with our darkened intellect and our weak will. Whatever happened to us has all the earmarks of an abuse of freedom. We rebelled in Adam, who was the head of the human race, and the effects of his sin were passed on to all of us, except

Mary. That is what we mean by saying Mary was immaculately conceived. She was preserved free from the traces of original sin in virtue of the anticipated merits of our Lord's death on the Cross.

A little after the fall, God promised He would renew man. He said the seed of a woman would conquer the seed of Satan (GN 3:15). The seed of the woman would be Christ. In the divine plan, the very elements used for our destruction are used for our redemption. In the fall there was a disobedient man, Adam; a proud woman, Eve; and a tree. God would take the very elements of defeat, and use them as the elements of victory. For the disobedient Adam, there is the obedient new Adam, Christ; for the proud woman, Eve, there is the humble new Eve, Mary; and for the tree, there is the Cross. They will be our hope.

23

EFFECTS OF ORIGINAL SIN

There is a background about original sin, and we are concerned with how it affects us. Everyone is interested in psychology. We try to understand ourselves. We probe and analyze our anxieties and our conflicts. Some of us wonder why we are run down and others why we are wound up.

There are many explanations of these conflicts within us, but original sin alone gives us the basic understanding of human nature. No one can understand psychology unless he understands human nature and original sin. Somehow the abuse to our mind has been due to human freedom. We feel like a radio that is tuned in to two stations. We get nothing but static. We're tuned in to heaven; we're tuned in to hell. Ovid, the Latin poet, described it very well; he said, "I see and I approve the better things of life; the worse things of life I follow" (METAMORPHOSES 7.20). St. Paul also described our inner psychology when he wrote, *The good which I will to do, that I do not. And the evil which I will not, that I do* (RM 7:19).

We seem dual, pulled in two different directions as if we were a team of horses and one horse was going to the right and the other horse was going to the left. Our soul is like a battlefield on which a civil war is being waged. We feel split almost into many worlds. Some of us may even feel like the young man out of whom our Lord drove the devil. Our Lord said to the devil, *What is your name?* The devil answered, *My name is Legion; for we are many* (MK 5:9). Notice the conflict between "my" and "we." He was one; he was multiple. Even the best of us feel as if we are mountain climbers; we can see the summit and the peak toward which we are striving up above us, and then we look back and we see the abyss into which we might fall. Above is what we ought to be, and below is what we can become.

There are explanations given for this conflict within us. They are true to some extent, but they are only partial. One is psychological; one is biological; and the other is economic.

The partial explanation is the psychological, which tries to find out what has happened personally to us in the past. Some will say the reason we have this particular psychosis is because we were frightened when we were locked in a closet for bad behavior, or else our parents scolded us when we tried to manifest our interest in a possibly sexual pleasure. Hence, whatever is wrong with us has a personal background; therefore, to be cured of our difficulty, there must be an analysis of our subconscious mind. If we can bring out of the subconscious mind the source of this personal conflict, we will be cured.

This explanation has some merit, but it is only a partial accounting for the way we are. It is wrong to assume if we are to find the source of any particular person's difficulty we need to go into that person's background. No! Everybody has a conflict! It is not just our personality and our psychological background; something has happened to our nature. Do not think you have a temptation because there is something wrong with you. Do not believe you have a monopoly on temptation! Everybody is tempted. If we are to find the ultimate explanation, we must get beyond the person; we've got to get back to human nature. Something has happened to us and affected every single human being in the world.

Another partial explanation is the biological. There was a fall somewhere in the evolutionary process, and we all have the traces of our animal origin. This is hardly the explanation, because animals, left to themselves, never have anxieties. They may have natural fears, but they have no subjective anxieties in the strictest sense. Birds do not develop a psychosis about whether they will take a winter trip to California or to Florida. An animal never becomes less than it is, but a man can because he is a composite of both spirit and matter. What is wrong with man must be sought within man himself. Since man is spirit as well as matter, he can descend to the level of beasts, though never so completely as to destroy the image of God in his soul. It is this possibility that makes the peculiar tragedy of man. Man would never be frustrated or have an anxiety complex if he were an animal made just for this world. The desire for perfect happiness, which he does not attain, creates a seat of conflicts. The animal in us is not the cause; it is something more profound.

A third false partial explanation is the economic. Here it is assumed man has conflicts because of communism, capitalism, or poverty. Yet the world has never had so much wealth, and so much unhappiness. Never before has it had so much learning and so little knowledge of the truth. Never before has it had so much power and been so bent on the destruction of human life. Economic development is not the total cause of man's derangement. All the rich are not virtuous; all the poor are not sinners. If poverty were the cause of the way we are, then the rich should be paragons of virtue. Actually, the overprivileged and rich have more mental conflicts than the poor. Very often the more one is detached from our world, the healthier he is on the inside. The world has swindled the treasury of morality, creating a kind of poverty from which we suffer. Somehow or other we lost spiritual capital.

Looking back on the explanations, we have to conclude that God certainly did not create us fallen. There is a voice inside of our moral consciousness telling us our immoral and unmoral acts are abnormal. God made us one way, and we've made ourselves, in virtue of our freedom, another way. He wrote the drama, we changed the plot! We are not just animals who failed to evolve into humans; we are humans who have rebelled against the divine. If we are riddles to ourselves, we are not to put the blame on God or on evolution. We are to put the blame on ourselves. We are not depraved criminals, merely weak. We're not just a mass of corruption, for we bear within ourselves the image of God. We are very much like a man who has fallen into a well; we ought not to be there, yet we cannot get out. We are sick; we need healing; we need deliverance; we need liberation. We know we cannot give liberation and freedom to ourselves.

God has established a law. There will be a free moral universe. We can abuse our freedom, but we are not to blame God. When you buy an automobile, you always secure a set of instructions. The manufacturer tells you the pressure setting for your tires, the kind of oil you put in your crankcase, and the kind of gasoline you put in the gas tank. He has nothing against you because he gives you these directions. God has nothing against us when He gives us Commandments. The manufacturer of the automobile really wants to be helpful when he gives us instructions. He wants you to get the maximum utility out of your car, and God is anxious we get the maximum amount of happiness out of life. So He said, "I will tell you what you should do." We are free; we can do just as we please. We ought to put gasoline into the tank of our car, but we can put perfume in there. We can put in smell number 5, and there's no doubt that it is going to be nicer for our nostrils to fill the tank with perfume than with gasoline, but the car simply will not run on smell number 5. In like manner, we were made to run on the fuel of God's love and Commandments, and we simply will not run on anything else. We just bog down.

Here is another example which explains original sin and the conflicts within us. Suppose there was an orchestra before us with a distinguished conductor. A symphony was composed. All the musician had to do was to follow the marks. Each member of the orchestra was free to follow the conductor and produce harmony. Suppose one of the musicians deliberately played a false note, and then jabbed the violinist next to him and told him to play another false note. There's discord. Having heard that discord, the director can do one of two things. He can either strike his baton and say, "Play it over," or he can ignore it. It makes no difference which he does because that note is already going out into space, traveling at the rate of about eleven hundred feet per second, and on and on it goes, affecting even the infinitesimally small radiation of the universe. Just as the stone dropped in the pond causes a ripple, this discord affects even the most distant star. As long as time endures, somewhere in God's universe, there is a disharmony introduced by the free will of man.

Can that discord be stopped? Not by man himself, for

man cannot reach it. Time is irreversible, and man is localized in space. Is there any way of stopping the discord? If the Eternal came out of His eternity into time, He might lay hold of the false note. But would there still be discord in the universe? There could be harmony if God wrote a new symphony and made that false note the first note in the new harmony. Then there would be harmony again.

A long time ago God wrote a symphony and asked man and woman to play it. There was a complete set of instructions delineating what to avoid. They could obey the divine Director and produce harmony or they could disobey Him. The devil suggested, because the divine Director had marked the script and told them what to play and what not to play, He was destroying their freedom. They believed him and introduced a false note into the universe. Through the human race, this discord affected every single human being in the universe with this disharmony.

Repercussions were evident in the material universe: Thistles grew; beasts became wild; man had to earn his bread by the sweat of his brow; women brought forth their children in sorrow. A stream polluted at its source passes on its pollution through its length, so the original thought was transmitted to all in humanity. The discord could not be stopped by man himself because he could not repair an offense against the Infinite with his own finite self. The debt could be paid only by the divine Master, who is the Musician coming out of His eternity into time. There would be a world of difference between stopping a discordant note and stopping a free, rebellious man.

That's where the analogy breaks down. God refuses to be a totalitarian dictator and He refuses to abolish evil by destroying human freedom. God could seize the note, but

He would not seize a man. Instead of conscripting man, God willed to consult humanity again as to whether or not it wanted to be made a member of the divine orchestra once more. And so out from the great white throne of Light comes an angel, and it comes to a woman, whose name is Mary. And the angel asks Mary, "In the name of God, will you give to God a man; will you give to God this new note out of humanity with which He can write a new symphony?" This new man must be a man, otherwise God would not be acting in the name of humanity; but He must also be out-side of the current of infection to which all men are subject. Being born of a woman, He would be a man, and being born of a virgin, He would be a sinless man.

The virgin was asked if she would consent to be a mother. Her answer was *Be it done unto me according to thy word* (LK 1:38). Nine months later the Eternal established its beachhead in Bethlehem. He who was eternal appeared in time, and His name was Jesus Christ, God and man. He was God; thus, whatever He did has an infinite value. Though this human nature is His, it's sinless. He makes Himself responsible for all the sins of the world. As a rich brother takes upon him-self the debts of his bankrupt brother, so our Lord takes upon Himself all the discords in harmony—sins, guilt, and blasphemies—as if He Himself were guilty. He takes human nature, plunges it into Calvary to have our sins burned away. Since sin is in the blood, He pours out His blood in redemp-tion, for without the shedding of blood there's no remission of sin. Then on Easter Sunday He rises again with His glori-fied, sinless human nature.

This becomes the first note in the new creation, the be-ginning of the new symphony which will be played again and again by the divine Conductor. How are other notes added? We're the other notes if, like Mary, we freely consent to be added to this first note. We become added by the sacrament of Baptism, by which each person dies to the old Adam and is incorporated into the new Adam, Christ. These notes added to the first note constitute the new body of Christ, or what is known as His Mystical Body, the Church. This is what it means to be a Christian.

24

SANCTIFYING GRACE

Once upon a time there were two tadpoles amusing themselves under the water. One little tadpole said to the other, "I think I'll stick my head up and see if there's anything in this world besides water." The other tadpole said, "Don't be stupid! There's only what we know, just water." We often wonder, "Is there any power above the wisdom of the human intellect and above the power of the human will?"

There is something else in the world besides water or our weak human nature, and that is grace. Grace is not the name of a girl. Grace is this higher wisdom that can come to us. It means *gratis*. Since it is free, we cannot merit it in the strict sense. Grace appears repeatedly in the New Testament. In the Greek its name is *charis,* and it appears about 150 times. If there is another life above the purely natural, or the human, then it is possible for every Christian to lead a double life: a natural or human life, and a divine or spiritual life. In the book of the Apocalypse we read, *You call yourselves living and yet you are dead* (RV 3:1), meaning you are biologically alive but you are spiritually dead. We are constantly bumping up against walking corpses on the street. Their bodies are alive, but their souls are dead. As the life of the body is the soul, so the life of the soul is grace, or the partaking of the divine life.

Before we come to an understanding of what this divine life is and where it comes from, let us picture a three-story house. It has a cellar, a first floor, and a second floor. The cellar is a kind of a dark place where there is a lot of refuse. The first floor is fairly comfortable, and the second floor is magnificent. Now these three stories correspond to the three kinds of lives people may lead. The cellar corresponds to the life of the senses and emotions: food, drink, carnal pleasures, and the like. I'm not saying these things are wrong, just a form of culture. The great Harvard professor Pitirim A. Sorokin calls it the sensate culture. The first floor is the floor of reason, science, art, humanism, and culture. There is another story, the floor of grace, where there is a higher intellect, stronger will, new powers, new loves.

Some people who live in the cellar say, "Well, I'm satisfied here." They are kind of spiritual dropouts who refuse to walk up to the first floor and to enjoy those cultural pursuits which give man so much joy. There are those who live on the first floor of humanism, reason, science, and art. They, too, may object to rising to a higher level.

"In order to get up to that top floor, I have to walk, don't I?"

"I have to put forth a little effort, and I refuse to do that."

"You tell me there's great joy, peace, and happiness on the third floor. How do I know? I've never been up there!"

"I'm not going to endanger my heart by walking."

That's the attitude not only of those who live in the realm of the senses, but also of those who live in the realm of reason. The tragedy of life is not so much what people suffer; it's what they miss. That's the great sadness.

The catechism defines grace as a supernatural gift of God bestowed on us by Jesus Christ to save us. We will take out one word, "supernatural." "Supernatural" means the third floor in relationship to the second and the first, but it needs more of an explanation. Suppose flowers on an altar suddenly began to walk on their stems and walked out through our little chapel and came here into my study and stood before me. Suppose each one of their little petals bowed down and saluted me. Does the power of movement belong to a flower? It certainly does not. This gift exceeds the nature, power, and needs of a flower. In other words, it would be a supernatural gift. Suppose a dog came and listened to me for a moment and suddenly said, "Say, you missed a good point there. You should have quoted the *Pars Secunda* of St. Thomas Aquinas at this point. And I think if you had brought in this quotation from Shakespeare, it would have helped you very much." Does it belong to the nature of a dog to speak and to reason? This exceeds the nature, power, and the needs of a dog and would be a supernatural act for a dog.

Let's come to man. Every person is a creature of God. Suppose I suddenly became a child of God so that not just the life of my parents but the life of God came into me; so my reason had another light than just the light of reason, and my will had other powers than just my poor, weak human will. If I became a new creature so the body and blood of Christ somehow were in me, that would be, in the strict sense, a supernatural gift. I certainly do not deserve it. Furthermore, when this gift comes, it always changes our direction, because by our nature we are weak. We tend toward sin, doubt, and selfishness. If we are to change our direction, a new power is needed. Natural human beings continue in certain directions, like Paul would have continued his persecution; sinners would continue in their sin; agnostics would continue in their doubt, unless some superior power intervenes, and that is the power of grace.

Take one example of the changing of direction. The former editor of the Communist *Daily Worker* of London and his wife were listening to a radio program by a commissar of Russia. Suddenly the wife got up and shut off the radio.

She said to her husband—now remember they both were communists—"I don't believe he wants peace. I think he wants war! He's talking peace, but he means war."

He said, "Don't talk that way; you're not talking like a communist."

She said, "I don't care what I'm talking like."

He said, "If you continue to talk that way I shall report you to the party!"

She said, "Report me!"

"Why," he said, "you're beginning to talk as if you might become a Catholic!"

She said, "I am!"

He said, "Shake! So am I!"

Here were a husband and wife living together, sharing communist ideas, and suddenly they both changed, unknown to one another. What did it? A power outside of them, this power of grace.

There's no such thing as just becoming better in the natural order and suddenly, in the strict sense, meriting grace. Nature and grace are quite distinct. It's really the difference between making and begetting. When you make anything, you make something unlike you. When you make a table, the table does not share your nature. When parents beget a child, they beget something like themselves. When God made us, God was our Creator, but when He begets us as children, then He is not just our Creator, He is our Father. When grace comes into us, as our blessed Lord said, the sap passes through the vine into the branches, and the same sap from the vine passes through the branches. We begin to share the nature of our blessed Lord, so He pours out His nature upon us. St. John said, *Of His fullness we have all received* (JN 1:16). When we respond to grace, then we become something like a pencil in the hand. A pencil in the hand, as long as it is directed by the hand, will do anything the hand wants. We are the instruments of God, and we obey His will just as the pencil obeys the will of the hand. When there is total obedience, there is sanctity. That's what a saint is. A saint is one who is as available to God as a pencil is to my hand.

What does grace do to our human nature? Grace makes the body a temple of God; that is one of the reasons for purity. A temple is a place where God dwells. Remember when our blessed Lord went into the Temple of Jerusalem? When the Pharisees asked for a sign, our blessed Lord said, *Destroy this Temple and in three days I will rebuild it* (MK 14:58). He was not speaking of the earthly temple. He was speaking of the Temple of His body, because God dwelled in the human nature of Christ. By participation He dwells in us. The body is sacred and we have reverence for it. The principal effects of grace are in the intellect and in the will.

The intellect is the faculty of ours by which we know; the will is the faculty by which we choose. The object of the intellect or reason is truth; the object of the will is goodness or love. When grace comes into the intellect, it comes as a kind of a light. It is rather difficult to describe what it does to the human mind. Picture sunlight shining through a stained-glass window. Notice how it is diffused and brings out all of the colors. That's what grace does to the intellect; it gives a new vision. Faith becomes to reason something like the telescope is to the eye: It does not destroy the eye, it perfects it. When faith gets into us, we have a new certitude quite beyond reason. All you get in these instructions are motives of credibility. Certitude has to come from faith, which has to come from God. Our blessed Lord said to Peter, *Flesh and blood have not revealed this to thee, but My Father who is in heaven* (MT 16:17). The certitude from faith is so great nothing can destroy it. Certitude is greater than the reasons for faith because the light comes from God.

We have many certitudes stronger than the reasons we can give. If we were challenged to prove we were legitimate children, it might be rather difficult. We do not have the documents. But nothing could shake our certitude. A learned man could give many reasons against the existence of God and the divinity of Christ to one of our children, but he could never destroy the faith of that child. Not only does faith give certitude, but it also gives us a new outlook, a new outlook on birth, suffering, death, joy, pleasures, literature, and art. Those who have what St. Paul calls the carnal mind cannot understand the things of faith; it's like trying to make a blind man understand color. Very often those who lack the gift of faith wonder why we are so certain.

"Why do we have this outlook on suffering?"

"Why aren't we depressed?"

"Why don't we contemplate suicide?"

It's simply because we see things much better. We have a light that they don't have. Perhaps we have already said that we have the same eyes at night as we have in the day, but we do not see at night. Why? Because we lack the light of the sun. Let two people look at the same problem. They see it very differently. It's because one has only his reason and his senses, and the other has faith.

There's also the human will. When grace comes into the will, it gives us new power, new strength that we never had before. It gives us a new ability to resist temptations. Too often in this world as soon as anyone becomes a slave of sin, we speak of him as having a compulsion. We say, "Oh, he is a compulsive drinker. He is a compulsive eater." That is true. The word our blessed Lord used to explain compulsion was "slavery." This does not mean these people have completely destroyed their freedom. There's always a little area of freedom left in an alcoholic, in a pervert, and in anyone who is given to the slavery of sin. These sins which started with free acts of our own may have weakened, but not destroyed, our will. It is possible for grace to establish a beachhead. Grace has its D-day, and God can get into any one of these people. When we're trying to cure people of vices, we can never drive out a vice; we can only crowd it out. How do you crowd it out? You crowd it out by putting in something else that is new. The grace of God comes in when we begin to love Him; then, these vices begin to be pushed out. Once a new love comes in, we are changed. I remember once dealing with an alcoholic woman, and I said to her, "You love alcohol more than anything else in the world. Because you love alcohol more than anything else in the world, I can't cure you until you begin to love something else more." So we prayed for grace and grace came in and she was cured.

This is what grace does to the poor, weak human will. Then it also gives power so we influence others. If there is any influence in these words of mine, it is not because of any knowledge or power that I possess. If I have any influence on you, it's because the Spirit and the grace of God are working on you. My words are nothing. Of course I did not begin these instructions without a prayer that the Spirit and the grace of God might give me strength, but if at any time you were changed, do not say, "Oh, Bishop Sheen, we are so grateful to you." Bishop Sheen did nothing. I'm only the poor instrument of the good Lord.

If you are changed, there's the difference now between your nature and grace. Before grace comes, you act in your own way; after you receive grace, you act in His way. That's the difference. Your conscience becomes quickened, and what before was very precious to you, now seems as nothing, and what before seemed as so much dross, now is precious. That's grace. Grace is supernatural power that illumines your mind to see things above reason; it's that supernatural power that strengthens your will to do things which before you could not do. It changes you from a creature into a child of God, and most of all it enables you to call God, Father.

PART IV

SACRAMENTS

I see we were wrong in saying:

"The Word became flesh and dwelt amongst us

Churchgoers, the respectable, the majority, and the good."

And I see that we are wrong today in changing the tune:

"The Word became flesh and dwelt among the Rebels,
the minorities

And the protesters."

We will be right again when we believe

God is the Father of all mankind,

And show Christ to all that they will see Him in their color,

And they will show Him to us, that we will see Him
in our color.

—FULTON J. SHEEN

25

GRACE AND THE SACRAMENTS

Grace divides the world into two kinds of humanity: the once born, and the twice born. The once born are born only of their parents; the twice born are born of their parents and of God. One group are what might be called natural. The other, in addition to having nature, share mysteriously in the divine life of God.

Let me tell you two incidents about grace. I went to preach a sermon in a Parisian church. I stayed in a tiny hotel near the Opéra Comique, and in a small side room there was an Englishman playing a piano. I listened for a while, responded with compliments, and invited him to dine with me.

In the course of the dinner he said, "I have a problem I would like to present to you. I have never met one good man or one good woman." I thanked him for the compliment. He told me that a year ago he saw a woman trying to break a lump of sugar into a cup of coffee. He went over to her and broke the lump. She told him how cruel her husband was and he said, "Come and live with me."

"I'm tired of her now; I get tired of them all after about a year. I wrapped up her clothes this morning, left them at the concierge, and told her to leave, but she left me this note saying that if I do not continue living with her, she will commit suicide by throwing herself into the Seine. My problem is, may I allow her to continue living with me to prevent her from committing suicide?"

I said, "No, you may never do evil that good may come from it, and what is more important, she will not commit suicide."

It got late.

He said, "Where are you going?"

I said, "I'm going up to Montmartre."

He said, "I was just beginning to think you were good, now you're going up to the hellhole of Paris."

I said, "There's something else on the hill of Montmartre besides dives and dens; there is the beautiful Basilica of the Sacred Heart. Hundreds of men pray every night in perpetual adoration of our Lord and the blessed Sacrament. Come with me."

We went up together. He asked, "How long will you stay?" I said, "I intend to stay all night, but I will leave when you want to go." He stayed all night. I suppose there were about eight hundred to a thousand people spending the night there in prayer. We left the next morning after I had read Mass.

He said, "This is the first time in my life I ever came in contact with goodness."

He asked me to stay in Paris for a few days and teach him. I arranged to meet him that night. At the appointed hour he came into the courtyard with another woman, not the woman involved in the story.

He said, "The three of us will go out to dinner." I said, "No, tonight I want to see you."

Then I called him aside. I said, "You received a great grace yesterday; you got the first dim contact with goodness, love, and holiness. Tonight you have to make a choice: Either you are going out with this woman, or you are going out with me. Which will it be?"

He walked up and down the courtyard for a few minutes and then came back to me.

He said, "Well, Father, I think I'll go out with her." That is the end of the story. The impulses of grace he received could have developed him into a saint, but it was like the story of our Lord looking over Jerusalem: I would, thou wouldst not (MT 23:37).

Let us take another incident. I used to do parochial work in St. Patrick's Church, Soho Square, London, England. I opened the church door one cold Epiphany morning in the month of January, and a limp figure fell in. It was a young woman about twenty-three years of age.

I said, "How did you happen to be here?"

She said, "I didn't know where I was, Father. Oh, Father, I used to be a Catholic, but not anymore."

I said, "But why are you here? You seem to be a little bit intoxicated. What are you running away from?"

She said, "From men, each of whom thinks I love him."

I asked her name, and when she told me I pointed to a billboard on the other side of the street.

I said, "Is that your picture over there on that billboard?"

She said, "Yes, I'm the leading lady in that musical comedy."

The woman was very cold. I made her a cup of coffee and asked that she come back before matinee.

She implored, "I will on one condition, that you do not ask me to go to confession."

I said, "Very well, I promise you won't have to go to confession."

She came back before the matinee.

I said, "We have a beautiful Rembrandt and a Van Dyck in this church. Would you like to see them?"

As we walked down the middle aisle, I gave her a gentle "push" into the confessional. I did not ask her to go, but she went to confession. The actress became a nun in a convent of perpetual adoration in England.

Here are two stories of responses to grace. In both instances the human will was free. In the one there was a correspondence; in the other, a rejection. We receive millions of these graces called actual graces. Everyone receives them. You need not be a Christian. Every Muslim, Buddhist, and communist in the world receives actual grace. Here we are speaking of what is called habitual grace, a more permanent grace, which creates a likeness that remains in us. How is this grace communicated to us? Perhaps you've seen signs on roadways, they are often painted on rocks, which read JESUS SAVES. Yes, indeed He does, but the very practical question is, How?

We have a span of twenty centuries between the life of our Lord and our days. Yes, He is God, but how does He infuse His divine life and power into our souls? He does it by what are called sacraments. We define the word "sacrament" in a very broad way. In Greek it means mystery. A sacrament is any material or visible thing used as a sign or a channel of spiritual communication. God made this world with a sense of humor. We say a person has a sense of humor if he can see through things, and we were always to see Him through things like the poets do. We would look out on a mountain and think of the power of God; on the sunset and think of the beauty of God; on a snowflake and dwell on the purity of God. Notice we would not be taking this world as seriously as the materialists, to whom a mountain is just a mountain, a sunset is just a sunset, and a snowflake is just a snowflake. The serious-minded people of this world write only in prose, but those who have this penetrating glance of perceiving the Eternal through time, the divine through the human, have what we call the sacramental outlook on the universe.

There are certain signs and events in our daily life which are a kind of natural sacrament. Take for example a word. A word has something audible about it and, at the same time, something invisible. If I tell an amusing joke, you might laugh, but if I told it to a horse, a horse would not even give a horse laugh. Why? You get the meaning because you have a soul to reason and an intellect. A horse lacks the spiritual, perceptive power and does not get the meaning. A handshake is something visible, material, and fleshy. There is also something spiritual about it; namely, the communication of greeting, welcome, and the communication of personal warmth. A kiss is a kind of sacrament; it is something visible, and at the same time something invisible; namely, the communication of love.

Have you noticed how much our modern architecture is devoid of all decoration? What a contrast to the cathedrals, where there were all material things, even cows and angels, sometimes little devils, peering around corners. The ancient architecture was always using material things as signs of something spiritual, and today our architecture is flat, nothing but steel and glass, almost like a cracker box. Why? Our architects have no spiritual message to convey. The material is just the material, nothing else; hence, no decor, significance, meaning, or soul. I wonder if decor and decoration in architecture have not passed out of the world at the same time politeness has. We certainly are not as polite in this century as we were in another century. Possibly the reason is because we no longer believe people have souls; they are just other animals and are to be treated as means to our ends. When you believe in addition to a body there is a soul, then you begin to have great respect and reverence for a person.

How do we ever contact the life of Christ and His grace? Christ Himself was the great Sacrament because He was the Word made flesh, He was the God-man. We would have seen a man, but we would have known He was the Son of God. Christ is the supreme sacrament of history. His human nature was the sign of His divinity. We saw God through His body; we see eternity through His time; and the living God in the form of a man who was like to us in all things, save sin. Our blessed Lord took His human nature to heaven. Once He is glorified there, as we said in speaking of the Ascension, He is our Mediator, our Intercessor, who can have compassion for us, and on us, because He passed through our temptations, sufferings, and trials. He is God as well as man and is going to pour down upon us from heaven His truth, His power, His grace, His life. How will He do it? He will not do it through what we might call His bodiliness, because that is already glorified in heaven. He will do it through things and also through human nature. He will use certain things in this world as extensions of His glorified body. These things might be water, bread, and oil as channels for the communication of His divine life.

Why did He institute these sacraments? His life is so rich it has to have various manifestations in life, like the life of a sun. The sun is so bright that if we are to understand its inner beauty we have to shoot the sunlight through a prism. When we do it splits into the seven rays of the spectrum. Our blessed Lord shoots His divine life through the prism of the Church and it splits up, not into the seven rays of the spectrum, but into the seven sacraments of the Church.

Another reason He used sacraments is to spiritualize our material world. God not only redeems man, He redeems things. We lay hold of material things like water, oil, and bread and make them serve God. Too often they have not been used for divine purposes. We have a body and soul. We get all our spiritual thought through the senses. Why didn't God use things that appeal to our senses, some material signs which would be revelations of this grace that He is pouring into our souls? For example, it would be wonderful if He used water to indicate the great sin we inherited from Adam being washed away. Bread would be a very good sign of nourishment. Oil strengthens us in the natural order. It might be a very good sign for strengthening our souls. Now divinity uses humanity and material things that there might be something transhistorical, transcosmic, so the divine life of Christ will pour into our souls. Christ in heaven contacts us in this day and age through seven sacraments.

There are seven conditions for leading a physical life, and there ought to be seven conditions for leading a spiritual life. Five of these conditions are individual, and two refer to society. In order to live a physical, natural life, I must be born; I must grow to maturity; I must nourish myself; I must heal my wounds; and I must drive out traces of disease. Then, as a member of society, there must be a propagation of the human species and there must be government.

Over and above this human life is the divine life, and there are seven conditions of leading a divine life. If I am to live the Christ life, I must be born into it, that is the sacrament of Baptism. I must grow to maturity, and accept the responsibilities of life; that is the sacrament of Confirmation. I must nourish myself, sustain this divine life; that is the sacrament of the Holy Eucharist. I must heal the wounds of my soul caused by sin; that is the sacrament of Penance, or Confession. I must drive out all traces of the disease of sin found in my senses; that is the sacrament of the Healing of the Sick. As a member of society, there must be a propagation of the Kingdom of God, the growth of the Mystical Body of Christ; that is the sacrament of Matrimony. Finally, there must be divine government; there must be Holy Orders or the sacrament of the episcopacy and the priesthood.

The reception of grace in these sacraments is very effective in our souls because it is Christ who confers the grace. The divine life of Christ is poured into our souls by the mere fact we receive the sacrament. We must not put an obstacle in the way of receiving the sacrament. It is Christ who baptizes. It is Christ who forgives sins. There are ministers, bishops, and priests, but we lend Christ our eyes, hands, and lips. It is He who gives the grace. Even though you receive the sacraments from an unworthy priest, it would still be a sacrament because the sanctification does not depend upon the priest. Sunlight comes through a dirty window, yet the sunlight is not polluted. A messenger may be very ragged, but he could still bear the message of a king.

So you see the Church, the Mystical Body of Christ, takes care of you from the cradle to the grave. It meets you in all of the events and circumstances of life, and your sanctification does not depend upon our preaching; it depends on Christ Himself. This is the sweet mystery of life, the sacraments.

26

BAPTISM

Baptism is the sacrament that incorporates us into the Mystical Body of Christ, the Church, and is called the door of the Church. There is just a faint parallel to be drawn between the Church and a nation. Most of us did not wait until we were twenty-one, then study the Constitution, the history of the United States, and decide to become American citizens. We were born out of the womb of America. In the strict sense, the Church itself is first, Christ's Mystical Body. Baptism incorporates us into it; we are born out of the womb of the Church.

As we explained, we do not become members of the Church as a brick is added to brick in a house. We become incorporated to the Church as cells expand from central cells. But you may ask, "What difference does the pouring of a little water make?" The water alone probably makes little difference. Take the water in a steam engine. When you combine it with the mind and spirit of an engineer, it can drive a steam engine from one end of the country to the other. When water is united with the spirit of God, it is capable of making us something that we are not, partakers of His divine nature.

Remember the beautiful description of baptism given in the Gospel of St. John:

> And there was a man of the Pharisees, named Nico-demus, a ruler of the Jews. This man came to Jesus by night and said to him: Rabbi, we know that thou art come a teacher from God; for no man can do these signs which thou dost, unless God be with him. Jesus answered and said to him: Amen, amen, I say to thee, unless a man be born again, he cannot see the king-dom of God. Nicodemus saith to him: How can a man be born when he is old? Can he enter a second time into his mother's womb and be born again? Jesus an-swered: Amen, amen, I say to thee, unless a man be born again of water and the Holy Ghost, he cannot enter into the Kingdom of God. That which is born of the flesh is flesh: and that which is born of the Spirit is spirit. Wonder not that I said to thee: You must be born again. The Spirit breatheth where he will and thou hearest his voice: but thou knowest not whence he cometh and whither he goeth. So is every one that is born of the Spirit. (JN 3:1–8)

Our Lord is speaking of a second birth completed by two agencies: water and the Holy Spirit. Water by itself can exer-cise no spiritual influence, but it is a material sign of what is communicated invisibly and spiritually in the soul, thanks to the words of baptism: "I baptize thee in the name of the Father and of the Son and of the Holy Spirit."

Water is a good sign for the sacrament of Baptism. It signifies a washing, and baptism washes us from our sins; furthermore, water is transparent to light. It signifies how

light can be communicated, the light of faith into the soul.
The Greeks used to say that all life came from water. Their
biology may have been wrong, but theologically they were
sound, for all divine life really does begin with water. Notice our blessed Lord said to Nicodemus that unless he was
born again of baptism in the Holy Spirit, he could not enter
the Kingdom of heaven. We should not be surprised at this.
After all, we cannot live a human life unless we are born of
the flesh, and we cannot live a divine life unless we are born
of God.

We are, as some philosophers have said, *capax Dei*: We are
capable of God. Nature is full of examples of such capacities; all seeds are of this nature. They are dead until favorable circumstances of soil quicken them into life. The egg of
a bird has in it the capacity to become a bird, like the parent,
but it remains a dead thing if the parent forsakes it. There
are many of the summer insects which are twice born; first
of their insect parents, then of the sun. If the frost comes in
place of the sun, they die. The caterpillar already has a life
of its own, but enclosed in its nature is a creeping thing with
a capacity for becoming something higher and different. It
may become a moth or a butterfly. But in most the capacity
is never developed. They die before they mature. Circumstances do not favor their development.

These analogies show how common it is for capacities of
life to lie dormant and how it is for a creature in one stage of
existence to have a capacity for passing into a higher stage.
A capacity can be developed only by some agency outside
of it and adapted to it. In this condition man is born of his
human parents. He is born with the capacity for higher life.
There is in him a capacity for becoming something different and higher. That capacity lies dormant and dead until

the Holy Spirit comes and quickens it. The influence has to come from without; there must be the efficient touch of the Holy Spirit, the imparting of His life. The capacity to be a child of God is man's, but the development of this lies with God. We have to be quickened from without. We cannot give physical birth to ourselves, and we cannot give divine birth to ourselves.

When this sacrament is received, what are some of the effects? One of the principal effects is that it remits original sin, the sin of nature which we have inherited from Adam. If we are adults who have never been baptized before, baptism remits not only original sin but all of our personal sins. Imagine a great sinner being baptized on his deathbed. Suppose he dies immediately after baptism. He has no sins to go before the judgment seat of God, and the reason is he has just been born. We are not to presume that God will give us this grace on our deathbed. Baptism is something that makes us pass out of one land into another.

It is like the passage of the Jews over the Dead Sea from the slavery of Egypt to the land of freedom (EX 14:5-31). Baptism is a passage, for we are transmuted from the kingdom of earth to the Kingdom of heaven. We no longer belong to the race of Adam; we belong to the race of the new Adam. We pass from one master to another. In the ceremony of baptism the one who was baptized is asked, "Dost thou renounce Satan?" Are you willing to pass from the overlordship of Satan to the overlordship of Christ? We die in baptism to our old nature. In the early Church, baptism was often given by immersion. St. Paul tells us when we are baptized we are buried with Christ (RM 6:4); it is like our old Adam being crucified. When we are baptized, which corresponds to the Resurrection, we receive the newness of the life of Christ.

There are in the world really not a multiplicity of races and nations. There are two humanities: One is the humanity of Adam and the other is the humanity of Christ. One is the unregenerate humanity and the other is the reborn, spiritualized humanity of those who are incorporated into the Mystical Body of Christ.

There is no such thing as being baptized into a certain sect. For example, no one is baptized a "Holy Roller." No one is baptized into the "Foursquare Gospel." No one is baptized into the "Triangular Church." As St. Paul says, *For all you who have been baptized into Christ, have put on Christ* (GA 3:27). We are baptized into Christ's Body, which is the Church. There is only one body. That is why it is not necessary for us, if we are absolutely certain of the baptism of anyone outside the Church, to rebaptize that person. It makes no difference who baptized. It is only important that the one who baptized outside of the Church have the intention of doing what the Church intends to do. Today we cannot be sure there are many who believe in the divinity of Christ, original sin, and when they baptize have the intention of doing what the Church intends. We are all baptized into the one Church, the one Body of Christ, whether we know it or not.

There are many who do not have an opportunity to be baptized. It must be noted there are three kinds of baptism. In addition to the baptism of water, there are also the baptism of desire and the baptism of blood. Baptism of desire takes place when a person who has never received baptism, who loves God and desires to be ardently united with Him, has sorrow for sins and is resolved to be baptized. There must indeed be many pagans and Buddhists, Confucianists, and all peoples who have had a desire, according to the light they have received, to be united with God and have followed

His Commandments and would willingly accept anything God revealed to them. They have baptism of desire, and they are incorporated in some way to the Mystical Body of Christ.

In addition, there is the baptism of blood. Suppose you were receiving instructions in a land where there was persecution. The soldiers of a dictator came to you and asked if you intended to join the Church. You answered in the affirmative. They would then sentence you to death. Rather than deny the faith you had and the hope you might be baptized, you submit to death. This is what is known as baptism by blood, because here there is the supreme witness to Christ by blood since there is a supreme love of Christ. I was once instructing a person; we came to the subject of baptism.

She said, "I have never been baptized. Suppose I should die tonight, what would happen to me?"

"Well, you certainly desire, do you not, to receive baptism?"

She answered most ardently, "I can hardly wait!"

She did die that night. She had baptism of desire.

Another difficulty, how about children who, through no fault of their own, die without baptism? Are they punished and sent to hell? No. Unbaptized children are not sent to hell, nor are they punished. Their capacity for the supernatural order was never actualized, but they have all of the natural happiness that is possible for them, and that state we call limbo.

Another effect of baptism is the infusion of certain virtues into the soul. These virtues are seven: faith, hope, charity, prudence, justice, temperance, and fortitude. The first three—faith, hope, and charity—relate us directly to God so that we believe in Him, hope in Him, and love Him. The other virtues are concerned with the means by which we come to God. We are prudent about the use of this world in order to attain the Kingdom of God, and so on for the other virtues. These virtues are infused into the soul. The best way to understand a virtue is in the form of a habit. There are two kinds of habits: acquired and infused. An acquired habit is playing tennis, or playing a violin. An infused habit is swimming, for a duck. These virtues are infused into the soul. It is as if we woke up one morning and discovered we could play musical instruments which before we never touched. Then we would have an infused virtue in the natural order which was not our own. When we are baptized, the virtue of faith is infused. When children come to us in our parochial schools, small though they be, they are immediately receptive to all the teachings about God, our blessed Lord, and the Church. They already have the faith. We do not have to prove the existence of God to them. We merely have to give reasons, developments, and explanations of the faith already in them.

A brief word about faith, hope, and charity. Faith is not a wish to believe or a will to believe something contrary to reason. Faith is not living as if something were true. Faith is the acceptance of a truth on the authority of God revealing as manifested in the Church and in Scripture. God alone causes faith in the believer. Faith is not the acceptance of abstract ideas. It is so often said, "Oh, by faith you have to accept a number of dogmas." No! Faith is participation in the life of God. In faith two persons meet: God and ourselves. Our affirmation of faith does not come because we see a truth clearly; it comes from the vision of Him who reveals truth. We know He cannot deceive or be deceived. Faith is not contrary to reason. Faith perfects reason. Faith is to reason much like a telescope is to the eye. A telescope enables us to see new worlds and stars by our unaided eye. Faith enables us to see truths which we could not see by our reason alone.

Human reason is stronger with faith than without it, just as our senses are stronger with reason than without reason. Reason is to be perfected by faith. A person who loses faith will discover his reason does not exercise itself as well. It's very interesting to read the writings of those who once had faith and lost it. Their minds are wandering and confused. We have the same eyes at night as we have in the daytime, but we cannot see at night. The reason is we lack the additional light of the sun.

Let two people look out on a Host. One sees bread and the other, with the eyes of faith, sees our blessed Lord. One has a light which the other has not. We thank God for revealing to us this beautiful sacrament of Baptism, which gives us this light and makes us His children. The ceremonies of the sacrament are beautiful. Assist sometime at a baptism, and a priest will explain all the ceremonies as they take place. They are beautiful, like putting on the white robe. Dante spoke of it saying purgatory was a place where we go to wash our baptismal robes. Would to God we could always keep clean that robe of innocence we receive in baptism before God and man.

27

CONFIRMATION

The greatest untapped reservoir of spiritual power is found in the Christian laity. It is mainly through the laity that the Church enters into the world. Laymen and laywomen are the meeting place of the Christian and the non-Christian. They are the bond between the sacred and the profane, the religious and the secular. The laity fulfill their Christian vocation in the world. When they come to church they receive life, truth, and grace, but they receive them for service in the world. In the world this Christian truth, grace, and life of theirs come into an encounter with others who may lack it or its richness. A Christian vocation is the exercise of the ordinary manifestations of life so the glory of God is made manifest.

There are two dangers. One is that the Christian laity may form a kind of a ghetto, considering their religious activities to be confined only within the Church in keeping the Commandments. There may also be Christians huddled together in a kind of an igloo, completely divorcing faith and action. The other extreme would be to become so worldly they can do nothing with it.

The result of the separation of religion and the world is

that culture has been emancipated from Christ and become demonic. If the laity are to be effective, they have to be conscious they are members of the people of God; they belong to a worshipping community. They must be theologically literate. As St. Peter said, that they should be able to give a reason for the faith in them (1 P 3:15). They must communicate with the world as Christians. They are involved with the world. As John Donne so beautifully put it:

> No man is an island, entire of itself; every man is a piece of the continent, a part of the main; if a clod be washed away by the sea, Europe is the less, as well as if a promontory were, as well as if any manner of thy friends or of thine own house were; any man's death diminishes me because I am involved in mankind. And therefore never send to know for whom the bell tolls; it tolls for thee.
>
> (MEDITATION 17, *Devotions upon Emergent Occasions*)

No one can expect to fulfill his Christian vocation or attain any kind of personal integrity in the modern world who is not at home with computers, slums, racism, world affairs, with everything. It is the laity who stand at that point where the Gospel intersects the world. As the Cross stood at the intersection of the cultures and the civilizations of Athens, Jerusalem, and Rome, the laity cross all frontiers, and they do this in the name of Christ. As we see the laity come into church on Sundays, we ask them, Do they really love one another? Are they a unified element in the community? Are they coming together just to fulfill an obligation, trying to avoid a mortal sin rather than to strengthen a life they ought to spread? Are they seeking selfish sanctification, forgetting our blessed Lord said, *For their sake do I sanctify myself* (JN 17:19). Will they be very much like everyone else around them, except for just this weekly habit of coming to church? When others look at this band of the faithful, will they say, "I ought to be like them; I ought to have their love, truth, and inner peace." Too often it's just the opposite.

The laity will have to come to a comprehension that our blessed Lord was crucified not in a cathedral between two candles but in the world, on a roadway, in a town garbage heap, at the crossroads where there were three languages written upon the Cross. Yes, they were Hebrew, Latin, and Greek, but they could just as well have been English, Bantu, or African. It would make no difference. He placed Himself at the very center of the world, in the midst of smut, thieves, soldiers, and gamblers. He was there to extend pardon to them. This is the vocation of the laity: to go out into the world and make Christ known.

Where will the laity find their power, wisdom, and courage as witnesses for Christ? If they are left to their own power, they would be as weak as the Apostles were; nine of them away from the garden, and three in the garden sleeping. Above the natural life there is a divine life. There should be a sacrament, some visible sign by which they contact the power of Christ, some channel that will pour away from Calvary down into their own souls and make them strong.

Go back into the natural order and you will recall that for living a person must be born; he must grow to maturity and assume the responsibilities of the society in which he lives. Above the natural life there is a divine life. We must be born to that divine, supernatural life, and that is the sacrament of Baptism. The sacrament inducting us into the higher supernatural life is the sacrament of Confirmation.

We are born spiritually in one sacrament, become citizens of the Kingdom of God, and we are drafted into God's spiritual Army into the lay priesthood of believers. Confirmation, like any other sacrament, is modeled upon the life of our blessed Lord.

Our Lord had a double priestly anointing corresponding to two aspects of His life. The first was the Incarnation, which made Him capable of being a victim for our sins. He took upon Himself a human nature with which He could suffer and redeem us from our sins. As God, He could not suffer; as man, He could. This first aspect of the life of our blessed Lord culminated in His Passion, Death, and Resurrection. The second anointing was the coming of the Holy Spirit in the Jordan River, which ordained Him for the mission of preaching the apostolate. The culmination for the Church was Pentecost. The descent of the Holy Spirit on our Lord in the Jordan had a double effect. It prepared Him for combat. The Gospel states, *Jesus returned from the Jordan, full of the Holy Spirit, and by the Spirit He was led out into the wilderness where He remained forty days tempted by the Devil* (LK 4:1-2). When He received the Holy Spirit, He entered into the conflict with Satan, who offered Him three easy ways from the Cross.

The Holy Spirit prepared Him for combat and for preaching the Kingdom of God. When our blessed Lord appeared at Nazareth, He said,

> The Spirit of the Lord is upon Me. He has anointed Me, sent Me out to preach the Gospel to the poor, to restore the brokenhearted, to bid the prisoners go free, and the blind to have sight, to set the oppressed at lib-

erty, to proclaim a year when men find acceptance in
the Lord. (LK 4:18-19)

After our blessed Lord received the Spirit and fulfilled
these two missions, He instituted the sacrament of Confirmation, by whose power, energy, and strength the Kingdom
of God passes into our souls. The ordinary minister of this
sacrament is the bishop. In cases of extreme necessity, as illness, a pastor may administer the sacrament. The one about
to be confirmed kneels before the bishop, who extends his
hands and prays:

> Almighty, everlasting God, Who hast deigned to beget
> a new life in this thy servant by water and the Holy
> Spirit, and hast granted him remission of his sins, send
> forth from heaven upon him Thy Holy Spirit, with His
> sevenfold gifts: The spirit of wisdom and understand-
> ing. Amen. The spirit of council and fortitude. Amen.
> The spirit of knowledge and piety. Amen. Fill him with
> the spirit of fear of the Lord, and seal him with the
> sign of Christ's cross, plenteous in mercy unto life ev-
> erlasting. Through the selfsame Jesus Christ, Thy Son,
> Our Lord, Who liveth and reigneth with Thee in the
> unity of the Holy Spirit, God eternally. Amen.

Then the bishop dips his thumb in holy chrism and
anoints the forehead of the one to be confirmed. He gives
the name, saying:

> [Name], I confirm thee with the chrism of salvation. In
> the name of the Father [making the sign of the cross]

and of the Son [making the sign of the cross] and of
the Holy Spirit [making the sign of the cross].

Then he gives the one confirmed a slight blow on the
cheek, saying, "Peace be to you." The reason for a slight blow
on the cheek is to remind the one being confirmed that he
must be prepared to suffer all things for the sake of Christ.
This sacrament may be received only once, because it leaves
an indelible mark upon the soul, as do the sacraments of
Baptism and Holy Orders. There are many who neglect its
inspiration.

Let us recall an interesting story from the Old Testament.
Remember the ancient prophet Eliseus, who went to visit a
widowed woman whose sons were about to be sold into slavery because she had no money? He asked, *What do you have in
your house?* She said, *Just a little oil.* He told her to go out and
borrow empty vessels from the neighbors. When they were
gathered, he told her to begin pouring out the little oil she
had into the empty vessels. She began pouring, but the oil
did not stop! And she filled one vessel, then another, and another until she said to her son, *Give me yet another vessel.* The
son said, *There are no more.* And the oil stopped (2 K 4:1–7).

The oil in sacred Scripture very often corresponds to
the Holy Spirit, and the lesson is that the spirit we receive
depends upon our emptiness. The increase of power from
the moment we receive the sacrament depends upon our capacity to respond to Christ. There is no limit to God's love;
there is no limit to His power to bless. He gives in an overflowing measure, far beyond our expectations, far beyond
our deservings. We may stint the blessings for ourselves by
not being in a fit state to receive them. We constantly see in
the history of the Church many blessings are forthcoming

just provided we would de-egotize ourselves. The power of the laity to bear witness to Christ, to be His soldiers in the world, depends upon their humility, their emptiness.

There is another lesson. A Sunday school teacher came before an empty room and said, "Where's the class?" The priest said to her, "You'll have to go out and gather a class." With a little exertion in the streets, she had a class. There are empty vessels all around us that can be filled with the love of Christ. Are there any empty vessels in your home or among your neighbors? If you are a lawyer, do you know empty vessels in your profession? And as a doctor, and as a nurse, are there many whose lives are aimless and destitute?

A lawyer died in Berlin as an unbeliever. He had a Catholic partner. When his friend became ill, the Catholic lawyer visited him and said, "You are about to die; you ought to make your peace with God." And the dying partner said to him, "If Christ in your Church has meant so little to you during your life that you never once spoke to me, how can it mean anything to me at my death?" A serious realization of the sacrament of Confirmation will make one seek to save souls. If we save a soul, we have a very good chance of saving our own. Confirmation is the great social sacrament. It binds us to the world, our neighbor, and humanity. It binds us not only to love God but to love even those people who are seemingly unlovable.

What does "identification" mean? I can tell you what it means by telling you how I failed. I visited a leper colony in Africa where there were about five hundred lepers. I brought five hundred small silver crucifixes with me. The first leper who came to meet me had his left arm off at the elbow. He held the stump of the arm up, and around the shoulder was a rosary. He extended his right hand. I never saw such a mass of putrid, foul corruption as I saw in that leper's hand. I held out the silver crucifix and let it drop. It was almost swallowed up in that volcano of leprosy. I took this symbol of Christ's love for man, this symbol of God's identification with suffering humanity, and I refused to identify myself with one who was perhaps bearing on his body less putrefaction than I had in my own soul. I was the five hundred and first leper and the worst of all because I had refused to identify myself with this brother of mine. The thought came to me of the terrible thing I was doing. I pressed my hand in his, hand to hand, and for all of the lepers in the camp. Because of the sacrament of Confirmation, I have to love all mankind. As a priest, I have to identify myself with them.

Identification can carry over into your own life if you keep the symbol of fire before you. Fire has two great qualities: light and heat. The light is the symbol of truth; the heat is the symbol of love. Too often we separate light and heat. We have the truth but we have little zeal and love. The enemies have no truth, but they have zeal and love for their cause. Confirmation would bid us to keep our truth and the love of truth together. That's what our Lord meant when He said, *I have come to cast fire upon the earth, and what will I but that it be enkindled* (LK 12:49).

28

HOLY EUCHARIST

The whole world hungers for God. St. Augustine said, "Our hearts were made for Thee, O Lord, and they are restless until they rest in Thee" (CONFESSIONS I.I). When our blessed Lord saw a very hungry crowd, He said, *I am sorry for the multitude. They have nothing to eat* (MT 15:32). What He gave them on that occasion is the subject of this lesson, the sacrament of the Eucharist.

In order to lead a physical life, we must be born to it. To lead a supernatural life, we need the sacrament of Baptism. Once we are born, we must grow physically. Spiritually, we must achieve maturity and accept responsibilities. For that we need the sacrament of Confirmation. Now we come to the new element in life. If life is to live, it must nourish itself. If divine life is to live, it needs its nourishment; for that we need the Eucharist.

The Eucharist is the greatest of all the sacraments because it contains in a substantial way the person of Christ, the Author of life. It is the one sacrament to which all of the other sacraments look. Imagine six arrows in a circle all pointing to a center. The center is the Eucharist; the six arrows are the other sacraments. The Eucharist is the sun around which the other sacraments revolve as planets. All other sacraments share in its power, and they perfect themselves in the celebration of the Eucharist. It is a sublime sacrament that human reason could never guess. Divine love is far deeper than we know.

The aim of this encycledia is not to tell you what you must believe, but to explain the faith to you. We begin describing and explaining the Eucharist through the analogy of biology. All natural laws are reflections of spiritual laws; it is not the other way around. The spiritual is the voice and the natural is the echo. Take the law of gravitation. It is a physical law which describes the way all material objects tend toward the earth as its center. In addition, there is a spiritual law of gravitation by which all things are drawn to God. Material gravitation is really a reflection of spiritual.

We come to another law in the order of biology. It is the law of communion. To live we must eat. All life lives through communion with some other form of life. There's nothing on this earth that does not obey that law in some way or other. Plant life does not commune with another kind of life. It is dependent upon something else for its existence. Plant life goes down to the earth for water, phosphates, and carbonates, and draws much life from the sun. If these chemicals and the sun were blotted out, depriving plant life of communion, it would perish.

Plant life is a communion with lower life, but when we get to animal life the law becomes clearer. There's still greater need of nourishment. It needs nourishment from the mineral order like sunlight and air, but the nourishment of the animal comes from plant life. From the very moment the animal comes into being, there is a quest for nourishment. Its fundamental instinct is to seek food. The animal

roaming in the field, the fish swimming in the ocean, the
eagle in the air, all are in search of daily bread. Without ever
knowing it, they acknowledge the law that life is impossible
without nourishment, life grows only by life, and the joy of
living comes from communion with another kind of life.

When you come to man, the same law applies. He has a
body just as animals that clamors for more delicate food.
Our bodies are not content, as the plant, to take food from
the ground raw, uncooked, and unseasoned. They seek the
refinement of a higher creature, acknowledging the universal law of life: Every living thing requires nourishment. Life
lives by life, and the joy of living is enhanced by communion with another form of life. Here we come to a difference:
Man has a soul as well as a body. Since his soul is spiritual,
does it require spiritual food? There's nothing on earth that
can completely satisfy the soul hunger of man because it is
an unearthly hunger. Everything in this universe demands
nourishment suited to its nature. A canary does not use the
same kind of food as a boa constrictor because its nature
is different. Man's soul is spiritual and demands spiritual
food. What will that food be?

Our blessed Lord saw thousands passing in a Passover
caravan, hurrying on to Jerusalem. They were toiling up the
hill in small groups. Some of them were very spent from
long walks, particularly mothers dragging their children
and the old, who longed for refreshment. Our blessed Lord's
heart went out to them. He proposed to feed them. Andrew,
the Apostle, pointed to a boy who had five barley loaves and
two fishes. These, our blessed Lord took. Notice the way
the Gospel describes what our Lord did and the parallel between this description and the Last Supper. We are quoting the Gospel of Mark: *And He took up the five loaves and two*

fishes and looked up to heaven and blessed and broke the loaves and gave to His disciples (MK 6:41). With these five barley loaves and two fishes, our blessed Lord fed the multitude of thousands, creating a miracle of multiplication. A grain of wheat multiplies in the ground. The bread and fishes, by a divinely hastened process, are multiplied until, the gospel says, *everyone had his fill* (MK 6:42). Do you suppose that if our blessed Lord gave out money instead of bread that the gospel would have said that everyone had his fill?

The effect of this miracle was stupendous because they saw the bread and the fishes increasing. The people saw the possibility of making our Lord a king who would bring prosperity and plenty. What people want, even from God who walks this earth, is economic prosperity. It was almost like the temptation of Satan on the mountain. Remember, Satan asked our blessed Lord to turn the stones into bread, to make Himself an economic provider (MT 4:3). The people wanted our Lord to be an economic, political king who would fill their gullets and stomachs. If He did that He would have power according to them. Our Lord, knowing they wished to make Him king, fled into the mountains alone. They could not make Him king, He was born a King!

This flight from political kingship might have disillusioned Judas. Do you know the first record that we have of the fall of Judas takes place when our blessed Lord announces and promises the Eucharist? The fall of Judas comes when our blessed Lord gives the Eucharist at the Last Supper. It was the Eucharist that disillusioned Judas. Then Judas knew our Lord was not going to be an economic king.

The next morning Christ was found at Capernaum. The people were curious about how He got there. When they asked Him, His answer was to reprimand them because they were identifying religion with soup kitchens. He said, quoting the Gospel of John, *Believe Me, if you are looking for Me now it is not because of the miracles you have seen, it is because you are fed with loaves and had your fill* (6:26). By these words our Lord indicated they had not taken the miracle as a sign of His divinity. They were looking for Him instead of to Him. Our Lord continued to reproach them, and these were His words: *You should not work to earn food which perishes in the using. Work to earn food which affords continually eternal life, such food as the Son of man will give you. God the Father has authorized Him* (6:27).

Our Lord was setting in contrast the bread that perishes and the bread that endures to life everlasting. He cautioned them against following Him as a donkey follows a master holding a carrot. To lift their carnal minds to eternal food, He suggested they seek the food the heavenly Father had authorized. This refers to oriental bread, which was often sealed with the official mark of the baker's name. The Talmudic word for baker is related to seal. Just as hosts used in the Mass have a seal upon them such as a lamb or a cross, so our Lord was implying that the bread He would give them was sealed by His Father.

They were not satisfied and wanted further proof the Father had authorized Him. He gave them bread, but that was not stupendous. They argued, *Had not Moses given them bread from Heaven in the desert?* (EX 16:1–5). Their argument was "What proof is there you are greater than Moses?" They minimized His miracle by comparing Him to Moses and by comparing the bread to the manna given in the desert. Our Lord had fed the multitude only once, and Moses had fed the multitude for forty years in the desert, so they made light of the gift. Our Lord took up the challenge. He said the manna they had received from Moses was not heavenly bread, nor had it come from heaven. Furthermore, it nourished only one nation for a brief space of time, and it was not Moses who gave the manna; it was His Father. Finally, the bread He would give would nourish unto everlasting life. Then He told them the true Bread comes down from heaven, and they said, *Give us this bread!* And He answered, *It is I who am the Bread of Life* (JN 6:34-35).

He makes the shadow of the Cross appear. Bread must be broken. He who came from God must die on the Cross as a result of the sins of the world. These are His words: *And now what is this bread which I am to give? It is My flesh given for the life of the world* (JN 6:51). Then the Jews fell to disputing one with another: *How can this man give us His flesh to eat?* (6:52). Whereupon Jesus said to them, *Believe Me when I tell you this; you can have no life in yourselves unless you eat the flesh of the Son of man and drink His blood* (6:53). Notice He is picturing Himself as one who gives Himself in death. The flesh and blood He will give them is not just that flesh and blood they see; it will be the flesh and blood that will be ascended into heaven at the right hand of the Father. He said He would give it for the world.

They begin to understand that these lambs they saw going up to Jerusalem to lose their blood were only symbols of the Pascal Lamb, the Lamb of God. Then He said they were to live by Him as He lived by the Father. His words were *As I live because of the Father, the living Father who has sent Me, so he who eats will live in his turn because of Me* (JN 6:57). Our blessed Lord is saying that life passes from Father to Son and will pass when He passes into His glory from Himself to us.

They knew it was strange. They all knew what He meant, that He was the Bread of Life and we would have to nourish ourselves on His life. They understood the reason Judas broke. Some of the disciples left and walked with Him no more, saying, *This saying is hard and who can bear it?* (JN 6:60). Then our blessed Lord turned to Peter the Rock and said, *Will you also go away?* (6:67). And Peter the Rock answered, *Lord, to whom shall we go? Thou alone hast the words of eternal life* (6:68).

Our Lord would never have permitted His disciples to leave if they misunderstood Him. What He promised that day He fulfills the night of the Last Supper. It suffices for the moment to recall this particular night. He gathers all of His Apostles round about Him. The next day He will die. He institutes a memorial of His death, Resurrection, and Ascension. He who said He was the Bread of Life now, in the words of the Gospel, took bread, blessed and broke it, and gave it to them, saying, *This is My body given for you* (LK 22:19). Notice He said over the bread, "This is My body." He did not say, "This represents My body" but "This is My body." He also said "given for you," given on the Cross. Taking the chalice of wine into His hands, He said, *Drink all of you of this, for this is My blood of the New Testament, shed for many to the remission of sins* (MT 26:28). Over the chalice of wine He said, "This is My blood," not "this represents," but it is. As the Old Testament was ratified with blood, now He ratifies the New Testament with His blood. Did our Lord mean what He said? We believe it. What makes our faith unique is this: We do not pick and choose among the words of our blessed Lord. When He said, *Whose sins you shall forgive, they are forgiven* (JN 20:23), we believe it. That is why there is the sacrament of Penance. When He called Peter the Rock, we believe it. When He said, "This is My body, this is My blood," we believe it. The law of communion continues through the universe. If the plants could speak, they would say to the animals, "Unless you eat me, you shall not have life in you." If the animals could speak to man, they would say, "Unless you eat me, you shall not have life in you." Christ speaks to us and says, "Unless you eat Me, you shall not have life in you." The law of transformation holds sway. Chemicals are transformed into plants, plants into animals, animals into man, and man into Christ. He gave His life to sustain our life, and the greatest joy in the world is communion with the very life of God.

29

THE EUCHARISTIC SACRIFICE

A great American patriot once said he regretted he had only one life to give for his country. He meant his love was greater than his sacrifice; his life could be given only once in time and could not be repeated. It is very different with the life of our Lord. Though the life was given once, it is eternally given and repeated in the sacrifice of the Mass. We are going to describe the Mass in terms of three of its principal parts: the Offertory, the Consecration, and the Communion.

First, the Offertory. This takes place when the priest offers bread and wine to God. Our blessed Lord, if we may draw an image, is looking out from heaven saying, "I cannot die again of the human nature I took from Mary. That human nature is now glorified at the right hand of the Father, the pledge and the promise of what your human nature is to be. But I can die in you and you can die in Me. Will you offer yourselves to me? I can add nothing to the sacrifice of My love except by and through you." Now we begin to offer ourselves to Him under the species of bread and wine.

Let me tell you how this was done in the early Church. If you would have come to Mass, you would have brought some bread and wine. You also might have brought some linen, fruits, wheat, oil, wool, and other things needed by the religious community, by the Church. The priest would have taken all of these gifts, piled them up at the side of the communion rail to distribute to the poor after Mass. But the bread and wine which was brought, he would use that for the Offertory of the Mass. We no longer bring either bread or wine, nor do we bring these other things, because today we live in a modern world where money is the medium of exchange. Instead of bringing bread and wine, we bring what equivalently buys bread and wine. The important thing is that when we offer ourselves to God, we do so under the appearances of bread and wine.

Why did our blessed Lord use bread and wine as the symbols of our Offertory? First, in order to signify our unity with one another and in Him, in the Mystical Body of Christ. Just as a unity of grains of wheat make bread, and just as wine is made up from many grapes, we, who are many, are one in Christ. Another reason is that perhaps no two substances in nature traditionally have so much nourished man as bread and wine. Bread is the marrow of the earth; wine, its very blood. In bringing bread and wine, we are bringing those substances which have most nourished ourselves, given us life. We are equivalently offering our lives on the altar. Wheat and grapes have to suffer a great deal to become bread and wine. Wheat has to pass through a winter, and then it has to be subjected to a mill and to fire before the wheat can ever become bread. Grapes have to pass through the Gethsemane of a winepress before they can become wine. We who offer ourselves to Christ are destined to sacrifice. Let us take those substances from nature which have given us life but indicate in their being the need of sacrificing and suffering in order to be united with Christ Himself. At the moment of the Offertory of the Mass, we are not passive spectators, as we might be in the theater. We are going to be actors in a great drama. We are standing on the paten that the priest is offering. We are in the chalice, participants; we are co-offerers to Christ, through Him to the heavenly Father.

If we understand the Offertory, we realize we have offered ourselves. What happens to us? The answer is given in the Consecration. The priest is only the instrument of Christ Himself at the altar. Christ is the Priest; Christ is the Victim. When the priest pronounces the words of Consecration, he is only giving to our blessed Lord his voice and his hands. At the moment of Consecration the priest says over the bread, "This is My body," and over the chalice of wine, "This is My blood." Then there takes place the mystery of transubstantiation. "Trans" means across, "substantiation" refers to substance. This mystery means the whole substance of the bread becomes the whole substance of the body of Christ. The whole substance of the wine becomes the whole substance of the blood of Christ.

Notice we use the word "substance." Just as a subject has a predicate, just as your personality wears clothes which are purely accidental to your personality because you can change clothes, so bread and wine have what are known as appearances, or predicates. After the moment of Consecration, the bread looks the same as it did before; the wine looks the same. The sensible appearances do not change, but the substance of the bread and wine change into the body and the blood of Christ. How do we know they change? Because our Lord said so. Is there any better reason in the world? Our blessed Lord said, *This is My body; this is My blood* (MT 26:26–28). We believe.

We have offered ourselves to Christ, and the Consecration is a repeating representation of the death of Christ. How is the death of Christ represented in the Consecration? Notice that the priest does not consecrate the bread and wine together. He does not say, "This is the body and blood of Christ." Notice that separate consecration is a kind of cleavage, a tearing asunder, a kind of mystical sword that divides the blood from the body of Christ, and that is how He died on Calvary. Hence, the Mass is called the unbloody sacrifice of Calvary, while Calvary itself was a real separation of blood from body.

But this is not the whole story of the Consecration. Remember we offered ourselves under bread and wine. See what has happened to the bread and wine? It is the body and blood of Christ. Christ is not alone in the Mass; we are with Him. What happened to us? We died with Christ. The words of Consecration have a secondary meaning. The primary meaning that we have given is very clear: "This is the body and blood of Christ." Mystically divided by the separate consecration of the bread and wine, our Lord renews the sacrifice of Calvary. The Vine sacrificed Himself; on the Cross the vine and branches, which we are, now sacrifice themselves in the Mass. The secondary meaning of the words of Consecration is about the branches united to the vine. We say to our Lord, "This is my body; this is my blood. All I am, my body, my blood, my intellect, my will; all of my desires, intentions, and motivations, all I am substantially is now thine. I die with Thee. Transubstantiate them so I am no longer mine, but Thine. All the species of my life, the mere accidents, what I do in life, my peculiar duties, let them remain; they are only the appearances. What I am in my essential relationships to Thee, make divine. I die with Thee, Christ, on Calvary!" That is the Consecration.

Now we come to the Communion. Remember in the Offertory we were like lambs being led on to Jerusalem, and in the Consecration we are those lambs who are offered in sacrifice. In Communion we find we did not lose anything at all. We did not die; we recovered life. We died to the lower part of ourselves in the Consecration of the Mass, and we get back our souls ennobled and enriched. We begin to be free and exalted. We find our death was no more permanent in the Consecration than was the death of Christ on Calvary. In Holy Communion, we surrender our humanity; we get back His divinity. We give up time; He gives us His eternity. We give up our sin; we die to it; He gives us His grace. We surrender our self-will and receive the divine will. We give up petty loves; He gives us the flame of love itself called Communion.

Holy Communion incorporates us to the life of Christ, to the death of Christ, and to the members of the Mystical Body, their joys and sorrows. In Communion we have unity with the life of Christ, the Christ born in Bethlehem, who lived in Galilee, who talked, who suffered, died, rose from the dead, is at the right hand of the Father, and is infusing His life into His Mystical Body. We receive divine life in Communion. Our blessed Lord said, *He that eateth Me, the same shall live by Me* (JN 6:58). Actually, He receives us and we become incorporated to Him. There's a kind of transfusion. Just as in the physical order there is transfusion of blood or life, so here there is a tremendous transfusion of divine life into our souls in Communion. At Communion we always have such a deep sense of unworthiness. The communion prayer is *Domine, non sum dignus:* Lord, I am not worthy.

In human love the beloved is always on the pedestal, the lover always on his knees. In divine love, we protest our unworthiness as we go to the Communion rail to receive the divine life because we died to our lower life in the Consecration. The divine Lover invites us to His banquet. He holds us in His embrace. If our faith were strong, we would crawl on our hands and knees to the Communion rail. Our Lord said, *He who eats My flesh and drinks My blood lives continually in Me and I live continually in him* (JN 6:56).

Communion is not only incorporation to the life of Christ, it is also incorporation to the death of Christ. Here is something that we very seldom think of. St. Paul wrote to the Corinthians, *It is the Lord's death you are heralding whenever you eat of this bread and drink of this cup* (1 CO 11:26). Why is there a death involved? Simply because we have not yet passed into glory. We have our old Adam with us, all of our sins, concupiscence, pride, covetousness, and avarice; and we have to die to all of these, as the Consecration suggested. When a farmer plows corn, he is very interested in life, but he is uprooting weeds. The condition of having the life of the corn is to bring death to the weeds. The condition of having the life of Christ is to bring death to the old Adam. In order to protect this divine life, we have to bring some kind of penance and self-denial to that which is lower. If our Lord died for us, then we have to die to ourselves. After the Resurrection it was the relics of His Passion and His Death He showed man.

Mary Magdalene wanted to achieve the glory of the Resurrection, and our Lord said, *Do not touch Me* (JN 20:17).

But He said to Thomas, *Touch My hands. Put thy finger into My hand. Put thy hand into My side* (JN 20:27). In other words, "Thomas, you may commune with My death to see that I am the Risen life." I believe the Church ordains fasting before Communion in order to be sure we will be incorporated in some tiny little way to the death of Christ before we receive His life.

Communion is not only incorporation to the life of Christ and incorporation to His death, but it is also communion with all of the other members of the Mystical Body of Christ. This is what we forget. When we receive Communion we are being united with every other member of the Church throughout the world. Your body is made up of millions and millions of cells. These cells are nourished by blood plasma, or lymph. It courses through all the gates and alleys of your body to nourish and repair. It knocks at the door of each individual cell. What blood plasma does to your human body is a faint echo of what our Lord does for His Mystical Body. The Mystical Body is made up of persons, not cells. Instead of human nourishment there is the divine life of the Eucharist, as the divine lymph or all of the cells or persons of the Mystical Body of Christ. St. Paul says, *The one bread makes us one body. Though we be many in number, the same bread is shared by all* (1 CO 10:17). The Eucharist makes the Church one.

The communion rail is the most democratic institution in the face of all history. We are communing at the rail not only with every member of the Church, but with the joys of the Church wherever they are in any part of the world and with the sorrows of the Church. Every Communion will make us more and more conscious of helping the Society of the Propagation of the Faith so the Body of Christ may grow and we may be more conscious of our communion with another in this Body of Christ. At Mass our Lord is on the altar.

Think of what our churches would be if we did not have a red tabernacle lamp telling us our blessed Lord was there in His Eucharistic presence. They would just be meeting houses or prayer halls. We would almost feel we were standing alongside of the empty tomb of Easter morn and an angel was saying, "He is not here." Thanks to the real presence of our Lord in our churches, the Eucharist is the window between heaven and earth. Thanks to the real presence, we look out to heaven, and heaven looks down to us. We can pray better there before our Lord, who is truly present in the blessed Sacrament; although the manner of presence is different, it is the Christ, our Savior, our Redeemer, and our love.

30

THE MASS

The Eucharist may be considered from the point of view of either a sacrament or a sacrifice. To understand this distinction, we go back to the analogy of nature. Every day of your life you partake of certain food, the products of wheat, vegetables, fish, and meat. They all enter into the sustenance of your life. Before they can nourish you, they must be submitted to some kind of sacrifice. Before they can be the sacrament of your physical life, they must die or be sacrificed. The vegetables must be torn up from the roots, submitted to fire and the purification of waters. Animals must be submitted to the knife. Death, in other words, intervenes before you can live. Even nature suggests that before you can have a sacrament, you must have a sacrifice. Before you can have Communion you must have the sacrifice, or the Consecration.

Running through nature is the law that we live by what we slay. These creatures submit themselves to our living; they are transformed into our higher life. This law seems to be applied even on Calvary. Looking at the Cross, we realize we live by what we slay. Who of us can claim innocence of the Crucifixion? Our pride is there in the crown of thorns, our avarice in the pinioned hands, our carnality in torn flesh. Though we are responsible for His death through our sins, He gives us His life. We live by what we have slain.

We said our blessed Lord came to this earth to redeem us. There's always been anticipation in history of this great sacrifice. Man, conscious of his own unworthiness, has taken wheat, grapes, bullocks, doves, and sheep, and made these things stand for himself. Then he destroyed them that there might be some proof before God that he was not worthy to exist in His presence. You see it was a vicarious sacrifice which stood for man. In the Jewish religion, sacrificial types were ordained by God Himself. One of them was the Pascal lamb. In all sacrifices, pagan and Jewish, the priest who offered was always distinct from the victim that was offered. If we call the priest the offerer, he is distinct from the fruit or the animal which was the offered. You could point to the priest on one hand, the victim on the other until our Lord appeared. Our blessed Lord was both priest and victim. He differed from every other sacrifice in the world since He offered Himself; He gave His own life. He was the offerer and the offered. This was still a vicarious sacrifice. He took our place as if the sins were His own. What is the Mass? It is the commemoration of the death and application of that sacrifice of the Cross to us.

This is rather a new idea to many; hence, we will have to use the analogy of Memorial Day. All peoples have kept a memory of the soldiers who died in battle to evoke piety and love of country. In the United States, we decorate soldiers' graves on Memorial Day, recalling the sacrifice which they made that we might live and be preserved in freedom.

Our blessed Lord died as the great Captain of our salvation. He did not come to live; He came to die. The purpose of His coming, to offer Himself in our stead, was to undo our infinite guilt. His death was more important than the thirty-three years of His physical life, because it was His death that purchased our salvation. The bloody sacrifice on the Cross began when He instituted the Last Supper. Before He institutes this memorial, Scripture states: *Jesus already knew that the time had come for His passage from this world to the Father. He still loved those who were His own, whom He was leaving in this world. And He would give them the uttermost proof of His love* (JN 13:1).

He proposes to give the uttermost proof; the Last Supper looks forward to His Cross. He is not going to leave the memory of His death to the chance recollection of men, because He knows men have short memories! He is going to, Himself, institute the precise memorial. On this night before He dies, at the Last Supper, He institutes not a Memorial Day, but a memorial act.

Here we must recall the words of our Lord at the Last Supper: *Then He took bread, and blessed and broke it and gave it to them saying, This is My body given for you.* Continuing Scripture: *Then He took a cup and offered thanks and gave it to them saying, Drink, all of you of this, for this is My blood of the new testament, shed for many to the remission of sins* (MT 26:26–28).

When the substance of the bread became the substance of the body of Christ, the substance of the wine became the substance of His blood. He says to His Church, and I am quoting Scripture, *What I have just done do you in your turn in commemoration of Me* (LK 22:19). Certainly these words mean if the Apostles were to do what He did, they had to be given the power to do it.

On the night of the Last Supper, when our Lord instituted this commemoration of His death, He was looking forward to Calvary on the next day. The Cross would not be

a distinct sacrifice; it would not be an entirely different oblation, but a new presence of the same sacrifice. This Last Supper was the unbloody presentation of His sacrifice, and the
next day, when our blessed Lord went to the Cross, would
be bloody. What we have to emphasize here is our Lord said,
"Do this. Repeat it. Prolong it. Extend it through space and
time that all may share in My sacrifice." When we do this,
we have the Mass.

Here we invoke another analogy, and all analogies are
incomplete, but here we use the analogy of a drama. Suppose some great playwright wrote a magnificent drama. It
might conceivably be the story of how a whole community
of people suffering from leprosy was cured of that disease,
how they were restored to peace and unity among themselves, and how they all began to live in charity. Suppose
this drama was well written, presented, and acted. It would
be a shame if only the people of one city and in one theater
in one moment of time saw it. What a tragedy if that drama
should have no other recall than what four dramatic critics
wrote about it, telling about the characters, quoting a line
here and there.

Do you think our Lord went through this tragedy of Calvary only once and intended to leave no other memory than
what four writers—Matthew, Mark, Luke, and John—might
say about it? Of course not! Just as theater producers would
organize road companies of that drama, so our blessed Lord
organized road companies. The great tragedian, Christ, offered His life for the sins of the world in accordance with
the script written by His heavenly Father. Immediately afterward, in accordance with His instructions, the tragedy
of Calvary is repeated throughout the world thanks to the

road companies playing to packed houses every day. This reenactment of the sacrifice of Christ on the Cross applied to our day and our lives is the Mass. In the Mass the Mystical Body of Christ offers through Him, and with Him, the sacrifice of Calvary. As our blessed Lord in the Last Supper looked forward to the Cross, so in the Mass we look back to the Cross and the Last Supper.

Which brings up two questions: How does the sacrifice of the Cross differ from the sacrifice of the Mass? Are the sacrifice of the Cross and the sacrifice of the Mass the same? Let us take similarities, then differences. There is the same priest in both, Christ, and the same victim in both, Christ. Both on the Cross and in the Mass, our Lord is both the offerer and the offered. That is why Scripture says:

> Having therefore a great high priest that hath passed into the heavens, Jesus the Son of God: let us hold fast our confession. For we have not a high priest who cannot have compassion on our infirmities: but one tempted in all things like as we are, without sin. Let us go therefore with confidence to the throne of grace: that we may obtain mercy and find grace in seasonable aid. (HEB 4:14-16)

Note the continuing exercise of His priesthood. In the Mass He offers His sacrifice to His Father. He is pleading as High Priest on our behalf. Imagine our blessed Lord in heaven holding out His scars, saying to His heavenly Father, "See what I suffered for men." As we have asked, "If the sacrifices of the Old Testament gave outward purification, shall not the blood of Christ, who offered Himself through the

Holy Spirit, purify our consciences to serve the living God?" Our Lord is the Priest and the Victim. Between our sins and His glory, He interposes His eternal sacrifice.

You ask, "What is the role of the earthly priest when he stands at the altar?"

When I offer the holy Mass, I am merely the instrument of Christ. He offers the Mass. He's the offered. Every priest is the sacramental image of Christ, in whose person, and with whose power, he utters the words of consecration. We cannot repeat it too often: Christ is the Priest; Christ is the Victim. When we are ordained we receive a power to act by the power of Christ and in His name. We lend our Lord our tongue, we give Him the use of our hands, but the sacrifice is His. He is the Priest; He is the Victim.

What are the differences? The sacrifice of the Cross was a very bloody sacrifice, and the sacrifice of the Mass is unbloody. On Calvary, those who stood near saw red rivers of redemption flowing through hands, feet, and side, but in the Mass there is no physical crucifixion. The Crucifixion is symbolically represented under the species of bread and wine. A second difference, on the Cross our Lord was alone; in the Mass the Mystical Body is with Him. On the Cross, our Lord was alone; He redeemed us all. By that sacrificial act He put a great deposit in a bank for the spiritually poor of the world. It will only be through the coming of the Spirit that we will be able to draw on that deposit.

Since the Holy Spirit came and the Church began to offer the Mass, our Lord is not alone, we are with Him. He, the Head, makes use of His Body. The Mystical Body is united with Christ, the Head, the offerer; the Mystical Body is united with Christ, the Head, as the offered. When we offer the Mass, the prayers are in the plural. For example, "We thy servants, Lord, and with us all Thy holy people offer to Thy Sovereign Majesty this sacrifice." In the Mass the Lord is no longer the sole Priest, no longer the sole Victim. He has associated with Him us earthly priests, who are the instruments of His power. He also has victims associated with Him, namely, the sacrifices and the battles against the old Adam and the crucifixion of our lusts and concupiscence, in fact, all the trials of the Mystical Body of Christ.

The Mass then is not a souvenir. The Mass is a vision; it is an action in time and in eternity. In time, because we see it taking place before our eyes on the altar. It is also in eternity as regards the value of redemption. All of the merits of our Lord's death, Resurrection, Ascension, and Glorification, are applied to us. We unite ourselves with the great eternal act of love, the Mass.

If, when the blessed Mother, St. John, and Mary Magdalene were at the foot of the Cross they had closed their eyes and merely concentrated on the tremendous mystery of love being enacted before their eyes, they would have been assisting at the Mass. If we at the Mass close our eyes and concentrate on that mystery, we would equivalently be with Mary, Magdalene, and John at the foot of the Cross. The Mass is not a new sacrifice; it is the representation in space and in time of redemption. Why should we be penalized by the eternal because of the accident of time? Are there women today who want to be Veronicas and to offer veils to the suffering Christ? Are there men like Simon who want to help Him carry the Cross (MT 27:32)? Do we want to take our own sufferings to have them united with Him that they might be considered part of our expiation for sins?

It is said today that science may someday be able to go back and pick up all the sounds ever spoken and made in the universe because they exist someplace in space. We might recover the voices of Alexander, Gregory, Damascene, and even the voice of Christ. Compare going back, finding, and repeating the very sacrifice of the Cross, of taking the Cross of Calvary, transplanting it into New York, London, Tokyo, and Berlin, and applying the benefits of redemption to our souls now. What a mystery of love! This is the Mass.

31

SIN

The three previous sacraments discussed were baptism, confirmation, and the Eucharist. All of them refer to a life above the physical; namely, the participation in the divine life. By baptism we are born to the divine life; in confirmation we grow and accept the full responsibilities of union with our Lord, and in the Eucharist, our union with Him reaches its peak and ecstasy.

The sacrament of Penance, or Confession, refers to the sins committed after baptism. It is the great sacrament of the mercy of God. If we may use the word as an indication of how realistic God is, once we are born to divine life, we should live in it. But some fall away lightly or seriously. God, in His mercy, has instituted this sacrament by which the sins committed after baptism may be remitted.

No human being could ever have thought of this sacrament, for it is something like the Resurrection; we rise after we are dead. It is a journey back again to God. It enables us to get rid of infections before they become chronic diseases and epidemics. It is not an unpleasant and necessary sacrament to be viewed merely as a humiliation. Penance is the inflowing of God's mercy, an opportunity for the increase of the grace of Calvary. It is a medicine for the soul, the healing of our wounds, a homecoming, an undoing of the past, an opportunity to get a fresh start in life, a kind of secondary baptism. Sometimes reconciliation is sweeter than an unbroken friendship. If we had never sinned, we never could call Christ, Savior. Confession is the sacrament which restores us to the fellowship of the Church, to God's community, to His *qahal,* to His Mystical Body. Before we can tell you about penance we must introduce the word "sin." George Bernard Shaw once said that the modern man is too busy to think about his sins. Perhaps Shaw should have said modern man keeps nervously busy so he will not think about his sins. Every sinner is an escapist just as Adam was when he hid from God.

The sins we are going to discuss are not original sin but personal sins. We have spoken about original sin and said it was not personal, it is the sin of human nature because we are the descendants of Adam. We are involved in it like a citizen of any country whose head has declared war. It gave us even a tendency toward sin, but inclination to sin is not sin. It became possible for us to turn sex into lust, thirst into intemperance and alcoholism, hunger into gluttony, and prudence into avarice. Through sin we became almost like those who were given the inheritance of a great estate but with the mortgage, too. Our nature is spoiled before we received it.

Now we come to the sins for which we are personally responsible; they are sometimes called actual sins. Why is sin possible? Because we are free. You can tell a man he ought to do something, but in his will he can resist. Sin lies in the abuse of freedom. It has something to do with a wrong or an evil choice. We never sin without the will. We can take two attitudes toward freedom, both of which are wrong. We can exaggerate human freedom; we can minimize it.

When we deny that we are the creatures of God and subject to His law, we exaggerate freedom. This was the essence of the temptation of the devil to our first parents. He said, *You will be likened to gods* (GN 3:5). In other words, "You will not be creatures; you will be creators." We exaggerate freedom when we say, "I love myself, my own will. I am my own law. I determine what is right and wrong. I shall treat my neighbor as an inferior, as a plaything for my pleasure, as a means to my profit. I am the end of my own existence." That is the abuse of freedom you find in those who live without God.

On the other hand, sin is possible when we minimize freedom. This comes about when we deny there is any such thing as guilt. We minimize freedom when we say all guilt is morbidity; it is a psychological complex, or guilt is just a hangover from religious, family, and moral taboos. Those who minimize freedom always expect to be praised when they are good, but when they do evil they say, "Oh, no, it really is not my fault. I was under a compulsion," thus denying responsibility. Nobody is bad; no one is a juvenile delinquent; they're only sick!

"You get too fat? You can't help it; you're a compulsive eater!"

"You drink too much? You can't help it; you are a compulsive drinker!"

"You steal? You can't help it; you are a compulsive thief!"

You see, behind that word and behind all other escapes there is the assumption "I am determined."

"I am determined by environment."

"I am determined by my grandparents."

"I am determined by something inside or outside of myself."

This denial of guilt is serious. Indeed, there are some manifestations of guilt. When Lady Macbeth washes her hands repeatedly, we have a morbid manifestation of guilt, but real guilt prompted that morbidity; namely, the murder of the king, in which she was involved. In the past, it was customary for a man to blame something outside of himself: economics, politics, bad environment, poverty, society, grade B milk, insufficient playgrounds. In all instances guilt was transferred from the individual outside of himself. A popular excuse is to say, "No, man is not guilty at all. The fault is not in the stars, but wholly in our unconscious. We cannot help being the way we are."

Some very serious effects follow this denial of personal guilt. The aim of it, as you see, is to make everybody "nice." The worse sinners are nice people, but by denying sin they make the cure of sin impossible. Sin is very serious, but it is more serious to deny sin. If the blind deny there is any such thing as vision, how shall they ever see? If the deaf deny there is any such thing as hearing, what chance is there of being cured of their deafness? By the mere fact we deny sin, we make the forgiveness of sins impossible! Those who very often deny sin become scandalmongers, talebearers, and hypercritics because they have to project their real guilt to others. This gives them a great illusion of goodness. The increase of faultfinding is in direct ratio and proportion to the denial of sin. In some persons sin works like a cancer, undermining and destroying the character for a long time without any visible effects. When the disease becomes manifest, some souls give up hope, which they should not.

Then there comes despair, something that demands the

infinite. Animals never despair simply because they do not know the infinite. Seldom will a man openly revolt against the infinite. If he has revolted and sinned and still does not accept the fact, he tries to minimize the gravity of the sin by excuses, just as Cain did. Modern man has lost the understanding of the very name of sin. He puts the blame on someone or something else: on his spouse, work, friends, and on tensions. Sometimes, by ignoring the real guilt, he may become either psychotic or neurotic. It is awful when despair takes possession of souls. Traveling at seventy miles per hour in an automobile is already an excessive speed, but if twenty miles per hour more is added, the danger mounts. Unrepented sins beget new sins, and the dizzying total brings despair! Then the soul will say, "I'm too far gone!" The drunkard becomes afraid of a sober day that will make him see his own state. The greater the depression the more a sinner needs to escape through further sins until he cries out with Macbeth in his despair, "I had lived a blessed time, for from this instant there's nothing serious in mortality; all is but toys. Renown and grace is dead" (*Macbeth* 2.3).

Despair often turns into fanaticism against religion and morality. A man who has fallen away from the spiritual order will hate it because religion is a reminder of his guilt. Some souls reach a point where like Nietzsche they want to increase evil until all distinction between right and wrong is blotted out. Then they can sin with impunity and say with Milton, "Evil, be thou my good." Expediency can now replace morality, cruelty becomes justice, and lust becomes love. Sin multiplies in such a soul until it becomes the permanent state of Satan. As Seneca said, "Every guilty person is his own hangman." Shakespeare said, "Conscience doth make cowards of us all" (*Hamlet* 3.1). What are we to do in the face of this sin? Continue to deny it? Is it not much better to try to define it and understand it?

We have indicated sin is not a manifestation of animal instincts; it is not an eruption of the subconscious. It is not something that has happened because we were loved too little by a grandmother or loved too much by a grandfather. It is an act of freedom by which we throw the whole harmonious nature out of joint. It is not just self-interest, but it is the affirmation of self at all costs.

Here we are assuming the very elementary concept of sin, so let us begin with some analogies from the physical and biological order. Sin is disobedience to the laws of God in the physical universe. Suppose someone builds a skyscraper out of plumb. The building will not stand because he refused to respect the law of gravitation. In a broad sense of the word, he sinned against the physical law. On a higher level, common sense is also a reflection of the divine law. I am free to drive my fist through a windowpane. My punishment is a cut and bleeding hand. I have violated a law and see the consequences.

Go into the biological order. Why does anything die? It dies because there is a domination of the lower order over the higher order. When do plants die? When the chemical order begins to dominate plant life. Fire kills a plant. Fire belongs to the lower order. How can an animal die? It can die through the domination of plant life over animal life, as through poisonous plants. Death is the domination of a lower order over a higher order. When does the soul die? Whenever there is the domination of the lower order over the higher order: the ego over the community, flesh over the spirit, time over eternity, the body over the soul. Then there is the death we call sin. Scripture equates death in the biological order and sin in the moral order: *The wages of sin is death* (RM 6:23).

Sin is a deliberate violation of the law of God. If you buy an electric coffeepot, you will find instructions in the form of a commandment. The instructions may read, "Put not the plug into the electric current when thy pot is empty." Suppose you say, "Why should anybody tell me what to do? He's violating my constitutional rights!" You forget the coffeepot manufacturer gave you instructions for perfect use. When God made us, He gave us certain laws, not to destroy our freedom but so we might perfect ourselves. When we violate those laws, we hurt ourselves. We break a relationship. In the parable of the Prodigal Son, the father said of the Prodigal, *He was dead; now he is alive!* (LK 15:24).

What is sin for the Christian? It is the breaking of a personal relationship. For those who are in the state of grace, it is a kind of crucifixion; it is the wounding and the hurting of the one we love. Why are we sorry for our sins? Not because we have broken a contract, not just because we've broken a law, but because we have hurt someone we love. Only when we discover God and, above all, His mercy in Christ, do we begin to understand sin fully. It takes love in order to make us understand sin. That seems strange, but it is true. Regardless of how great the sin, there is always mercy. To be a sinner is our distress. But to know we are a sinner is our hope, and the hope is the sacrament of Penance.

32

SIN AND PENANCE

We said from the natural point of view, sin is a violation of the law of God. Every sin has a triple effect: It divides a person from himself, his neighbor, and God. From himself because it makes the soul a kind of a battlefield. After a sin one always feels like a menagerie full of wild beasts. Then sin alienates a man from his neighbor. A man who cannot live with himself cannot live with his neighbor. Cain, after his sin, asked, *Am I my brother's keeper?* (GN 4:9). Finally, it estranges us from God and gives us a sense of loneliness. In some way we dam up the mind which ought to have communion with God.

There are mortal and venial sins. Here we speak of personal, or actual sins. The difference between the two is very easy to understand. We speak of someone receiving a mortal wound in the physical order, one that kills him. If he is not seriously wounded, that would be equivalent to a venial sin. In a mortal sin, for those who are in the supernatural order, grace is killed and divine life is extinguished. In the supernatural order, a mortal sin is not just a violation of the law of God; it is a crucifixion. As we read in the epistle of the Hebrews, *Would they crucify the Son of God a second time?*

(HEB 9:25–28). Sin is a second death because it is the death of divine life. When we fall into mortal sin, we lose all of the merits we gained before. We can regain them after a sacramental confession just like a tree can revive in the springtime after a very hard winter.

A venial sin does not kill the divine life but wounds it slightly, like the tensions between friends that endanger the friendship but never completely break it. When you love someone, you never make any distinction between mortal and venial sin. It is quite wrong to say, "Oh, is it a mortal sin? If it is, I will not do it. If it is a venial sin, I will."

Three conditions must be fulfilled for there to be a mortal sin: There must be grievous or serious matter, serious and sufficient reflection, and full consent of the will. If you stole an apple from a neighbor's orchard and he had dozens of trees, that would not be grievous matter. It may not be a sin of commission, but can be a sin of omission, like not going to Mass on Sunday. There must always be sufficient reflection or full advertence to what one is doing. During Lent, if you eat meat on Friday thinking it's Thursday, there's no mortal sin. There must be full consent of the will. Fear, passion, and force can diminish consent, but they do not destroy it. It is not always easy to know whether one has fulfilled these three conditions, and the best way to do so is to confess them as dubious and ask the priest for his judgment. In mortal sin there is a double element, a turning to creatures and a turning from God.

To remedy all of the sins and atone for those committed since baptism, our blessed Lord has instituted the sacrament of Penance. The matter that we submit in this sacrament constitutes our sins, which we submit to the Church's judgment. The other side of the sacrament is the words of the priest when he absolves us. He says, *Deinde, ego te absolvo a peccatis tuis in nomine Patris et Filii et Spiritus Sancti. Amen.* "I absolve you from your sins in the name of the Father and of the Son and of the Holy Ghost. Amen."

Our Lord, and not the Church, instituted the sacrament. It did not exist in the Old Testament, though in the Old Testament there was an acknowledgment of sins before God. When Adam had eaten the forbidden fruit, God said to him, *Hast thou eaten of the Tree of the knowledge of good and evil?* (GN 3:11). God knew that he had. Why did He ask? In order to elicit a confession. God said to Cain, *Where is thy brother?* (GN 4:9). He tried to elicit a confession from Cain. Cain refused to go to confession because he answered, *Am I my brother's keeper?* (4:9). Through the Old Testament every sinner had to bring a sin offering, which was burned in public as if to publicly admit his guilt. John the Baptist heard the confession of sins (MT 3:6).

All of these were types of the sacrament to come because forgiveness is possible only through the Passion, merits, and death of our blessed Lord. He certainly had the power to forgive sins and He did. Remember the man who was let down from the roof, the man who was sick of palsy? Our blessed Lord said to him, *Thy sins are forgiven thee* (MK 2:5). And the Pharisees that were standing about said, *Who can this be that He talks so blasphemously? Who can forgive sins but God only?* (2:7). They were right; only God can forgive sins. But how did He do it? He did it through a human nature.

God can communicate power to other human natures if He communicates the power of forgiveness to His Church. He conferred it on Peter when He gave him the power of keys, and He said to Peter, *Whatsoever thou shalt bind on earth is bound in heaven. And whatsoever thou shalt loose on earth is loosed in heaven* (MT 16:19). Power was given to Peter alone and is ratified in heaven. Our blessed Lord also gave Peter and the Apostles an extension of that power. Breathing on them as a symbol of the Holy Spirit, our blessed Lord said to Peter and the Apostles after the Resurrection, *Receive the Holy Spirit. When you forgive men's sins they are forgiven. When you hold them bound, they are bound* (JN 20:23).

Our blessed Lord was saying all power given to Him He now passed on to them. The very words He used to Peter and the Eleven, or to His Church, implied hearing confessions. If they did not hear confessions, how would they know which sins to forgive and which sins to retain? They could only make a judgment on the given material.

Why did our Lord institute a confession and the telling of sins? Why shouldn't we bury our heads in our handkerchiefs and tell God we're sorry? There is no test of sorrow if you are the judge. What would happen to justice in our country if all judges and courts when they had murderers, thieves, and dope addicts before them handed out Kleenex? Sin is pride; telling of it is the humiliation and reparation for the sin. In the natural order, does not a hurtful thing hurt more if it is shut up, like a boil or a tooth that aches? We lance boils to release the pus. So our Lord said He would lance souls in order to release the evil therein. The soul wants to throw off everything harmful. An avowed sin loses its tenacity, revealing its horror. A suppressed sin comes out in complexes. When we keep the cap on our soul and do not allow what is in us to come out normally, when we suppress guilt, then it begins to come out in a thousand abnormal ways.

God was merciful in instituting this sacrament. But you may ask, "Why should I confess my sins to a priest? Maybe he's not as holy as I am." That could be true, since we hear the confessions of many saints. Though you are holier than the priest is, you do not have more powers than the priest does. You may be a far better citizen than the mayor, but he has powers you do not have. Our blessed Lord gave the power to His Church. He did not give it to people. Thus, a priest is the authorized minister of the sacrament. Furthermore, the priest does not absolve you. A man cannot forgive sins. The priest in the sacrament is only the instrument of Christ; he gives and loans our Lord his voice. Christ forgives, and the words of absolution mean "I, Christ, absolve you from your sins."

Then, why be ashamed to confess the sins to the priest? He's bound by what is called the *sigillum,* or the seal of confession. He is only the instrument of our Lord; the sins he hears are not his own; they are not a part of his knowledge. In this instance he was the ear of Christ. He may not divulge any sin you confess, even under the pain of death. Suppose I kept money in a drawer in my desk, and every day somebody came in and stole some money out of the drawer. Then the person came to me for confession. I could tell that person to return the money because there must always be a validation of what was wrong, but because I learned something in the confessional, I would never again be allowed to lock my desk drawer. None of your sins will ever be told, nor can we even speak to you about them outside of confession. If you come and confess that you stole money, I could not go up to you at a later time and say, "Remember you told me about the money that you stole from that pickle factory? Did you ever return it?" That information is not mine; it belongs to God.

Another reason for confessing sins to a priest is this: No sin is individual. Each sin diminishes the Mystical Body of Christ and hurts the Church. It is fitting that a representative of the Mystical Body of Christ restores you again to its unity and fellowship. In the early Church even the penances were public to indicate in a very serious way the injury done to the *qahal,* to the Mystical Body of Christ, to the Church.

Let us come into the actual practice of confession. Before you go into the box you examine your conscience. You begin with a prayer to the Holy Spirit to enlighten. Remember it is only in the face of God, and in particular before the crucifix, we discover our true condition. We judge ourselves not by our own standards, or by public opinion, but by the standards of God Himself. You may examine your conscience according to the Commandments. This is not always the best way, because it reduces our Christian life to cold duties and we're apt to become legalistic and calculating. We could examine our conscience in the light of virtue and in light of the seven capital sins. In any case, we have to examine our sins according to their number, kind, and circumstances. When you confess sins you never involve any other person. You cannot say, "I was angry, but you ought to know my wife!" Such a confession would not be sincere.

This is a story and it is only a story. One day a group of lumberjacks from Canada came to confession. They had not been to confession in about ten years or more. They all lined up outside the box, one after the other. The first one went in. He had not examined his conscience, so he said to the priest:

"Father, I have committed every sin a man can commit."

The priest asked, "Did you ever commit murder?"

"No," he said, "I did not. That is one sin I never committed."

"Well," said the priest, "you go outside the box and examine your conscience again; the number, kind, and circumstances of sin."

As he went out of the box, he saw the long line of lumberjacks outside, and he said to them, "No use tonight, boys, he's just hearing murder cases!"

Now we go into the box and begin the confession. Immediately we kneel down, bless ourselves, and say, "Bless me, Father, for I have sinned." Then we state how long it has been since our last confession in a definite period of time, such as weeks, months, or years. Suppose we have someone who has not been to confession in fifty years. Suppose he's eighty years old. What kind of a confession can he make? He cannot remember all of the number of sins and the like. His confession might be something like this:

> Father, it has been fifty years since I last went to confession. During twenty years of my life I never went to Mass. I never frequented the sacraments. I never made my Easter duty. I did not fast. Many times a day I took the name of God falsely, I used it falsely. I also took false oaths in court about five times. I was disobedient in a very serious way to civil authorities, twice. I assisted an abortion, twice. I murdered, once. I was an alcoholic for ten years. I had immodest thoughts, certainly every day for about thirty years, immodest actions with myself many times for about ten years.
>
> While living with my first wife, I was guilty of adultery many times over a period of three years. While my first wife was living I married again, so I lived in adultery for about five years. Now she is dead.
>
> During this time, in business, I cut corners; I underpaid my employees; I thought only about making money. I never gave to any charities, except when I was forced to out of public shame. I particularly regret,

once, refusing to send one hundred dollars to the Holy Father for missions of the world when I had plenty of money.

I gave myself over to an excessive spirit of amusement and parties. I can never recall once in my life ever having helped someone in distress. I never gave up my evenings once to help the Church. I completely neglected my wife as regards esteem and affection. I never sent my children to a religious school. I left them to do as they pleased and I became angry with them for their impiety and now I am suffering.

For these and all sins of my past life, those which I do not remember, but as God sees them, I ask pardon of God and you, Father.

This is a confession of a man away from the sacrament fifty years.

33

PENANCE

Continuing the sacrament of Penance, we review the essential acts of Penance: the confession or the telling of sins, contrition or sorrow, and satisfaction for sins. We have partially treated confession, or the actual telling of sins. What are the differences among literary, psychoanalytic, and sacramental confession?

Let us take literary confession, such as in Jean-Jacques Rousseau. Those who write modern confessions do not confess sins for the same reason we do in the sacrament. Rousseau had great pride in revealing himself. This sentiment is almost implied in modern confessions: "See what a rogue am I?" Not only is there pride, but there is also an intent to arouse similar emotions, feelings, urges, concupiscence, and passions in the mind of the reader. Every disclosure of vice contributes to the increase of pleasure. When St. Augustine wrote his confession, there was great shame, not pride. He did not tell any of his grave sins. One would almost think, reading *The Confessions of St. Augustine,* that the worst thing he ever did was to steal an apple, which he made stand for all of his grave sins. Then, he said he wrote his *Confessions* so everyone might know the mercy of God. If you would ever like to read the finest piece of analysis of soul ever done, read *The Confessions of St. Augustine*.

We come now to the other objection. What is the difference between telling one's sins in confession and telling sins to a psychoanalyst or to a psychiatrist? There are many differences. In psychoanalysis there is an avowal of the attitude of mind and particularly an avowal of unconsciousness. Confession, on the contrary, is an avowal not of a state of mind but of a state of conscience; it is an avowal of guilt. Confession is the communion of the conscience and God. The mere revealing of one's subconscious is never very humbling. Most people when they describe their state of mind to a psychoanalyst will often end it up by saying, "Doc, did you ever hear a case like this before?" They are very proud of it.

Another difference between the two is everybody wants to do their own telling, knowing better than anyone else their guilt. "Let me tell it" is a primary right of the human heart. Confession satisfies that. Every decent mind resents probing by alien minds. Each wants to swing open the portals of personal conscience with no one breaking down doors from the outside. The very uniqueness of personality gives us the right to state our own case in our own words, and that is what happens in confession. We are our own witnesses. We are our own prosecuting attorneys. We are, to some extent, our own judges. No soul likes to be studied like a bug!

Another difference concerns the person to whom the avowals are made. Confession is always made to a representative of the moral order. The analyst represents not the moral order, but the emotional order. When you go to a representative of the moral order, you go there to be made better, to have your sins forgiven, not to have them explained away. In confession, the relationship between the confessor and the penitent is utterly impersonal. The very structure of the confession protects the penitent from revealing his identity: There's a screen; there's a veil; nothing can be passed, and the priest cannot see through. The penitent may go on impersonally for a valid confession and indifferently to any priest. It makes no difference to which one he goes. The guilty conscience wants to avow his guilt not to a theorist of a particular system, but to a mediator, a divinity. The Church asks that a priest who absolves the penitent be in the state of grace, a participant himself of divine life.

Psychoanalysis never raises the question of the moral fitness of the analyst. He may be beating his wife at home. But the Church always raises that question seriously. We are never made worse by admitting the need for absolution. We are not made worse by admitting we are all brokenhearted when we go to confession. We face our guilt and sin because we have the great advantage of being able to let God into our broken hearts.

In natural confession the penitent is never cited and forced to go. He receives no summons, but he goes of his own accord; he is not accused, he accuses himself; there are no outside witnesses, he witnesses against himself as the culprit. Therefore, there is no question of vindictive justice, as there is in civil courts. The reason one goes to confession is in order to be healed, to be reincorporated to Christ, and also to receive His mercy.

When we go to confession we are apt to forget sins. If we inadvertently forget to mention even a grave sin, there is no need to go back to confession. It is forgiven in the intention to confess the sin, but we should mention it explicitly in the next confession. No one seems to realize the great advantage there is in confession as regards character building. It confers grace, gives power to the will. An unbeliever once wrote, "The custom of monthly confession is a magnificent safeguard for the morals of youth. The shame engendered by this humble confession perhaps saves a greater number than the holiest of natural motives."

Now assuming the confession is made, we come to the second act of the sacrament, namely, contrition or sorrow. "Contrition" means to break, to crush, from the Latin *conterere*. Contrition is not a worldly remorse, related only to the past. It is not related to a standard, not related to God, not related to the divine life of Christ. Contrition is a wish that what was done be undone and does not make any reference at all either to neighbor or to self. The great difference between the two is evident in the case of Judas and Peter. Both sinned. Our blessed Lord said both would sin. He called Peter a devil (MT 16:23), and Scripture says Judas himself became possessed by the devil (LK 22:3). Why was Peter forgiven and Judas was not? It was because Judas repented unto himself (MT 27:3). That is the exact expression of Scripture. Peter repented unto our Lord. Judas had remorse; Peter had sorrow or contrition. Contrition is a sincere interior attitude or disposition of the soul.

Some say, "All that a Catholic has to do when he sins is to go to confession, admit his sins, and he comes out white as snow." Oh, no, he does not! The mere confession of sins without sorrow and a firm purpose of amendment does not make a valid confession. The absolution of the priest is not efficacious unless there is serious sorrow. Under certain

conditions one can have remission of sins without the telling of sins. Under no condition is absolution effective without sorrow.

Here is a story which indicates and reveals how important sorrow is. According to this fiction, a man, who was
a pickpocket, went to confession, and during confession,
which happened in the priest's own room, the man stole the
priest's watch. Then at the end of confession, he said, "Oh,
Father, I forgot to tell you, I stole a watch."

The priest said, "You must restore it to the owner."

The man said, "Father, I will give it to you."

"No," said the priest, "I do not want it. You must give it
to the owner."

"Well," said the man, "the owner won't take it back."

"In that case," said the priest, "you may keep it."

There was no sorrow, and there must be sorrow and
penance.

Remember how much our blessed Lord emphasized, *The
Kingdom of God is near at hand. Repent! Repent and believe the
Gospel* (MT 3:2). Our blessed Lord said sorrow was so important He introduced the Kingdom of God with it and repentance. As He said, *The Kingdom of God is near at hand. Repent
and believe the Gospel.* This was the first sermon of Peter; it
was also the first sermon of John the Baptist, and it was
the last sermon our blessed Lord preached. Sorrow is absolutely essential. Why is God not indifferent to sin? Because
God is holy. He makes a distinction between the sinner and
the sin. He wants to separate the two: the disease and the
patient, the error and the student. Therefore, we must be
sorry. In passing I might say a Catholic suffers more when
he sins than one who does not have the faith, because of his

greater love. He understands better the love of our Lord and redemption in the Church.

Imagine two men marrying two old shrews. One of the men was never married before; the other was married to a beautiful, kind, lovely, devoted wife who died. Which of the two men do you think suffered the more? Obviously, the one who knew the better love.

Catholics are in great agony when they sin, and not for any other reason than because they hurt someone they loved. Though we suffer more, we never fall into despair. That is the difference with the world. Our sorrow is not only a grief directed toward our Lord; it is also a detestation of sin with the purpose of not sinning again. Sorrow is of two kinds: It is imperfect and it is perfect. Imperfect sorrow is the sorrow that we have because we dread the loss of heaven and we fear hell. The perfect sorrow is the sorrow that we have because we offended God. When you go to confession, while the priest is giving you absolution, you recite the Act of Contrition. Notice that the Act of Contrition combines both kinds of sorrows:

O my God, I am heartily sorry for having offended Thee, and I detest all of my sins because I dread the loss of heaven and the pains of hell; but most of all because they offend Thee, my God, Who art all good and deserving of all my love. I firmly resolve, with the help of Thy grace, to confess my sins, to do penance, and to amend my life. Amen.

Perhaps I can illustrate these two kinds of sorrows by telling you about twin children. They both disobey their

280 YOUR LIFE IS WORTH LIVING

mother in an equal way. One of the children goes to the mother and says, "Oh, Mommy, I'm sorry. Now I can't go to the picnic, can I?" That is imperfect contrition. The other one throws her arms around the mother and begins to cry and says, "Mommy, forgive me! I love you!" That is perfect contrition.

Imperfect contrition is sufficient to receive absolution in sacramental confession. But suppose you are in a state of sin and you cannot go to confession. Suppose you are in a plane that is falling, or you are a soldier going into battle, or you are in any state of grievous sin, and there is no way of going immediately to confession. What should you do? You make an act of perfect contrition. A perfect contrition will remit sins provided you have the intent to go to sacramental confession at the earliest opportunity. Along with this sorrow there is the purpose of amendment because we say we promise to amend. The purpose of amendment is not the certitude of amendment. That would be presumption. St. Paul says, *If any man thinks he can stand let him take heed lest he fall* (1 CO 10:12). What is meant by a firm resolve not to sin is the sincere desire with the help of God's grace to do all in our power not to fall again.

We examine ourselves and think up ways of avoiding the fall. When we are in the state of sin, when we are absolved as a result of sacramental confession, we take the firm purpose not to sin again. The way to make up for sin is to do away with many of the occasions of sin and to make up for the sin as soon as possible. If we are nasty and sarcastic, we must make up for it. Many people will cut others to the quick with nasty remarks and never once ask pardon. They just forget and let it pass. This disposition does not indicate a firm purpose of amendment. If you have stolen something, you have to return it. If you have been guilty of calumny, rectify it. Then, I say, you avoid the occasions of sin through certain reading, companionship, or visits; you avoid them to prove the sincerity of your sorrow. Sorrow is Eros, the god of flesh in tears. Sorrow is an intention to abandon the ego. It is hard, and sometimes it is like being skinned alive.

To conclude the subject of sorrow you might ask me, "Which is more common in confession, perfect or imperfect contrition?" In my experience, I would say perfect contrition, because most people are sorry for their sins because they dread the loss of heaven and fear hell and have hurt our Lord. After all, it is the Cross that reveals the dimension of sin. No one ever thoroughly sees sin in its utter nakedness until he understands redemption. Take the errors, stupidity, and crimes of every day. People summarize them by saying, "Oh, what a fool I made of myself!" There is a world of difference between that and "Oh, what a sinner am I!"

When we go to confession there is always a crucifix in the confessional box. As we kneel there we see Goodness nailed with the Cross. Remember, we priests have to go every week. We are sinners, too. When we see the crucifix before us, we see our own biography. There is no need of anyone writing my life! There it is nailed to a cross! I can read my thoughts in that crown of thorns; the nails are like so many pins, the parchment and the skin. There I am as I really am. Far be it, therefore, from any of us to say, "Oh, we are not as bad as those who crucified our blessed Lord." Let us not forget they did not crucify our Lord, except physically. Sin crucified Him! In that we are all equal, we are all representatives. When we go to confession, we gather up all the rubbish of our lives, the kind of rubbish that we have thrown down into the cellars of our lives as we throw rubbish down into the cellars of our houses. And we take it all up and lay it at the feet of our Lord.

If you have ever walked Saturday afternoon or evening to a large city church with rows of confessionals on either side, you have seen feet protruding from the little curtains of the confessionals: big feet, little feet, male feet, female feet. They belong to people who have finally come to disown their sins. The only part of them which is revealed to the world, which sticks out from under the curtain, is the feet, the lowliest part, the symbol of the absence of pride. When a Catholic goes to confession, instead of putting his best foot forward, he puts his worst foot forward. Every penitent who has ever made a confession, as he enters the box has said, "I may fool others, but what a fool am I to fool myself, and what a sinful fool I am to think I can fool God."

34

SACRAMENT OF THE SICK

Shakespeare speaks of the ills "that flesh is heir to" (*Hamlet* 3.1). It is of those ills and sicknesses that we speak in the sacrament of Extreme Unction. The sacrament is also called the sacrament of the Anointing of the Sick. Sickness does many things to us physically and psychologically by cutting us off from many occasions of sin. The will to sin is certainly weakened by physical infirmity. Sickness also manifests the uniqueness of our personalities. We begin to realize that "I am I"; self is confronted with self, the soul sees itself. Sickness breaks the spell defining pleasure as everything that we ought to do to go on building bigger barns since life is worthless unless it is thrilling. We readjust our sense of values and begin to understand the words of our Lord *What doth it profit a man if he gains the whole world and lose his immortal soul?* (MT 16:26).

Then it can end in death. There is a world of difference between the way the pagan faces death and the way the Christian does. The pagan fears the loss of the body; the Christian fears the loss of the soul. To the Christian, the physical life and the world are not everything. This world is only scaffolding to him; it is scaffolding up through which souls climb to the kingdom of heaven. When the last soul shall have climbed up, then it shall be torn down and burned with fervent fire. Not because the world is base, but because its work is done.

There is another difference between the pagan and the Christian as regards death. A Christian never feels his whole being is threatened by death; a pagan does. A pagan is always moving forward toward death as if he were walking toward an abyss. The Christian is walking backward from death. He starts with the fact "Someday I'm going to die; someday I must render an account of my stewardship. Knowing I will die, I now prepare my life so it may enter the Kingdom of heaven." The worst thing that can happen to a Christian is not death. The greatest tragedy is not to have loved enough.

Let us study the background of a sacrament our Lord instituted, the sacrament of the Anointing of the Sick. Many of the prophecies told about our blessed Lord revealed and heralded Him as the healer of the sick. In countless places in the New Testament we read such statements as these: *Jesus went about teaching and preaching the Kingdom of God and curing every kind of disease and infirmity* (MT 4:23). Then again we read in Mark, when our blessed Lord was at Gennesaret, as Scripture states, *And they began bringing the sick to Him, beds and all wherever they heard He was. And they begged Him to let them touch even the hem of His cloak, and all that touched Him recovered* (MK 6:56). Like the woman suffering from hemorrhage for twelve years—remember, she said, *If I but touch the hem of His garment I shall be healed* (MK 5:28). The Gospel does not tell us all the miracles of healing, but St. John ends up his gospel by saying that if he had written down all of the miracles our blessed Lord had worked, the world would not be large enough to contain the books thereof. The point is our blessed Lord, as the Son of God made man, had the power to heal the sick.

After the Resurrection, our blessed Lord communicated power to His Apostles, and here I am quoting the Gospel of Mark: *Lay hands upon the sick and make them recover* (MK 16:18). Then again in the Gospel of Luke we read, concerning the Apostles, *They worked cures everywhere* (LK 9:6). How did our Lord communicate this power? How did He tell the Apostles to cure? He told them to do so by using oil, because the Gospel tells us, *And they anointed with oil many sick people and healed them* (MK 6:13). Our blessed Lord instituted this sacrament of the Healing of the Sick, or what is called Extreme Unction, and passed it on to His Church. We find the early Church was using the sacrament just as we use it now. St. James, one of the Apostles, writing in his epistle says:

> Is any man sick among you? Let him bring in the priests of the church and let them pray over him, anointing him with oil in the name of the Lord. And the prayer of faith shall save the sick man. And the Lord shall raise him up: and if he be in sins, they shall be forgiven him. (JM 5:14-15)

That is the earliest description that we have of the sacrament of the Anointing of the Sick. Notice that our blessed Lord told His Apostles to use oil. Just as our Lord in other sacraments used bread and water, He uses oil, because oil was used to strengthen the body. Athletes very often would rub their bodies with oil, and our Lord used it for the sacrament. Where does this oil come from? The bishop on Holy Thursday blesses it. There are three kinds of oils that are blessed on that day. The oil for this particular sacrament is distributed to various parishes. And during the year the priests anoint the sick with this oil. When the bishop blesses and consecrates these oils, he says this particular prayer over the oil:

> With this heavenly anointing let none be medicined
> but that he shall find protection within and without,
> gone all pain and sickness, gone every ailment of soul
> and body.

Should there be a sacrament for the sick just as there is for the wounded? There is a world of difference between being wounded and being sick, between being cut by a knife and having smallpox. Our blessed Lord has instituted a sacrament for our spiritual wounds, namely, the sacrament of Penance. He has a sacrament for the sickness of the body, the body that is united to the soul. The beauty of this sacrament is that though the grace is communicated to the soul, it influences the body in a very special way. This sacrament does not act in the way in which the divinity of our blessed Lord influenced the humanity that He took from His blessed Mother. No! But in some mysterious way the results of our blessed Lord's Passion are poured through the soul into the body, since you cannot think of any part of the body that has not been a vehicle of sin.

This particular sacrament wants to do away with all traces of that sin and in some way restore the body again to health if it be God's will. You cannot think of a single sin that did not come through the body, not a one. Envy? That certainly came through the eyes. For example, you saw how much better the Joneses were doing and you had to keep up with the Joneses. Pride? Your ear might have been involved. Someone said that you were smart or beautiful. Drunkenness, adultery, robbery, and blasphemy all in some way involve the body that is the object of this sacrament, even your feet. You walked into an occasion of sin. Even your nose! Your nose could have contributed to vanity; you may have smelled good cooking and ate too much. Considerable vanity could be involved in the use of perfume.

When a sin gets into the soul through the body, it always leaves a trace, much like certain diseases. They leave little remembrances behind, not the kinds of remembrances we'd like to have. Viruses leave vestiges of themselves. That is why certain diseases are not contracted again. Some diseases leave important marks, sometimes embarrassing marks, like smallpox. Sin comes into the soul through the body, and after a while the body becomes like a chimney through which fire and smoke are emitted from the hearth. The chimney becomes full of soot. Ships going through the ocean attract many barnacles. Sewers become clogged. You just cannot have sins pouring through the eyes, ears, nose, and the feet without these senses becoming clogged, sooty, dirty, and barnacled.

The Church purifies the avenues of sin: the eyes, ears, nose, hands, lips, and feet. The purification takes place by the anointing with oil and words of the priest. First the priest anoints your forehead, saying:

> Through this holy anointing
> may the Lord in his love and mercy help you
> with the grace of the Holy Spirit. Amen.

Then the priest anoints your hands, saying:

> *May the Lord who frees you from sin*
> *save you and raise you up. Amen.*

When the sacrament of Extreme Unction, or the Anointing of the Sick, is given to a priest, he is always anointed on the backs of his hands. The laity are always anointed on the palms of their hands. The reason why the priest is anointed on the back of his hand is because the palm of his hand was anointed when he was ordained a priest.

Extreme unction is given only in serious illness. The one who receives it must be in some danger of death through sickness. There need not be the certitude of death. The sacrament of the Anointing of the Sick may not be given to soldiers going into battle. They are in danger of death, but not from sickness. If they are wounded, they can be anointed. This sacrament should not be delayed until the patient is unconscious and can no longer join in the prayers. It should be given while he can lift up his soul to the healing power of Christ, who is refreshing his senses and his soul and his sins. The sacrament does not mean that the person is going to die. There are many that believe that when a priest is called to administer this particular sacrament, the patient is beyond hope. The Council of Trent refused to consider Extreme Unction only as a sacrament for the dying.

In the administration of this sacrament there is no mention of death. It is not necessarily the sacrament of the dying; it is the sacrament of the sick. Here is a prayer the priest recites after he has anointed the hands, feet, and other members of the body. Listen to this prayer; note carefully that the word "death" is not used. Note the burden of the prayer is the restoration of the sick person:

> Cure, we beseech Thee, O our Redeemer, by the grace of the Holy Spirit, the ailments of this sick man [or woman], his wounds, and forgive his sins. Deliver him from all miseries of body and mind and mercifully restore him to perfect health, inwardly and outwardly, that having recovered by an act of kindness he may be able to take up his former duties. Thou, who with the Father and the Holy Spirit, liveth and reigneth God, world without end. Amen.

Though the sacrament is given at a critical time, it is more concerned with sickness than with death. The sacrament could be called the sacrament of the Anointing of the Sick. Grace is always received by the soul. We are a unit, a composite of body and soul, and here this sacrament has a very special repercussion upon the body. To use a modern word, we might call it the psychosomatic sacrament, the sacrament of body and soul. It looks to the healing of the body not clinically, because the Church regards the body differently than medicine. To the Church, the body is not just an organism; it is also the temple of God, the residence of divine life. That is why St. Paul says the body is for the Lord.

Therefore, this sacrament looks to the body. It seeks to give it relief so it will not impede the soul's love of God. We fail if we do not see the beauty of this sacrament. I wonder if we really express the faith that we should have. Did St. James speak of the great faith demanded when the sacrament is received? (JM 1:5–8). The divine Physician comes to us, and we should look less to our disease than we look to Him. The sickness does not preclude the possibility of death, because we are all under the penalty of death. If we are in danger of death, then we receive the sacrament of the dying, which is viaticum. The viaticum is the Eucharist that is given to the dying. "Viaticum" means on the way you take the Lord with you.

If it be God's will that death be not postponed, then we see in the sacrament, because our senses have been cleansed, an incorporation to the death of Christ. We were baptized in His death. The Eucharist reminded us of His death. We are incorporated in a special way. We say with our Lord on the Cross, *It is finished* (JN 19:30). Our death is united to His and we're also united to His Resurrection. This sacrament prefigures the anointing of future glory. It applies the resurrection of the body in anticipation by applying it to our thoughts and desires. We can go before God with all of the avenues of our bodies cleansed.

This beautiful sacrament throws out a bridge between earth and heaven. The saddest of our suffering is wedded to the yearning for God. If you want to witness this sacrament, just go with us priests into the sickroom as we minister to the dying. Pray you may never die without this sacrament.

35

HOLY ORDERS

May I tell you a story about a bishop and a priest as a fitting introduction to a sacrament concerned with the government of the Church, namely, Holy Orders?

A fellow prisoner of the bishop told this first story to me. The good bishop was put into a Chinese communist prison. Through persecutions and beatings, his weight fell to about ninety pounds. Covered with vermin, prison sores, wearing a black stocking cap and a black kimono, he was unable to walk by himself. He always had to be supported by two fellow Chinese prisoners. Providentially, however, he was the only one in prison that was ever given bread and wine. The communists did not know why they gave it to him. If they knew he was going to read Mass with the bread and wine, they certainly would never have given it to him. This person in prison with him told me no Mass in a Gothic cathedral, with all the pomp and splendor of liturgy, could ever equal the beauty of that Mass said by the bishop as he leaned against the prison wall with the tin tray before him, moving his fingers, saying over the bread, "This is My Body," and over the wine, "This is My Blood." Then secretly afterward passing out Communion to those who shared his faith.

He was put in the death march, where later on he perished. A communist colonel, who was in charge of the march, put a sack around his neck. It weighed about thirty pounds. It was tied so that as he marched the rope would gradually tighten, the sack would become heavier, and the bishop would eventually be choked to death. When the march began, this fellow prisoner told me he broke ranks and went up to the communist colonel and shouted at him, "Don't do that! Look at the man!" It was kind of an *Ecce homo*. The communist colonel looked at him as if for the first time in his life he really saw suffering, and said to the one who interrupted him, "Get back in line, you dog!"

The death march began. This friend of mine said he tried to peer through the marching lines of the prisoners to see if he could catch a sight of the bishop supported by two fellow Chinese prisoners. After about a mile he saw him. The bishop was still standing, but the sack was not on his back. The sack was on the back of the communist colonel.

I asked, "What happened?"

He said, "I think he was edified by the patience and resignation of the good bishop. As a result, the communist colonel was arrested and sent to prison."

In a second story, communists told a priest to strip himself. He stripped himself to a point where he had left only his shoes and stockings. They started beating him about the head and the body with rods. He leaned over and began taking off his shoes and stockings.

They said, "Leave them on! Why do you want to take them off?"

He said, "Because I want to die like our Lord."

Where do bishops and priests come from? They come from a sacrament. It will be recalled there are two social sacraments: Matrimony and Holy Orders. In the natural order man and woman propagate the human species through the sacrament of Matrimony. There must be government. In the divine, supernatural order, in the Mystical Body of Christ, there must be government, and the sacrament of government of the Mystical Body is Holy Orders. In this government there are degrees, order, hierarchy. The division of these orders is principally three: diaconate, priesthood, and episcopacy. The night of the Last Supper, and all during His public life, our blessed Lord chose human instruments to mediate between Him and the world. As Scripture says, *They are to be the ministers and dispensers of the mysteries of God* (2 CO 3:6). Again, in the epistle of the Hebrews we read, *For every high priest taken from among men is ordained for men in the things that appertain to God, that he may offer up gifts and sacrifices for sins* (HEB 5:1).

We are dispensers of the great mysteries of God. Why did He not choose angels? Because sympathy, compassion, and suffering together with One who has already suffered would be lacking to an angel. Is not this the whole principle of the Incarnation? Did not our Lord come down, take upon Himself our human nature, become a kind of a slave? As Scripture says, *In order that He might have compassion on us, share our woes, share our wounds* (HEB 4:15). No one could ever say God does not know what it is to be human. Even the one very thing lacking in His nature, the quality of femininity, He compensated for by calling Mary to suffer at the foot of His Cross in His Passion. Our Lord was able to choose us because He shared something in common with us.

As Cardinal Newman has put it, God chose us weak creatures "for the sake of those with whom we deal." He has sent forth for the ministry of reconciliation not angels, but men. He has sent forth your brethren to you, beings of your own bone and flesh. It is your brethren He has appointed, sons of Adam, to preach to you, the same by nature, differing only in grace and in power; men exposed to the same temptations, same warfare within and without, and with the same deadly enemies: the world, the flesh, and the devil. They have the same human wayward hearts, differing only as the power of God has changed and ruled. We are not angels from heaven that speak to you, but men whom grace has made to differ from you.

What a strange anomaly. All is perfect, heavenly, and glorious in the dispensation which Christ has vouchsafed to us except the persons of His priests. He dwells on our altar, the Most Holy, the Most High. The angels fall down before Him. Yet the priests, consecrated apart with their girdle of celibacy and maniple of sorrow, are sons of Adam, sons of sinners of a fallen nature. Every priest is a kind of a mediator between God and man, bringing God to man and man to God, continuing the priesthood of our blessed Lord. Our Lord was not a priest because the Father eternally begot him. Our Lord was a priest because He had a human nature, which He could offer up for our salvation. We are something like Jacob's ladder, which reaches up to the heavens and at the same time is placed on the earth. Every priest is a kind of other Christ, having vertical relations to Christ in heaven and horizontal relations to men on earth.

Bishops are the successors of the Apostles. In sacred Scripture one finds our blessed Lord giving them many powers. Our Lord said like Him that they are the lights of the world; like Him, they are the shepherds of Christian people; like Him, they are the doors through which the flock will enter into the Holy City. A bishop is consecrated, not just primarily for a diocese; he is consecrated primarily for the world, because our Lord said to His Apostles, *Go ye into the world* (MK 16:15). Only for jurisdictional reasons does a bishop have a diocese, but his primary responsibility is the world.

The missions of the Church are not foundlings on the doorsteps of a chancery office. All peoples of the world weigh upon a bishop's heart. What would you think of a person who was so concerned with his own heart that he tied tourniquets around his arms and legs? If he were asked his reason, he might say, "I find my blood is going out to the extremities of my body; it is wasting strength. Since I want to preserve my strength, I'm going to keep all the blood in my heart." After a while the heart would not function. If a bishop of the United States cut himself off from the extremities of the Mystical Body of Christ, from Africa, Asia, and Latin America, speaking here of a bishop of the United States, his own diocese, his own episcopacy would suffer. The right and left sides of the heart have no communion directly with one another; they have communion only because the blood passes through one side of the heart, traverses the entire body, and then comes up to the other side. Every bishop, every diocese in every parish, has communion with itself and communion with the entire Mystical Body of Christ.

Whence comes this call to the priesthood and to Holy Orders? Sacred Scripture tells us we must be called by God as Aaron was. No one takes this office unto himself. God does not always choose the best. St. Paul says, *Not many wise, not many noble* (1 CO 4:7–13), because the power is actually not in us; the power is in Christ. He can choose, and that is why

He calls weak vessels, frail earthenware, to be the bearers of His treasure.

This vocation that comes to us is rather silent for the most part. God never comes down, shakes our bed, and says to us, "Come on, get up! I want you to be a priest." It is a long, persistent calling instead. I can never remember a moment in my own life when I did not want to be a priest. The prayer of my First Communion was that I would be a priest. All the time I was studying I always felt unworthy, and I feel more unworthy now. After all, the more we bring a painting to the sunlight, the more the imperfections are revealed; the closer we look at ourselves in the light of the great High Priest whom we are to represent, the more foul we see ourselves. The treasures God has put into our hands and the little interest we have drawn frightens us.

Each one of us is something like Simon Peter. Remember Simon was the name he had from his family; Peter was the name our blessed Lord gave him. In each of the priests there is this double nature. There is the Simon nature we derive from our parents. Our poor, weak, human body, mind, and will, this is what God uses. Then there is the Peter nature: the call from God, and the infusion of divine powers, to forgive sins, to be a priest, to renew the sacrifice of Calvary. All the while we feel our great powers, we feel our great weaknesses. We hope people realize the Simon nature in us must not blind them to the Peter power.

It is interesting to recall how St. Peter, at the end of his life, changed and became more humble. In the first epistle, written a few years before his death, he began by calling himself *Peter, apostle of Jesus Christ* (1 P 1:1). The last epistle, written very shortly before his death, began *Simon Peter, ser-*

vant and apostle of Jesus Christ (2 P 1:1). At the end of his life he came back to his weak Simon nature, and united in both, his priesthood and his episcopacy, the union of the human and the divine, ended by calling himself the servant. We are servants of Jesus Christ.

Our service is an arduous one. It involves labor in the fields in the daytime and serving at night. There is no such thing as saying at the end of a day, "Well, I've done my duty for today." Rather, our Lord said we have to call ourselves unprofitable servants (LK 17:10). The less there is of self-satisfaction in our lives, the more zeal there is in His service. If we count the converts we have made, we're very likely to begin by thinking we made them instead of our Lord, Himself. We cannot say, "I built three rectories, now the bishop ought make me a monsignor." He still has to keep in mind that he is an unprofitable servant. Labor union rules are not sufficient for us, we belong to a different union, where love is the standard of measure.

When we think of all our Lord has done for us, we really can never do enough. The word "enough" does not exist in love's vocabulary. It's very much like telling a mother who has spent all night alongside the bed of her sick child that she has done enough. We know we are called the ambassadors of Christ, but we are also the victims of Christ. We know very well our blessed Lord refused to distinguish between work and extra work, between being on duty and standing by, between walking one mile and another mile, between giving our coat and giving our cloak. No errors of self-complacency are divinely permitted; no self-pity, no pluming ourselves on our administrative talent; we are worthless servants when we have done our best. To our dear Lord alone belong the merit and the glory of our services. To us belongs nothing but the gratitude and the humility of being pardoned rebels. To sum it all up, we are the ambassadors of Christ, and we are the channels of His power. Our principal and great act is holy Mass.

When reading the Mass, we take our blessed Lord upon the Cross out of that locale to Paris, Cairo, Tokyo, and the world's poorest mission. Our work is to extend Christ's forgiveness of our sins and to give His blessing with our poor hands. We mount the altar wearing our chasuble. Hanging on to that chasuble are the millions of souls in the world who know not Christ Himself. When we take a Host into our hand, we have to see our fingers heralded from slavery in the salt mine of Siberia. We have to see our feet as bleeding feet of refugees tramping westward toward barbed wire beyond which lies freedom. When looking at the candles, we think of the glow of the blast furnaces tended by gaunt men who have had their lives devastated by those who deny economic justice.

Our eyes look at the Host wet with the tears of the widow and suffering of the orphan. The stole about our shoulders is like the stole of the Old Testament priest we see bearing the stones of the twelve tribes. We see them as living stones, the burden of all churches and the world's people. We drag humanity to the altar and join heaven and earth together. We merge our hands into Christ's hands, for He lives on to make intercession for us.

We say with Peter, *I will follow Thee wherever Thou goest* (MT 26:33), and yet we do not. We see sunlit meadows, and alongside of those meadows are our desolation, weariness, and loneliness. We feel tired; our feet ache; our bodies rebel; and our spirits waver. There are times we want to sit down and pluck flowers and admire the view. We are tempted to lose patience with our Lord's calm, slow, and never-faltering step. When we stumble, we are tempted to lie where we have fallen complaining we cannot go on any further. We tell ourselves we were not meant to be saints, yet we know we are. Pray for us.

36

THE SACRAMENT OF MARRIAGE

Marriage is a sacrament and an unbreakable bond until death. The Pharisees asked our blessed Lord if it was right for any man to put away his wife for any cause whatsoever. He answered,

> Have ye not read that he who made man from the beginning, made them male and female? And he said: For this cause shall a man leave father and mother and shall cleave to his wife, and they two shall be in one flesh. Therefore now they are not two, but one flesh. What therefore God hath joined together, let no man put asunder. (MT 19:4–6)

Our blessed Lord was speaking of marriage from the beginning. And when the question of divorce arose, He said, *I tell you that he who puts away his wife and marries another, commits adultery. And he, too, commits adultery who marries her after she has been put away* (MT 5:32).

These words sound like a great judgment upon civilization where in the United States there is one divorce for every 2.3 marriages, and remarriages after such divorces. It must not be thought divorces and remarriages are wrong just for Catholics. They are especially wrong for Catholics, but they are a violation of the natural law of God by everyone, whether he is Tibetan, Muslim, or Christian. Original sin and the deluge did not lock out the divinely established order of man and woman. We are interested for the moment in the human natural order. Marriage was instituted not by man, but by God. He made it a union, not a contract. In marriage two persons become one. They become spiritually, mentally, and physically united. There are judges who will grant divorces, but how does God look upon them? After the divorce they aren't two separate individuals as they were before the marriage; they are fragments of a joint personality, like a babe cut in two.

Marriage between a man and woman is meant to be enduring by the nature of love. There are only two words in the vocabulary of love: "you" and "always." "You," because love is unique; "always," because love is enduring. No one ever said, "I will love you for two years and six months." All love songs have the ring of eternity. Why is jealousy in the human heart? To be the safeguard of monogamy and an enduring marriage! Consider the nature of love in the human order. There are three terms: the lover, the beloved, and love itself. Suppose love had only two terms: my love and thy love. There would be separateness, impenetrability. There has to be a third element, just as two vines, if they are to be one, must be united in the soil. Two hearts are united because of the love that is outside them. Then the impotence of the "I" to completely possess the "thou" is overcome by the realization that there is something beyond turning the "I" and the "thou" into "our" love. People who are in love always speak of "our" love. They say to one another: "Thou art more than thou alone, and my love no longer founders on thee because it reaches out beyond thee to all that is worth loving. When we embrace, we embrace more than one another. In embracing one another we give testimony of that by which we are embraced, namely, by the love of God."

As the book of Genesis put it, *Man and woman both He created them* (GN 1:27). Notice they complement one another, never once admitting a separation. God makes man; God makes woman from man. God is present at the creation of the world, and man is present, though in ecstasy, at the creation of a woman. Because man comes directly from God, he has more initiative, power, and creativeness. Woman coming from God through the ecstasy of man has intuition, response, acceptance, submission, and cooperation. Man lives more in the external world because he was made from dust. He is close to nature. It is man's mission to rule over it. A woman lives more in the internal order, because she was created from an inner, human life. Man is more interested in the outer world. Man talks more about business, and woman talks more about persons. They complement one another in a divine way. The book of Genesis says, *It is not well that man should be without companionship. I will give him a mate of his own kind* (GN 2:18). The divine creation of two sexes is suggested as essential for fellowship. A helpmate does not mean inferiority; differences complement one another, like a bow and a violin. Marriage is not just a contract; it is a union made by God that endures until death.

There is a natural order and a supernatural order. We live in the order of the human and the divine. In addition to physical life there is supernatural life, which is grace. Our intellects are illumined with faith, and our wills are strengthened with power in the divine nature. Our blessed

Lord makes marriage a sacrament. To those who are united in His Church, He gives grace, strength, and power to live out their mutual existence. Every sacrament has two elements. The visible is the exchange of consent signified by the joining of hands and witnessed by a priest. Invisible grace is communicated for their married state. This grace symbolizes another marriage, the marriage of Christ and His Church, which is the meaning of sacramental marriage. Considerable explanation is written all through the epistles of St. Paul. For example:

> For no man ever hated his own flesh, but nourisheth and cherisheth it, as also Christ doth the church: Because we are members of His body, of his flesh, and of his bones. For this cause shall a man leave his father and mother: and shall cleave to his wife. And they shall be two in one flesh. This is a great sacrament: but I speak in Christ and in the church. (EP 5:29–32)

He also said, *Husbands love your wives as Christ loves the Church* (EP 5:25). We come to a profound reason. St. Paul describes it as a high mystery.

The marriage of baptized persons in the Church signifies another marriage. All through the Old and New Testaments, God expressed His relationship with us in terms of nuptials. In the Old Testament, God always spoke of Himself as the Bridegroom, the husband of Israel, which was the *qahal*. Israel, or the chosen people, was considered by God as the Bride of God. There are many passages in the Old Testament showing how God could find no other symbol of His love for Israel and for the vehicle of His revelation than the symbolism of married love.

In due course, God becomes man. Would our Lord ever call Himself the Bridegroom? Yes, He did in such a very natural way. One of the occasions was when He was asked why His disciples did not fast as the disciples of John the Baptist did. The answer of our Lord was *Can you expect the men of the Bridegroom's company to go fasting when the Bridegroom is still with them?* (MT 9:15). The Bridegroom should be taken away. John the Baptist called himself a "friend of the Bridegroom" (JN 3:29), a kind of best man. I think that there is beautiful mystery hidden in the marriage feast of Cana. Our Lord began His public life by assisting at the marriage feast, showing His relationship with His Church could be exactly like the relationship unfolded in the Old Testament. The old *qahal* of Israel became the new Church, or the new Israel. Through redemption and Pentecost, we had the continuation of this symbolism. Eve was the continuation of man, bone of his bone, flesh of his flesh. The continuation of the new Adam is Christ.

A human marriage is like the union of our Lord and the Church. When the bridegroom and bride stand at the altar, we read the marriage ceremony informing them: "You, the bridegroom, stand for Christ, and you, the bride, stand for the Church." Marriage becomes beautiful when this mysterious grace is conferred upon them. Scripture tells us just as Christ is the head of the Church, so man is the head of a woman: *That man is the head of woman in exactly the same way that Christ is the Head of the Church* (EP 5:23). The husband is to sacrifice himself for the wife. He was the head by dying, sacrificing Himself, and pouring out His blood. The headship is based upon self-forgetfulness for the sake of the beloved. The wife is related to the husband in the same way the Church is related to our blessed Lord, through love, service, and devotion. The husband is the head of the woman just as Christ is the head of the Church. This becomes sacrifice, not superiority.

There is another divine reason why the marriage of baptized persons is unbreakable. They symbolize the unbreakable, eternal union of our Lord and the Church. When the Son of God came to this earth and took upon Himself a human nature, which flowered into His Mystical Body, the Church, He took it not for three years, but for all eternity! A husband takes a wife as Christ took the Church, until death does him part. To symbolize the enduring union of the espousals between Christ and His Church, they are to love one another until separated by death.

Hidden in this lovely description of the symbolism of marriage is the fact there can be only one Church. Remember in Scripture, the Church is the Bride of Christ. Do you think our Lord could have many brides? That would be spiritual adultery! There is one Spouse; there is one Church, and that union continues forever. Thus, the marriage of husband and wife is unbreakable in the sacramental order.

Here is a little theoretical problem which helps bring out this truth. Suppose John and Mary were married at a Nuptial Mass, went to the church door, and separated. They never saw one another again. Could that marriage be dissolved? Yes, under certain conditions. That is called a marriage *ratum sed non consummatum,* a marriage ratified in the Church but never consummated by union of two in one flesh. The union of a husband and wife in a marriage only ratified but not consummated is something like the union of the individual soul and Christ by grace. The individual soul, often, is separated from Christ through sin. A marriage ratified and consummated has the symbolism of the union of

Christ and His Spouse, the Church, and those two can never be separated. Their marriage is absolutely unbreakable.

How beautiful marriage is in the Church. Fidelity is an eternal engagement with the future. The soul knows that it cannot be saved unless it is faithful to the spouse, even in the midst of trial. If God's love is never withdrawn from His Church, then the love of husband and wife is never withdrawn one from another. Their love is a proclamation to the world of another marriage, the marriage that gives us joy and happiness, the beautiful union of Christ and His Bride, the Church.

PART V

WORLD, SOUL, AND THINGS

I see that though the doubters have choked the spiritual life,

As the Philistines choked the wells of Abraham,

Yet, if we but dig, as Isaac did,

We will find the underground waters of life

Still there buried and undestroyed.

—FULTON J. SHEEN

37

SEX IS A MYSTERY

The two words most often used and abused in our modern world are the words "freedom" and "sex." "Freedom" is often used to signify the absence of law, and "sex" is often used to signify the absence of restraint. We will commence with three popular expressions about the subject of sex and then apply some thinking to these expressions.

The first popular expression is "Sex is not anything to be ashamed of." It is right if sex means the human race reproduces in a way giving pleasure. It is wrong if it means carnal license, the mess the sex instinct has us in today with uncontrolled use of pornographic literature as if these things are nothing to be ashamed of.

Let us take a second one: "We must be self-expressive." It is correct if it means we are to perfect our personalities. It is wrong if self-expression means to allow the sex instinct every satisfaction at all times and under all circumstances. We must analyze the full significance of the term "self-expression." Can you imagine a soldier in battle deserting the line and then running back to safety, meeting a superior officer, and the superior officer saying to him, "I am so glad you were self-expressive. We have inherited a number of old

Victorian ideas about a man staying in the battlefield." Certainly we are to follow the idiom "Be yourself," but we have to remember what we are. We are human beings.

Then a third expression often used today is "God would never have given us this particular instinct unless He intended us to use it!" Certainly we have a right to use it according to our nature. Our nature is rational; we have to live according to purposes and goals. We are to use our instincts according to the order of reason and not according to mere instinct. We have a hunting instinct, but we are to use it appropriately. Just as dirt is matter in the wrong place, so lust is the sex instinct in the wrong place.

We quote the sociologist Dr. Pitirim A. Sorokin, who writes:

> Those families among us who frequently change husbands and wives, who fail in their duties to their children, and adopt the moral code of the gutter are pushing us along the road to chaos. Greece, in the third and second centuries before Christ, brought sex into the open. We know because there were men in those days, too, who prided themselves on their objectivity as they calmly recorded the distressing picture of whole families getting together to indulge in promiscuous behavior. Adultery and prostitution were so common that those who indulged were regarded merely as interesting fellows.

Now note how this sociologist concludes:

> But such a society was not able to summon the backbone to resist in the face of war or to endure the auster-

ity program that might have salvaged that overblown economy. Soon the glory that was Greece was over and the mighty Acropolis was only a hillside strewn with ruined marble. (*Social and Cultural Dynamics*)

It would be well for any country which stresses the flesh too much to remember this lesson of history.

Let us take an entirely different point of view. There's a certain amount of sympathy to be extended to those who protest against the way purity and chastity have been stressed. Too often it is negative. Almost all talks on chastity begin with "Don't do this" or "Don't do that." It would seem as if it were almost a negative virtue rather than a positive one. No, Christianity bids us, "Look at things in a God-like way" and "What do we learn by studying man?" We see every human being has two strong and fundamental instincts: one is hunger, the other is sex. God implanted both of these. Thanks to hunger we preserve individual life. Thanks to sex we preserve social life. God had to associate great pleasures with these two instincts in order to assure a continuation of both personal life and the human race.

Naturally, there will come deviations, excesses with either of these instincts. Man may eat too much; he may drink too much; and his body will get fat. Or there can be excesses of the sex instinct; there can be deordination. Just as one may produce bad health from abusing the hunger instinct, one can develop a carnalized mind. One would not generally put garbage into the stomach, but too often one will put garbage into the mind.

Now looking at it positively: Youth are not to think, therefore, that this urge they have is wrong. It's God-like; it's heaven-sent; it's good! It is never wasted, even when it is controlled, because the energy that might go out physically is sublimated and may come out in another way mentally and spiritually, as it most often does.

Let us try and treat this subject in a dignified and positive fashion. We begin by asking: What is purity or chastity? Purity is reverence paid to the mystery of sex. If we used the Greek word, we would use the word "sacrament." You remember in the supernatural order every sacrament has two elements: one material, one spiritual; one to be seen, heard, or touched, and the other, which is divine. In the natural order, sex is a mystery because it has these two characteristics. Sex is something known to everyone and hidden from everyone. The known element in everyone is either male or female; the invisible, mysterious element of sex is its creativeness, a sharing in some way of the creative power of God.

God's love made Him a Creator. God has poured love into man and woman to make them cocreators with Him as a free gift. We have certain movements in our bodies not subject to freedom. Breathing, digestion, and circulation are to a great extent unconscious and involuntary; they go on independently of our will. But to create a poem, a statute, or a child is a free act. God gave the divine commission, *Increase and multiply* (GN 1:28). We are sent into this world to pass on a torch, the torch of life, and God has put that into our hands to burn controlled unto the purpose and destiny fixed by Him. Purity is reverence paid to the mystery of sex, and the mystery of sex is creativeness.

All creativeness is surrounded with awe and given to man and woman. There has been an association of religion with the unity of man and woman, not only in Christianity, but also among all pagan peoples. They believed this great power of creativeness should be surrounded in some way by religious sanction. If we understand the mystery correctly, we mortals supply act, bread, water, and words just as man and woman supply the flesh and God supplies the mystery. There's a sense of mystery, reverence, and awe that makes young men and women shrink from a too precocious surrender of the secret. One of the reasons why man is naturally chivalrous toward a woman is not because he believes she is physically weaker but because of the awe he feels in the presence of mystery.

Why can't sex be used outside of marriage? Because certain powers are to be used only in certain relationships. What is lawful in one relationship is not lawful in another. A man may kill another soldier in a just war but not in his private capacity as a citizen. A policeman can arrest someone as a duly appointed guardian of the law fortified with a warrant. The creativeness of man and woman is lawful under a relationship sanctioned by God called marriage. Purity will never separate the two. The things which God has joined together will not be separated. Purity is not just physical intactness. In a woman, it is the firm resolve never to use the power until God sends her a husband; in a man, it is a steadfast desire to wait upon God's will that he have a wife to use for God's purposes.

Purity begins in the will and from there flows outward, cleansing the imagination and, finally, the body. Life is impure only when the will is impure. You see purity is the sacristan and guardian of love. We do not want to see an American flag under someone's feet because there's a mystery to that flag; it symbolizes something else. The pure are shocked at the impure because impurity is the prostitution of the sacred, and it makes the reverent irreverent. The essence of all obscenity is the turning of the inner mystery into a jest. There is a hidden presence of God in every person and a hidden divine presence in the Bread of the altar. Each person becomes a kind of a consecrated Host. Not as the Bread of the altar, but because chastity, or purity, is a consecrated affection. Notice we are making it positive, not negative. A young man goes with a young woman and is dedicated to her ideals and to their marriage. Love inspires charity, chastity, and purity.

We want to describe the danger of isolating sex from love and its purpose and creativeness. Suppose a director of an orchestra becomes very conscious of his hands, focusing on how he is going to hold the baton. Do you think it is going to have an effect upon the music? Suppose he concentrates on the music, the orchestra, and the production of harmony. Everything fits into place. He is unconscious of the hand.

When sex becomes a part of love and the purpose of life, it is a dedication and fits into the whole. Sex is not something isolated from life. Self-control is subordination of a part to a whole to serve a higher enthusiasm. Purity properly understood matches love and the sex instinct. Frequent Holy Communion is the best guardian of chastity, because sex is placed in the context of love.

We've already said chastity is the vestibule, the sacristan of love. When we become in love with our Lord, when we have a sense of this tremendous ecstasy from Holy Communion and from oneness with our Savior, then every part of us, our hunger instinct and sex instinct, becomes a part of that love. Love awakens chastity; it is not the other way around. From the time we are children just reaching the age of reason into old age, it is the love of God that makes every other kind of love, even the love of husband and wife, understandable. He who loves honesty never has to be told not to steal. He who loves his neighbor never has to be told not to cut his throat. Any of us who love God, human persons, and the mystery of creativeness never have to be told not to do something. We are in love with the mystery. Sex is the reverence paid to the mystery of creativeness.

38

BIRTH PREVENTION

The subject is birth control, but the words are a misnomer because those who practice it don't believe in birth or in control. We shall never use these words again. We propose to answer objections about the subject and purpose of marriage.

Married couples will often say, "We cannot afford more children." Those who make this statement probably never think of the terrible principle that they are annunciating; namely, the primacy of the economic over the human. Put that into practice in other walks of life. Suppose a husband says that he can no longer support his wife. Should he be entitled to shoot her?

What is forgotten here in giving primacy to the economic is that we receive blessings as we put ourselves in the area of God's love. A waif on the street does not receive food, clothing, and shelter as a child in a family because that waif is outside the environment of love. To the extent we put ourselves outside the environment and area of God's love, we exclude divine assistance that would otherwise come to us. Those who put primacy upon the economic are really not interested in saving or earning; they are interested in spending which dictates the frustration of life. Idle passions and a desire for more credit, clothes, and selfishness dictate their philosophy. They believe they are free to manipulate life apart from God's laws because the laws of fruitful marriage bind only Catholics.

They say that Catholics are opposed to any frustration of human life in marriage, but it must be remembered those who are not Catholics are no freer to violate God's natural laws than anyone else is. It just happens the Catholic Church is defending a natural law. There are some that believe opposition to the frustration of love, the principle that marriage is destined to be fruitful, is purely and solely a Catholic doctrine. Suppose a vast majority of people went around with their eyes blindfolded and their ears plugged up. We would soon have a Papal encyclical in opposition, and the Church would say, "It is not right to blindfold your eyes or to plug up your ears. Reason tells you the eyes were made for seeing and the ears were made for hearing. You must allow these organs to work out the function for which God created them."

Many would say, "Oh, the Catholic Church is opposed to eye control."

"The Catholic Church is in opposition to ear control."

God created male and female, husband and wife in a certain way, and their organs should be permitted to function. What are we going to make this world: a universe in which we pick up violins and bows never producing music; a universe in which sculptors pick up chisels and never touch marble to create a statue? Are we going to have trees blooming but never any fruit? Are life and love to be reduced to a kind of an epidermic content without any fruit or purpose?

We must always take the positive position and enunciate two sublime teachings: Love in marriage creates the deepest kind of unity, and deep unity of love by its very nature tends to an incarnation. This particular point proves there is not to be a union of sexes outside of marriage. Have you ever noticed Scripture does not speak of marriage in terms of sex, but always in terms of knowledge? The book of Genesis said, *And now Adam had knowledge of his wife, Eve, and she conceived* (GN 4:1). "Had knowledge of her." When the angel Gabriel announced to the blessed Mother she was chosen to be the mother of our blessed Lord, she asked, *How can this be since I have no knowledge of man?* (LK 1:34). Notice here there was no question of the ignorance of conception, but of some deeper mystery. St. Peter said, *Husbands possess your wives in knowledge* (1 P 3:7). Why is marriage spoken of as knowledge? Because one of the closest forms of unity in the natural order is that which comes from knowledge. You look out on a flower or a tree and you know these things. The closest kind of unity in the natural order is between the knower and the thing which is known. You cannot think of anything closer than the union of your mind and what you know.

Sacred Scripture compares marriage to knowledge because marriage produces unity and demands fidelity. When a man knows a woman, a unity is created between the two like the union of the mind and that which is known. They are two in one flesh; from that point on nothing happens to a woman that does not happen to the man. He made her a woman; she made him a man. Just as you are always indebted to your alma mater, which gave you knowledge about Shakespeare, one is always indebted to the one who created unity. The resulting psychic changes are great physically, too. The woman can never again return to virginity; the man can never again return to ignorance. From their oneness comes fidelity as long as either has a body. They can never put themselves back into the state that they had before. Therefore, it is not just an experience; they have a bond that continues to exist forever. In married couples this union is very deep. All love tends toward an incarnation.

We have spoken of the love between husband and wife creating a deep bond of unity through which love naturally is diffused. Everything that is good diffuses itself. The sun diffuses itself in light and heat. A flower diffuses itself in perfume. Animals diffuse themselves in the generation of their kind. Man is good; his mind is good, and his mind diffuses itself in thoughts. God diffuses Himself, not only in creation, but also from all eternity. God has an eternal Son. The source of all generation is in God. Procreation is an imitation of God, who from all eternity has an eternal Son to whom He can say, in the agelessness of eternity, *Thou art My Son, this day have I begotten Thee, this day without beginning or end* (HEB 1:5).

The power of generation eternal in the godhead is communicated to man's mind and communicated to the body of a husband and wife. As God Himself said, *Shall I, that make others bring forth children, Myself be barren?* (IS 66:9). The power of generation is a gift from above. The motive power of begetting children is in the Trinity and in the Incarnation, because all love ends in an incarnation, even God's. God so loved man, He became enfleshed in the human nature. What is our blessed Lord but God's love incarnate, God's love walking this earth in the form and habit of man? You see how beautiful love is? If one could give a definition of love in the light of the Trinity and the Incarnation, it might be that love is mutual self-giving which ends in self-recovery. Mutual self-giving because no one is good unless he gives. Love is mutual self-giving which ends in self-recovery. In the Trinity there is the giving of the Father to the Son and the Son to the Holy

Spirit. There is self-recovery as the Holy Spirit is the bond in the unity of love. There is mutual self-giving between husband and wife ending in self-recovery, which is the child.

The thrill of a farmer as he sees a grain of wheat he planted coming into life, the joy at seeing a geranium bud blooming on a tenement windowsill, the ecstasy of a saint at seeing a sinner responding to prayer and beginning to live in Christ are earth's witnesses to the inherent happiness that comes to anyone who sees life springing and sprouting. Love does not mean just the joy to possess; it means the will to see a new life born, to see someone created in one's own image and likeness. The child becomes the bond of union between the husband and wife, unveiling fatherhood in the husband and motherhood in the wife. A new relationship is created. Love becomes a kind of ascension from the sense plane and goes back again to God. The children are almost like beads in a rosary binding together the love of husband and wife. Love always demands something unrevealed; it flourishes only in mystery. One never wants to see the infinite denied, life's urge still, or a passion glutted. One wants to see an unfolding, enrichment, and enfleshment of love.

The mystery of motherhood and fatherhood unfolds when the children have to be trained. New areas of exploration are opened up. As each child is born it binds together husband and wife as a reflection of the binding love of the Holy Spirit in the Trinity. Each child has a soul to save, awakening sweet responsibility in the father and the mother. As Kahlil Gibran wrote, when he spoke of children in *The Prophet*:

> And a woman who held a babe against her bosom said,
> Speak to us of Children. And he said: Your children

are not your children. They are the sons and daughters of Life's longing for itself. They come through you but not from you, and though they are with you yet they belong not to you. You may give them your love but not your thoughts, for they have their own thoughts. You may house their bodies but not their souls, for their souls dwell in the house of tomorrow, which you cannot visit, not even in your dreams. You may strive to be like them, but seek not to make them like you. For life goes not backward nor tarries with yesterday. You are the bows from which your children as living arrows are sent forth. The archer sees the mark upon the path of the infinite, and He bends you with his might that His arrows may go swift and far. Let your bending in the Archer's hand be for gladness; for even as He loves the arrow that flies, so He loves also the bow that is stable.

In the story of life, God sets up the target; you are the bow, and your children are the arrows. You have a messianic mission to represent the conquest of love over the ego. Children symbolize the defeat of your selfishness; they represent the victory of charity. Every child begets sacrifice as a gift of God, becomes a pledge of one's own salvation. How happy you will be on judgment day when God says to you, "Your love has borne fruit." If God did not bless you with children, you can always rejoice that you sent your love back again to God.

39

THE FOUR TENSIONS OF LOVE

There is nothing more beautiful in this world than two people in love. For love to endure, we need to recognize some of the great spiritual and psychological differences between man and woman. Understand that some of the tensions, which are to be expected in married life and which can easily be resolved, are part of our fallen human nature.

The first tension is this: between wanting and not wanting love. You really never know one another until you are married. Courtship is a kind of a masked ball, and in marriage, we take off the masks and see ourselves as we really are. As Elizabeth Barrett Browning said in "The Lady's Yes":

> *"Yes," I answered you last night;*
> *"No!" this morning, Sir, I say:*
> *Colors, seen by candle-light,*
> *Will not look the same by day.*

There can be a change. The human heart can reach a point where it has too much love and wishes to be loved no longer. In the human order, there comes a tug between wanting and not wanting love. What is the mysterious chemistry inside of the human heart which makes it swing between wanting and not wanting love? Torn between longing and satiety, craving and disgust, desire and satisfaction, the human heart asks, "Why should I be that way?" When satiety comes, the "thou" disappears in the sense it is no longer wanted. When longing reappears, the "thou" becomes a necessity. Love too much, there is discontent; love too little, there is emptiness.

There is a reason why you feel this way. You were made for the great Sacred Heart of Love, and no one but God can satisfy you. Your heart is right in wanting the infinite, but your heart is wrong in trying to make its finite companion the substitute for the infinite. The solution of this tension is in seeing that disappointments are just reminders that love is God's love on pilgrimage. Both the being loved too much and the being loved too little can go together when seen in the light of God. When this longing for infinite love is envisaged as a yearning for God, then the finiteness of our earthly love reminds us of the words of St. Augustine: "Our hearts were made for thee, O Lord, and they are restless until they rest in Thee" (CONFESSIONS I.I). Just keep in mind that in every marriage a man and woman promise each other something only God can give.

There is another tension you will feel, and this is very basic to human nature: the tension between wanting to be one with another person and at the same time feeling so alone, almost alone together. There will come moments when your self is lost in another, and then afterward a terrific sense of being thrown backward on your own solitary personality. Why is this? The reason is because there is nothing material, fleshy, or carnal in the world that can unite. You just try making two blocks of marble one. Why can't you unite them? Because they are material! The flesh alone cannot unite. Only the soul, the spirit, can unite. If we learn together the Our Father, my knowledge of the Our Father does not deprive you from learning it. If we pray together, we are much more one than we could be in any material fashion. It is the spirit that unites. The flesh is the means to unity; you see it's not an obstacle to unity. Your flesh is a means to unity because it is bound up with the soul. To the extent that love loses its soul, it loses its unity and sense of oneness. When the spirit is gone, there is only boredom and fatigue.

Passion for a crescendo of intimacy until oneness is achieved cannot be completely satisfied in the physical order because after the act of unity there remains the status of two distinct personalities, each with its own individual mystery. You see the paradox? Souls of lovers aspire to unity, but the body alone, though it is the momentary symbol of that unity, is exclusive of unity. The flesh is impervious to that kind of unity which alone can satisfy the spirit. There is no marriage in the world free from this tension, and the tension increases as the body goes through the motions of love without the soul. You will find the tension of the body decreases as the soul loves.

There's an escape from this tension. We are not to be cynical about it. The greatest relief for this tension is the begetting of children. Seeming disproportion is felt between a passion for unity and the failure to make it permanent, which is compensated for by the child, who becomes the new bond of unity outside a father and mother. Husband and wife will never feel the emptiness one with another when their relations are filled up with a new body and soul so directly infused by God, the Creator. God made people right, and people are unhappy if they try to frustrate these laws.

Children are the answer to the paradox of the aloneness together. They are the link that binds the lovers together, body
and soul.

The next is a tension between the unending ecstasy of
love, which is dreamed about, and the way love actually turns
out in marriage. There are some that have become cynical,
which one should not. If one starts with the assumption the
other person is God, then one is doomed to drink the bitter
dregs of disappointment. We must not attribute too much
to the other party. If we do, we are going to feel let down because the other partner did not give all he promised to give.
Sometimes the other feels betrayed, deceived, disappointed,
and cheated. In other words, "I entered this marriage to be
supremely and infinitely happy, and you're not making me
happy!" The reason that kind of discontent comes over the
soul is because one expected something from marriage that
is not there.

Here is the answer: Remember, no human being in the
world is love. God alone is love. We creatures are just lovable and only to a limited degree. When the creature begins
to take the place of the Creator and is made to stand for
love, then marriage turns to hate. One marries expecting
a god, or a woman to be a kind of an angel. She turns out
to be a fallen angel, and the man turns out to have feet of
clay. When ecstasy stops and the band no longer plays, the
champagne of life loses its sparkle. There are some that will
call the other partner a cheater and a robber. Then they go
to a divorce court and they say, "We want a divorce because
we are incompatible." Was there ever in the world a perfectly
compatible marriage? No two people in the world are absolutely compatible.

Then they begin looking for new partners and go through

the same mistake, expecting another partner to give that which only God can give. They enter into new marriages. They do not find happiness. Why not? The reason the marriage failed was because they refused to see married love as vestibule to the divine. It is vain to think another love can supply what the first love lacked. Cows can graze on other pastures, but there is no substitute for a person to whom one has committed his whole being for life. Remember then that you are not to expect too much. What you want is in heaven, not here on earth. Your partner is a fraction; God alone is the whole. Do not expect the other partner to give you infinite happiness. There is a heaven, but it is not on earth.

Following is the tension between sex and love. When we speak of this tension, it must not be assumed the two are opposites; they are not. When we speak of them here separately, it is because we are referring to those who separate sex from love. In married life the two are to be united. Sex is the highest expression of the love between husband and wife. When the two are not correctly understood, or when they are divorced, then we find these differences: Sex seeks the part, love the totality. Sex is biological and has its very definite zones of satisfaction; love includes all of these but is directed to the totality of the person loved, the person made of body and soul, created to the image and likeness of God. Love sees the clock and its purpose; sex concentrates on the mainspring and forgets it was made to keep time. An organ does not include the personality, but the personality includes the organ, which is another way of saying love includes sex, but sex does not necessarily include love. Love concentrates on the object, sex on the subject; namely, on the self. Love is directed to someone else for the sake of the other's perfection; sex is directed to self for the sake of self-satisfaction. Sex flatters the object, not because it is praise-worthy in itself, but rather as a solicitation. It knows how to make friends and to influence people. The ego in sex pleads it loves the other person, but loves the projection of the ego and the self in the other person.

Sex is moved by a desire to fill a moment between having and not having. It is an experience like looking at a sunset or twirling one's thumbs to pass the time. It rests after an experience, being glutted for a moment, and then waits for reappearance of the new passion to be satisfied, sometimes on an entirely different object. Love frowns on this notion, seeing nothing but the killing of the objects loved for the sake of self-satisfaction. Sex would give birds flight but no nest. It would give hearts emotions but no homes. It would throw the whole world into the experience of voyagers at sea but with no ports. Instead of purifying a fixed infinite—namely, God—it substitutes the false infinite, never finding satisfaction. One of the reasons so many suffer from psychoses and neuroses is because they are in a fruitless and constant search for the infinite in the finite, for God in carnality.

How different real love is. Real love admits the need, thirst, passion, and craving, but it also admits a real adhesion to a value that transcends all space and time. In love, poverty becomes integrated to riches. In real love the need becomes the fulfillment and the yearning becomes a joy. Sex is without that joy of offering. The wolf offers nothing when it kills the lamb because the joy of oblation is missing. Sex receives so as not to give, but love is sole contact with another for the sake of perfection.

You will feel a tension between the romance and the marriage, between the chase and the capture. Is there any way to always have the thrill of romance and the thrill of the capture? Yes there is, but not in this world. The only real answer to this paradox of the chase and the capture is to be found in eternity. When your love leads you back to God, then you will capture something infinitely ecstatic, and it will take an eternity of chase to discover its meaning. Understand that and as husband and wife you will know all the love you have is just a spark to lead you up to the flame which is God. Your marriage will become like a tuning fork to the song of the angels, like a river as it runs into the sea, where the romance and the marriage fuse into one. Since God is boundless eternal love, it will take that eternal chase to sound its depths. Then, there will be a limitless receptivity and a boundless gift in heaven. You marry for love, and love leads you to God.

40

MARRIAGE PROBLEMS

It is often assumed life should be without trials and difficulties. Our blessed Lord did not predict it so when He said, *In this world you shall have tribulation* (JN 16:33). Even when one enters into a realm of love, such as marriage, there are challenges. This is what might be called a What-to-Do kit for problems in marriage. We shall consider two: when marriage dulls and when the other partner becomes impossible.

First, when marriage dulls. Everything in life dulls after a time. Love does not continue to be one abiding ecstasy. Since flesh is the medium of married love, it suffers the penalty of the flesh and gets used to affection. As life goes on, a greater stimulus is required to produce an equal reaction to sensation. The eye becomes used to beauty, the fingers used to the touch of a friend. The intimacy, which was so desirable, at times becomes a burden. There is such a feeling as "I want to be alone" or "I think that I will go home to Mother." These feelings strip the eye of rose-colored glasses. Bills begin to come into the kitchen, and love is in danger of walking out. The habit of love becomes boring and not an adventure. It is conceivable there might even be a yearning for a new partner. Then children come with multiplied accidents and diseases, which tend to bring the vision down from the clouds to realistic trips to the nursery. Sooner or later the emotional life asks, "Is love a snare, a delusion, a false promise? I thought this would be complete happiness; yet it has settled down to a routine."

At this point, those who think love is an animal evolution and not a gift of God falsely believe another partner could supply what is lacking. This fallacy forgets that the emptiness does not come from the other partner, but from the nature of life itself. Here is the reason for that feeling. The heart was made for the infinite, which only the infinite can satisfy. The first ecstasy of love given to a couple was to remind them love was a gift that came from heaven. Only by working toward heaven would they ever really discover it to be infinite. Remember when our Lord gave bread at Capernaum (JN 6:1–15)? Later on He spoke to those who received the bread about the Eucharist, the Bread of everlasting life, His very Self. He was using the bread as bait to make them interested in the Bread of Life, the Eucharist. Similarly, the human love God gives us is bait, a divine come-on so we might seek the flame, which is God.

When married life becomes dull, one has not hit the bottom of life; one has hit the bottom of one's ego. There's a world of difference between the two. One has not hit the bottom of his soul, only the bottom of his instinct; not the bottom of his mind, but the bottom of his emotional life. These trials are contacts with reality which God sends into every life. If life went on as a dream without any shock of disillusionment, who would ever attain perfect happiness? Who would ever want God? The majority of men would rest in mediocrity without this push for perfect love. Acorns are not content to be saplings; children have to grow up; and our love has to grow up. God keeps something back, namely, Himself in eternity. If He did not, we would never push forward! Every now and then we run up against a brick wall. In a crisis we begin to feel like nonentities with an overwhelming sense of nothingness and loneliness. We see that life is only a bridge to eternity. The crisis of nothingness is caused by the meeting of a fancied ideal, the reality of love as the ego feels it, and of love as it really is.

This sense of nothingness is not peculiar to marriage itself. It happens in the spiritual life. Priests, brothers, nuns, and contemplatives all reach this crisis. Prayers become dry and formal; there's danger that we may become used to touching the Bread of Life. The same emotional thrill in reading Mass does not happen when one is ordained forty years as there was at the first Mass. There may not be that same ecstasy in visiting the sick when one is ordained fifty years as there was on the first sick call. The nun who is teaching children for thirty years has to bring herself with extra prayer to realize that all those youngsters have been put before her as charges by Almighty God. It becomes difficult for all of us to meditate. Thanksgivings are apt to become shorter after Mass. We have our problems, too. It is a problem of love. How can I love better? How can I pray better? How can I establish greater union with God? The answer is by sacrifices.

Since we are concerned with the development of love life in marriage, we return again to marriage. We say just as there is such a thing in the spiritual life as the dark night of the soul, in marriage there is such a thing as the dark night of the body. Just as the dark night of the soul in the spiritual life needs considerable purification through self-denial to reach deeper insights of love, so does marriage. Whenever there is discontent, God is stirring the waters of the soul. He is reminding us the perfect love for which we crave is not here; we're on the road to it. Just as, for example, a mother eagle will throw her young out of the nest that they may learn to fly, God, in these moments of trial, gives wings to our clay feet. Dryness, either in the spiritual life or in married life, can be for salvation or damnation, depending on how it is used.

There are two kinds of dryness: there is the one which rots, which is the dryness of love without God, and there is the dryness which ripens when one goes through the fire and the heat of sacrifice.

In moments of dullness, in this crisis of nothingness, the idea of eternity has to be reintroduced. In the days of romance the eternal emphasis was on the ego's durability in love. In the crisis of nothingness and dullness the eternal element is God, not the ego. Love now says, "I will love you always, for you are lovable through eternity for God's sake." Love, which began with pleasure and self-satisfaction, changes into love for God's sake. The other person becomes less the necessary condition of passion and more the partner of the soul. Our blessed Lord said that *unless the seed fall to the ground and die, it will not spring forth into life* (JN 12:24). Nothing is reborn to a higher life without a death to a lower one. The heart has its cycles as well as the planets, and the movement of the heart is an upward spiral and not a circle turning. The crisis of nothingness needs its purification and its cross. The cross is not a roadblock on the way to happiness; it is a ladder up which one climbs to the very heaven of love. There is no need to run off to someone to analyze your mental state simply because you find life dull. Intensify your love of God and begin to look upon the other partner as a gift of God, and then love will not be dull. Then we will see every human creature bathed in the beauty of God's love.

The other problem of marriage and trial is when marriage becomes a cross and is *impossible*. Marriage is for better or worse, and sometimes it turns out worse. Suppose the husband or wife becomes a chronic invalid or develops antisocial characteristics, becomes a drunkard, cruel, unfaithful, a tyrant, or bossy. What are we to do? We always have to regard the other person as a gift of God. Sometimes God's gifts are sweet and sometimes they are bitter. If we are selfish, we have to get rid of the other partner. Why? Because the other partner is a burden! If we are Christian, we take on the burden as something coming from the hand of God Himself. As St. Paul said, *Bear the burden of one another's failings; then you will be fulfilling the law of Christ* (RM 15:1-6).

If you object and say, "God never intended that anyone should live under such difficulties," the answer is flatly, "Oh yes He does!" Our blessed Lord said, *If any man has a mind to come my way let him renounce himself, take up his cross, and follow Me. The man who tries to save his life shall lose it. It is the man who loses his life for my sake that will secure it* (MT 16:24-25). We would all like to have tailor-made crosses. We are very willing to take on the mortification and self-denial which we choose, but when God chooses it, then we say, "Oh no, I cannot take that cross!" What sickness is to an individual an unhappy marriage may be to a couple: a trial set by God in order to perfect them spiritually. Without certain bitter gifts of God, many of our spiritual capacities would be undeveloped.

The acceptance of such trials of marriage is not a sentence to death, as some believe. The soldier is not sentenced to death because he takes an oath to his country, but he admits he's ready to face death rather than lose honor. An unhappy marriage is not a condemnation to unhappiness; it is a noble tragedy in which one bears the slings and arrows of outrageous fortune rather than deny a vow made to the living God. If it is noble to be wounded for the country we love, then is it not nobler to be wounded for God? Then here is this verse of Scripture very few people think about and which is so important. It is in St. Paul's epistle to the Corinthians: *The unbelieving husband is sanctified by the believing wife and the unbelieving wife is sanctified by the believing husband* (1 CO 7:14). In other words, the merits, the prayers, the sufferings, the patience, the meekness of one pass into the other.

If the other partner, who is an alcoholic, was sick, would you take care of him? Suppose he had tuberculosis or a heart attack, would you leave him? If he has a moral heart attack, is he to be abandoned? By a moral heart attack I mean guilty of any one of the sins that make marriage so very difficult. If there's such a thing as the transfusion of blood from a healthy member of society to a weak member of society, why can't there be the transfer of sanctification? A wife can redeem her husband and a husband can redeem the wife. There is a spiritual communication that does not have much romantic satisfaction in it, but the returns are eternal. Many a husband and wife after infidelities and excesses will find themselves saved on judgment day as the faithful partner never ceased to pour out prayers for his or her salvation.

Let me tell you this story to indicate how the merits of one will pass into the merits of another. At the turn of this century, an ordinarily good Catholic girl and an unbelieving medical doctor were married in Paris. His name was LeSueur. He promised to respect the faith of his marriage, but immediately after marriage tried to break it down. In addition to practicing medicine he became the editor of an anticlerical, atheistic newspaper in Paris. His wife reacted and decided that she would study her faith. She built a library of apologetics and he built up an atheistic library in the same house. In May 1905, as she was dying, she said to her husband, "Felix, when I am dead you will become a Catholic and a Dominican priest."

He said, "Elizabeth, you know my sentiments. I have sworn hatred of the Church and sworn hatred of God, and I shall live in that hatred and I shall die in it!"

She repeated her words and passed away. Fumbling amid her papers, he discovered her will, which stated in 1905 she asked Almighty God to send her sufficient sufferings to purchase his soul.

Then, she added, "On the day I die I shall have paid the price. You will have been bought and paid for. Greater love than this no woman hath than that she should lay down her life for her husband."

He dismissed this as the fancies of a pious woman, though he loved his wife. In order to forget his grief, he took a trip in the southern part of France. He stopped in front of a church, to which his wife had gone for a visit during their honeymoon. She seemed to be speaking to him, saying, "Go to Lourdes." He went to Lourdes, but he went there as a rank unbeliever. He had written a book against Lourdes, proving miracles were fraud and superstition. As he was standing before the grotto of Our Lady, he received the gift of faith, so complete, so total, he never had to go through the process of juxtaposition and say, "Well, now that I believe, how will I answer this difficulty or how will I answer that difficulty?" He saw all he had believed in its utter error and stupidity.

The conversion of Dr. LeSueur was about as exciting as the news of the bombardment of Rheims.

Then time passed. In 1924 I made my retreat in a Belgium Dominican monastery under the spiritual direction of Father LeSueur, Dominican, Catholic, and priest, who told me this story. I tell you it is not often you can make a retreat under a priest who every now and then will say, "As my dear wife, Elizabeth, said." But the moral of the story is love is not completely and totally here. It is in God, and by loving God we save the other partner whether it be a bad wife or a bad husband. For once married they are two in one flesh.

41

COMMANDMENTS: 1-3

Have you ever been guilty of speeding? Did you ever shoot game out of season? Did it ever cause you great remorse? It is obvious that breaking the law is the same as wounding someone we love. The standard and norm of our morality is not just a law, but a person, not something prohibited, rather, charity and love. Some people will feel greater sorrow for sin than others will. It all depends upon how much we love.

Suppose you cannot sing and are put into a choir where everyone else can and the other singers are displeased with your performance. You hit a false note. The director of the choir would look at you with a very sour face. All the other singers would turn toward you and give you a dirty look. Why do they act that way to you? It is because they feel discord more than you do. You are not musical enough to appreciate it, but they are. There are some people who do not appreciate the love and the mercy of God and are not inclined to feel regret as those who have just a vague concept of deity. I do not mean to say they are without blame, just as there is a reality to you hitting a wrong note. I only say where there is a love of Christ, there is a refusal to do anything that would wound Him, and secondly, when we do hurt Him, we feel a greater contrition and sorrow. There is a difference between law and love, between sin in the natural order and sin in the supernatural order.

When we are governed solely by law, when we are not in the state of grace, and when we do wrong, we have a sense of guilt. When we are in the state of grace and sin seriously, we have a sense of pollution, shame, and defilement. The difference between the two is much like the remorse of Cain or Judas compared to the remorse of the Prodigal Son, who said he had sinned against his father. In the natural order we are apt to have a fear of temporal punishments, whereas in the supernatural order of grace, we are governed by a sense of God's holiness. In the natural order our sorrow often extends only to some sins, particularly the more shameful ones, not always to such sins as avarice or selfishness. When the Spirit of Christ penetrates us, we are sorry for our bad motives, our evil thoughts, anything that inspires bad actions.

In the natural order, grief for a fault or sin is often temporary, as it was in the case of the judge who heard Paul. Remember, sacred Scripture says something very striking: *The dog goes back to his vomit* (PR 26:11). Sometimes sinners go back again to their sin because they were not penetrated with a keen sense of the reality of their sin. If we live in the supernatural order, there is an enduring conviction of sin. We become very much like Peter. It was said he regretted his sin so much that he had furrows in his cheeks from the tears he shed for denying our blessed Lord.

Our aim is to imitate the life of Christ Himself. This does not mean we have to be born in a stable or visit Egypt, or dispute our teachers at the age of twelve, or change water into wine. It means each of us should do what Christ would have done in our place. We are not to copy Christ as a student will copy a great master in an art gallery, but we are to have the spirit of Christ in us.

We return to the law that should govern all of our moral life. We repeat, because it is so important, our blessed Lord said, *Thou shalt love the Lord thy God with thy whole heart and with thy whole soul and thy whole mind. This is the greatest of the Commandments. And the second is like to this, Thou shalt love thy neighbor as thy self* (MT 22:37-39). Notice all the Ten Commandments were summed up in love. You never can have love except by and through a person who is opposite you. Now who is the person opposite you? God and neighbor. That is why when we are in love with someone we speak of "our" love. There's a bond uniting the two of us so the basis of moral life is an earthly trinity. Just as there is the Trinity of the Father, the Son, and the Holy Spirit in heaven, so on earth there is a trinity of moral relations: I, thou, and God. Just as there is a dialogue between me and you and God, so there is the eternal dialogue of love: Father, Son, and Holy Spirit.

Our blessed Lord spoke of the heavenly Trinity as the model of this earthly trinity of love the night of the Last Supper. These were His words—He was talking about how He revealed the Father's love to us—and He said to His heavenly Father that *the love Thou hast bestowed on Me may dwell in them and I, too, may dwell in them* (JN 17:26). You observe the norm of our love of neighbor is not just the love we have for ourselves, but the love Christ has for us forming the foundation of love.

The two Commandments, love God and love neighbor, sum up the Ten Commandments, which refer to love of God and love of neighbor. The first three Commandments are related to God; the last six Commandments are related to neighbor. Between the first three and the last six comes the Fourth, *Honor thy father and thy mother* (DT 5:16). God put this in between the two because the parents in the home take the place of God, and obedience to parents is a very high form of justice related to neighbor and to God. When we disobey God, we are offending one of the first three Commandments about adoring God, keeping holy His name, and the Sabbath.

We are not concerned with telling you about sins or the vices you have to avoid. What interests us is to increase in you the love of God and to construct a positive, moral imitation of Christ. We will mention the sins in passing, but you will find them in any prayer book where there is an examination of conscience. This is not a complete enumeration of the sins against these first three Commandments (DT 5:6–15), but only some of them. Anyone would violate the general commandment of love of God, or the first three, if he refused to recognize God as Creator, Redeemer, and Sanctifier. If there were a hatred of God, failure to worship, failure to attend Mass on Sundays and holy days of obligation, or a rebellion against God for the trials and crosses He permitted; these would also violate the first three Commandments. If there were such things as idolatry, superstition, blasphemy, cursing, sacrilege, loss of faith, presumption, despair, dishonoring the Sunday, and the like; we are not just to avoid these sins, we really must know: Why should we worship God? Why should we honor Him? Why is His name holy? If we understand the First Commandment, to love God with our whole mind and our whole soul, perhaps we will not fall into any of these sins.

How do you think of God? Do you think of Him as someone on a throne Who gets angry if you do not go to Mass on Sunday or if you blaspheme? Do you think it makes Him unhappy when you do not pay any attention? Or do you think He is a benevolent grandfather Who's indifferent to what you do, Who likes to see you go places, do things, and have a good time regardless of how you do it? No, God is not like either picture. Does He lose something when we do not worship Him? Of course not; we do!

What is worship? "Worship" is a contraction of "worth-ship." It is a manifestation of the worth in which we hold another person. Worship is a sign of value. You applaud an actor on the stage. You may applaud an athlete. When you do, you're putting a value on his worth. What does it mean to worship God? It means to acknowledge in some way His power, His goodness, and His truth. If you do not worship God, what do you worship? Nine times out of ten it will be yourself. If there is no God, then you are a god. If you are a god, I am an atheist, because I cannot believe in that kind of a god. The basic reason there is so little worship of God today is because man denies he is dependent.

Why should you worship God? You have a duty to worship God, because you will be unhappy if you do not. Suppose you are a father. Your little boy brings you a little ten-cent knife he bought for Christmas. Do you value the little knife more than a box of very fine cigars from your insurance agent? If you are a mother of a little girl, have you received a handful of yellow dandelions from her and been more pleased than by a bouquet of roses from a dinner guest? Do these trivialities make you any richer? Do you need them? Do you need the knife? Do you need the dandelions? Would you be imperfect without them? No. Why do you love them? Because your children are worshipping you! Because they are acknowledging your love and goodness, and by doing so are perfecting themselves. They are developing along the lines of love rather than hate, thankfulness rather than ingratitude, and service rather than disloyalty. They are becoming more perfect and happy children.

Just as you do not need that little knife or those dandelions, neither does God need your worship. Their giving is a sign of your worth in your children's eyes, and prayer, adoration, and worship are signs of God's worth in our eyes. If you do not need your children's worship, why do you think God needs yours? Their worship is for their perfection, not yours, and your worship of God is for your perfection. Worship is your opportunity to express devotion, dependence, and love to make yourself happy.

A lover gives gifts to his beloved because in his eyes she is possessed of all gifts. The more he loves, the poorer he thinks his gifts are. If he gave everything, it still would not be enough. One of the reasons we take price tags off our gifts is because we do not wish to establish a proportion between our gift and our love. When a man gives a young woman gifts, his gifts do not make her more precious, but they make him less inadequate. By giving he is no longer nothing. The gift is his perfection, not hers.

Worship is our perfection, not God's. To refuse to worship is to deny a dependence that makes us independent. Worship is to us what blooming is to a rose. Our refusing worship would be like a rose cutting itself off from the sun and the earth, or a student denying history can teach him anything. To withhold admiration from one who deserves it is a sign of a jealous, conceited mind. Down deep in his heart a man who refuses to worship God knows he is not a creator; he even knows he could not be godless if there were no God. God made you to be happy; He made you for your happiness, not His. God would still be perfectly happy if you never existed. God has no need of love for His sake, since there is nothing in you that makes you lovable to God. Most of us are very lucky if we receive any affection from human beings. God put some of His love into us; thus, we can find everyone else lovable. By our sharing some of our love with them, they become lovable.

We love others because of need. We live in poverty; someone has to supply our lack. God does not love us because He needs us. He loves us because He put some of His love into us and made us valuable. When God asks us to love Him with our whole heart, our whole mind, and our whole soul, it is because He wants us to be happy.

42

COMMANDMENTS: 4–10

The first three Commandments speak of our duties to God and the last six of our duties to neighbor (DT 5:6–21). In between is the Fourth Commandment: *Honor thy father and thy mother,* because it is a bond between both God and neighbor. The justice we owe our parents is close to the justice we owe to God and related to the justice we owe our neighbor. After God, it was our parents who gave us life, and this Fourth Commandment is the Commandment which provides for the future of our civilization.

Napoleon was asked when the education of a child begins. He answered, "Twenty years before the child is born—in the education of the mother." This is true because the parents take the place of God in the home. A child is so much clay in the hands of the parents, who will decide its future. When God gave a child to the parents, He made a crown for that child in heaven, and woe be to the parents who do not fulfill the high destiny and vocation of that child. Among the gravest dangers facing children can be the examples of their parents. Delinquency begins at home. Parental delinquency becomes juvenile delinquency, and the divine law regarding the two has been clearly expressed in sacred Scripture. In the epistle to the Colossians (3:20-21) we read of the relationship children should have to parents, then later on, the relation parents have to children.

Children must be obedient to their parents in every way; obedience is a gracious sign of serving the Lord and obeying God Himself. Parents must not rouse their children to resentment or they will break their spirits. There must be gentleness that characterizes the mercy of God toward us.

What a beautiful lesson of obedience is given in the divine Child of Nazareth. There is no evidence He ever gave Mary and Joseph just the nominal right to command. Scripture says, *He lived there in subjection to them* (LK 2:51). Imagine, God subject to man! God, before whom the angels, principalities, and powers tremble, is subject to Mary and to Joseph, for Mary's sake. Here are two great miracles of humility and exaltation: the God-man obeying a woman, and a woman commanding the God-man. The very fact He became subject to her endows her with power and obedience that lasted for thirty years. By this long span of voluntary obedience, He revealed the Fourth Commandment as the bedrock of family life. How else could the primal sin of disobedience against God be undone except by obedience in the flesh of the God Who was once defied? It was Lucifer who said, *I will not obey!* (IS 14:12-14). Eden caught up that echo, and down the ages its inflection traveled, worming its way into the nooks and crevices of every family.

As parents surrender their legitimate authority and primary responsibility to their children, the state begins to take over. When the parents no longer bring up their children in the love and fear of God, and the children become juvenile delinquents; then the state takes over the home and takes over the children. Obedience in the home is the foundation of obedience in the commonwealth; conscience submits to a trustee of God's authority. The world has lost its respect for authority; since it was lost first in the home, and as the home loses its authority, then the state begins to become tyrannical. A bond is established between the home and the state. Democracy put man on a pedestal; feminism put woman on a pedestal, but neither democracy nor feminism can live a generation unless a child is first placed on a pedestal, and such is the significance of Nazareth. Our Lord warned about caring for the child. He said, *And if anyone hurts the conscience of one of these little ones that believe in Me, he had better have been drowned in the depths of the sea with a millstone hung about his neck* (MT 18:6).

It is not to be thought that obedience in the home does not include every other kind of obedience. This commandment embraces what is known as the virtue of *pietas,* or piety, and involves family, neighbor, and state. All authority comes from God; hence, this commandment obliges us to obey civil authority. Remember when Pilate boasted he had power to condemn our blessed Lord, our blessed Lord said he would not have the power unless it came to him from above (JN 19:10–11). Scripture tells us every soul must be submissive to its lawful superiors (EP 6:5). Authority comes from God only, and all authorities that hold sway are of God's ordinance. It is very beautiful to realize St. Paul and St. Peter asked for obedience to civil rulers even though the civil leader was Nero, who would put them both to death. You will find those who love God are always the great patriots. Whenever a decline of patriotism begins in a country, there is always a decline of belief in God.

In the other Commandments, the Fifth through the Tenth, our blessed Lord said that we were to love our neigh-

bor as ourselves. How do we love ourselves? We love ourselves very much. But there are also some things we do not
like about ourselves. We hate ourselves when we are boorish,
loud, and insulting to others, or make excessive demands
upon our neighbor, or when we tell untruths that hurt our
friends. You see we can love and hate ourselves.

We love what is good in ourselves and we hate what is
bad. We love what is good in our neighbor, and we hate what
is sinful in him. We love the sinner and we hate the sin. We
love the neighbor as a spiritual self, but we do not necessarily love him as a carnal self. Our blessed Lord tied together
love of Himself, love of neighbor, and love of ourselves.
There could be two great errors: one is to love God without loving our neighbor, and the other would be to love our
neighbor without loving God. We are often invited to take
part in brotherhood causes; there's much talk of the brotherhood of man. All that is very good and true, but how can
we be brothers unless we have a common Father? To leave
the Fatherhood of God out of the brotherhood of man is to
make us all a race of illegitimate children.

The love of neighbor is not to be standardized solely
upon our love of ourselves, but rather upon the way our
Lord has loved us. He says, *This is My Commandment, that you
should love one another as I have loved you* (JN 15:12). But who
is my neighbor? The one who lives next door? We can never
tell in advance who is our neighbor. The neighbor can be
a friend, just as our blessed Lord was a friend of Lazarus;
and the neighbor could be an enemy, as was the case of the
man who was injured on the road from Jerusalem to Jericho
(LK 10:30). The neighbor is the one who is in need of your
esteem. The saints have more of our esteem than do sinners,
but on this earth charity must be guided by the greatness of

either spiritual or corporal misery. If two are in misery and equally needy, then we can give to the one closest to us either by blood or by friendship.

We said the neighbor can also be the enemy, and our blessed Lord said, *But I tell you, love your enemies. Do good to those who hate you. Pray for those who persecute and insult you* (MT 5:44). Love of enemies is actually the touchstone to prove whether our love is truly divine. Our blessed Lord said before we bring a gift to Him at the altar, we should go and be reconciled with our brother if there is any conflict between us (MT 5:24).

We are related to our neighbor by mind, body, and things. We can be bound up with our neighbor in thoughts, desires, resolutions, the way we speak, and the way we listen. We can be related to our neighbor in body and in work. There can be pleasure through communication. We can be bound to our neighbor through money, land, and property, the whole economic order. These three—mind, body, and things—are the sources of the three major kinds of sin: pride, which refers to the mind; lust or impurity, which refers to the body; and finally, avarice, which refers to things.

Let us take up our relationship to the neighbor in temptations of the mind. Temptations are wholly in the mind. There are three elements to a temptation: suggestion, delight, and consent. You cannot sin in your mind until there is consent, which comes from the will. The suggestion may come from the eye, ear, memory, imagination, or suggestion, as Eve was tempted by the word of Satan. There can be delight, and that can even be physical. We can feel the repercussion of the thought in our body; it does not make any difference how long the feeling may endure; there is no sin until there is consent. We are not to think we are bad because we are tempted—that is only human; it is consent which is wrong.

Our relationship to our neighbor obliges us to speak the truth. No other moral virtue can grow up without truth. In the sacrament of Confirmation we receive the spirit of truth and membership in the Mystical Body becomes more intimate. The reason we are asked to be truthful is because the whole Incarnation is truth. Remember the inner word or the thought of God became flesh, became externalized. As the Son is the image of the Father, so what I say externally must be the image of what is in my mind internally. *The Word became flesh and dwelt amongst us* (JN 1:14).

All sins against truth are forbidden, like lying, boasting, defaming character, injuring another's good name, rash judgment, falsely accusing others, denying our faith even under persecution, hypocrisy, plus resolving to do something evil even when we are unable to carry it out. One can commit murder in thought though the thought never passes into act. The Commandments say, *Thou shalt not covet thy neighbor's wife. Thou shalt not covet thy neighbor's goods* (EX 20:17). Our blessed Lord said, *Any man looking after a woman and lusting after her hath already committed adultery with her in his own heart* (MT 5:28). You see, our blessed Lord does not wait until a thought passes into act. He's not interested just in hygiene; He keeps clean all the motivations of action. If all of the little rivers that run into the ocean are kept clean, then the ocean itself will be kept clean.

The body is deserving of respect because in the natural order, it is bound with the soul to constitute a person, and in the supernatural order, it becomes a temple of God where we are in the state of grace. Sacred Scripture says to us, *I appeal to you by God's mercies to offer your bodies as a living sacrifice, consecrated to God and worthy of His acceptance* (RM 12:1).

I believe we already said that very often people who enjoy excessive luxury of the body are naked on the inside. The more the soul is clothed with virtue, the less need there is of external display. We have to take care of our bodies not just for biological reasons, but in order to better maintain our spiritual, moral life. This does not mean sickness is incompatible with holiness. Sometimes sickness diminishes temptation, unites us with the Passion of our Lord, and assures us of the promise of glory if we suffer in His name. We have to remember every sin in the mind also can be an assault on the body. Thus, there will be no such thing as taking our own life, because that belongs to God. For a woman, there will be no such thing as abortion. There will be no taking the lives of incurable persons. There will be no evil thoughts or desires against the neighbor and no solitary sins, drunkenness and all the other sins against the body, which you will find mentioned in a prayer book. There will be no sins against our own body or against the body of the neighbor like murder, abortion, adultery, and prevention of the fruit of love.

We are related to our neighbor by things. Private property is the external guarantee of human freedom, and the right to property is personal, but the use of property is social. We are bound to our neighbor in charity to give alms. The superfluities of the rich are the necessities of the poor. Our blessed Lord said, *I was sick and you visited Me, I was thirsty and you gave Me to drink* (MT 25:35–36). There will be, as regards things, great charity, particularly to the missions of the Church in pagan lands. The Holy Father said, "This is the charity that surpasses all other charities, as heaven, earth, and eternal time."

All sins as regarding things will be avoided. There will be no stealing without restitution of what was stolen. If we do not know the person from whom something was stolen, then we will give a similar amount to charity. We shall repair for unjust damage, give full work for a day's pay. There will be payment by employers of a living wage and no cheating or cutting corners. Sacred Scripture says: *Thou shalt not have divers weights in thy bag, a greater and a less: Neither shall there be in thy house a greater bushel and a less. Thou shalt have a just and a true weight, and thy bushel shall be equal and true* (DT 25:13-14).

Thus, the Commandments.

43

THE LAW OF LOVE: TOTAL COMMITMENT

All we have discussed can be summarized in the difference between law and love. In the Christian way we are not governed by law at all, we should be beyond it. We seek not merely the keeping of the Commandments, but to be related to our blessed Lord. Is it hard? Is it possible?

Remember, one day a young man came to our blessed Lord and asked what he must do to be saved, and our blessed Lord said he must keep the Commandments. Our Lord mentioned about five or six of the Commandments, such as not stealing, not committing adultery, and the like. The young man said, *I have kept all these from my youth.* Our blessed Lord then added, *If you would be perfect, go sell all you have. Give it to the poor, then come follow Me* (MT 19:20–21). The young man left feeling sad, because he had great possessions. This troubled the Apostles. Must everybody sell everything to follow our Lord? They said, *Who then, can be saved?* (MT 19:25). Our Lord answered that it is not possible with men alone, by our own human power, but it is possible with God. All things are possible with God; we have His grace.

Christianity is hard from a worldly point of view, but it gives inner peace and joy to those who obey the law of love of our blessed Lord. When we understand the full import of the law, we hear our Lord say, "Give Me all, all of you. Give Me your whole self." Is that a loss? No, because He said, "I will give you a new self. I will give you Myself, My own will shall become yours."

We are trying to remain what we are and at the same time to keep a reasonable amount of peace. We want to be "good." We want our hearts and our minds to go one way; maybe it's after money, pleasure, or social prestige, and at the same time, we do want to behave honestly, chastely, and to keep the Commandments.

Our blessed Lord said, *A thistle cannot produce a fig, and a field that contains nothing but grass seed cannot produce wheat* (MT 7:16–20). If I want to produce wheat, the change has to go deep down below the surface. I have to be plowed up and to be resown. Our Lord said, *If you would be perfect, come follow Me* (MT 19:21), and again, *Be ye perfect as your heavenly Father is perfect* (MT 5:48). He meant we have to go in for the full treatment. It is hard, but hankering after it is a bit harder. When we get down to rock bottom, what are we afraid of? We are afraid to give our fingers to God because we fear He may take our hands. We have little secret gardens back in our hearts that we tend. The fruit is not His; it is ours. We wall it off from Him, sometimes a petty sin, a vice or selfishness, whatever it happens to be. We do not get the full joy of being a Christian. It's very hard for an egg to turn into a bird, but it would be much harder for it to learn to fly while remaining an egg. We are just like eggs now, and we cannot go on being just good eggs. A good egg is an egg that hatches.

Our blessed Lord insists upon a kind of a death; we have to renew in our lives exactly what happened in His. He is the pattern. He repeatedly said to Nicodemus and to us that if we are to live again, we have to perish in our old existence (JN 3:1–21). Is there anybody who hopes the real danger spots are rendered harmless because He is a kind Savior who takes hardened sinners back without questions? That person must read the text where He said He would not subtract one jot from the severity of God's law (MT 5:18). He had not come to abolish the law, but to perfect it (MT 5:17). Grace is not cheap. It cost our Lord His life. Can you think of anything more costly than what a man must pay on a cross? If we want peace, we have to pay the price. Without that death to the lower life, there's no peace; there's only fear and we live a kind of half existence.

Our blessed Lord said, *He who wills to do the will of the Father in heaven will know whether the teaching is from God* (JN 7:17). He means one of the reasons there are agnostics and skeptics is because they are not keeping the law of God. If we know His will, we will understand His doctrine. We may have entirely too much insistence upon a knowledge of Christian doctrine and not enough insistence on the doing. Our blessed Lord said, *If you do My will, you will know My doctrine* (JN 8:31). Only he who does the will earnestly and stakes his life on it will come to understand Christ and all that His redemption means. Our Lord is known only to those who venture, not to the cowards.

At first our blessed Lord is a disturber. He seems to irritate you and lead you into a kind of a crucifixion. You are an easygoing worldling and have settled down comfortably into your worldview, but if you are in earnest with Christ, you will have to give up that comfort because it is a false peace. The first advent of Christ into our lives is of one who upsets us, but once we give ourselves to Him, He becomes our defender. Before we have Christ, our hearts accuse us, we are unhappy with half measures. After we give ourselves to Him and His law of love, then our hearts are at peace. His attitude completely changes once we have changed ours.

This is another way of putting the difference between commandments and love: "Commandments only restrain me." We see them as hurdles and obstacles in the way of life. Those who live by the Commandments ask, "How far can I go?"

"What is the limit?"

"How close can I get to the abyss without tumbling in?"

"Is it a mortal sin?"

This is not the way of love; it is not the way of peace. It is the old Adam within me that talks this way about commands. When I merely obey commands, I am never there as a whole person. That's the psychological state of everyone who obeys a command, never the whole heart. When I love, I am a whole person, for love is a movement of my whole self; therefore, it can never be commanded.

Up to this point we have said the Christian doctrine of morality is a total commitment to Christ. We put on His mind, think His thoughts, love what He loves, and ask ourselves whenever we do anything, "Will this be pleasing to Him?" There's another side to the love of God; it is the love of neighbor. The two laws go together. Loving the neighbor is being a sin bearer.

Some years ago I remember meeting a woman who was distressed because her son had been put into prison. I think it was his fourth arrest for crime, robbery, and murder. She was bitterly ashamed and brokenhearted. I asked myself, "Why does she have all this shame?" And then the words of the prophet Isaiah came to me that had referred to our

Lord, and I might say of her, *She had borne his grief, carried his sorrows, and the chastisement of his peace was upon her* (IS 53:4–5). It would only be by her stripes that he would be healed. This good mother had very few sins in her life, certainly no serious ones; yet love made her exceedingly sinful for his sake. Immediately the mystery cleared up: the love a woman can experience for her son makes her one with him. His sin, disgrace, and shame are hers, which is the nearest thing that we can ever get on this earth to the love of God. We have to see that all of our sins, disgrace, and shame became His, which He bore in His own body upon the Tree.

This is what forgiveness cost and why grace and forgiveness are not easy. We are not to think that we are pious when we begin living our individual, holy lives apart from our neighbor, the world, and suffering humanity. That was the trouble with Simon the Pharisee. The sinful woman came into the house and poured ointment upon our Lord's feet. Simon was scandalized. He wanted no contact with a sinner; he was concerned about keeping the law for himself and maybe his own faults in inner peace. Our blessed Lord said to Simon, "Do you see this woman? Do you understand her? Her sins are part of the world's sins." He was taking on her sins, and the pouring of the ointment was a preparation for His Crucifixion and burial (LK 7:36–50). She was forgiven much, and forgiveness costs an awful lot.

Forgiveness is love in action, and love means sin bearing. Forgiveness can only be accomplished by sin bearing, which means a cross to God and to us! Our blessed Lord said, *If any man will be my disciple let him take up his cross and follow Me* (MK 8:34). The meaning of the Cross is love bearing the sin of the beloved because of oneness with Him. We can know the sin bearer, Christ, only as we bear the sins of others. We are redeemed in order to be redeemers, and we are not saved until God makes us saviors. A Christian has to go with our Lord into the Garden of Gethsemane and must pass from there to Calvary, filling up in his body what is lacking to the sufferings of Christ for the sake of His body, which is the Church.

We cannot, like Pilate, wash our hands and say, "I am innocent of the blood and sufferings of the world" (MT 27:24). If the Church is a church, it is a body of sin-bearing people who love with the love of God shed abroad in their hearts. They can forgive because they've been forgiven. They who have been loved can become lovers. Unless the Church of Christ is united by love with the whole of mankind, then the sin of the world is the sin of the Church; the disgrace of the world is the disgrace of the Church; the shame of the world, the shame of the Church; the poverty of the world, the poverty of the Church; then it is no Church at all. The Church is not, and can never be, an end in itself. It is a means of salvation for the world, not just our own sanctification. We cannot save ourselves alone. We pray in the context of "Our Father," not "My Father"; "Our daily bread," not "My daily bread."

The Church is the agent of salvation for mankind. It is not a refuge of peace; it is an army preparing for war. We seek security, but only in sacrifice; this is the mark of the Church and the hallmark of the Cross. If the sin of our modern slums and the degradation they cause; if the sin of our overcrowded houses and the ugliness and vice they bring; if the sin of unemployment with the damnation of body and soul; if the sin of the heartless and thoughtless stands out against the squalid and degrading poverty of Africa, Asia, and Latin America; if the sin of commercial trickery and dishonesty and the wholesale defrauding of the poor; if the sin of prostitution and the murder of women and children by disease; and if the sin of war that the others have bred; if all is not laid upon the Church as a burden, and upon us as members of the Church, and if we do not feel pain, we are not worthy members of the Church. We have missed our vocation. Christian morality is not just the keeping of the Commandments; it's love, total commitment, and taking upon ourselves the sins of others. This is the new law: Love God; love your neighbor.

44

DEATH AND JUDGMENT

Eventually, we had to come to the subject of death and judgment. If there is anything that characterizes life, it is the intolerance of boundaries. We all want the infinite. That is why we are disappointed frequently. We realize the tremendous disproportion there is between an ideal we have conceived and reality itself. But still we go on searching, because we have an infinite capacity for more. You cannot imagine yourself in possession of any good thing and not wanting more. Nature sets limits to the "more" of our bodies. There's a limit to bodily pleasures; they may even reach a point where they become painful and we become sick of them. There are no limits to the desires of the soul, which can never reach the point of satiety. There is no limit to a truth you could know, the life you can live, the love you can enjoy, and the beauty you can experience.

If this were all, we would be cheated. We would be frustrated just like a woman mad about fashions put into a room with a thousand hats but not a single mirror. Since you have a body and a soul, you can make one or the other master. You can make the body serve the soul, which is the Christian way, or you can make the soul serve the body, which is the miserable way. It is this choice which makes life so very serious. There would be no fun in playing games unless there was a chance to lose. There would be no zest in battle if crowns of merit rested suspended over those who did not fight. There would be no interest in dramas if the characters were puppets. There would be no point in life unless there were great and eternal destinies at stake in which we say aye or nay to our eternal salvation. Our blessed Lord put it this way: *And fear ye not them that kill the body and are not able to kill the soul. But rather fear him that can destroy both soul and body in hell* (MT 10:28). On another occasion our Lord said, *What doth it profit a man if he gain the whole world and suffer the loss of his own soul? What exchange shall a man give for his soul?* (MT 16:26).

There will come a time when this trial will be over. I know it is very difficult to convince modern minds, since they do not like to hear that life will end. Death is often disguised today by morticians. They would almost make you believe there was happiness in every box! They do not wish to face the fact of man's end. And have you noticed that modern minds feel awkward in the face of death? They do not know how to extend sympathy because they concentrate on the circumstances preceding death rather than on the eternal issues involved in death, namely, heaven or hell.

There are those who think death belongs to the biological order and that man dies just like pigs and roosters die and for exactly the same reason. But this is not true. Man has a soul, which is spiritual and immortal. The death of a man is not the same as the death of a beetle. An animal life is like a circle, unfolding from within and turning back upon itself. Man's life is like a trajectory that reaches out beyond time to someone else. The real reason for death is not in the natural order, but in the historical order. At the beginning of human history man sinned, and the penalty of sin is death. Scripture says, *It was through one man that guilt came into the world and since death came owing to guilt, death was handed on to all mankind by one man* (RM 5:12). Therefore, because of original sin, we die. If there were no sin, there would be no death. The Assumption of our blessed Mother follows her Immaculate Conception. The blessed Mother's body did not become subject to corruption, because she was preserved free from sin. The giving of the Eucharist implied the resurrection of the body, as we were united to His body and blood. Christ said, *The man who eats My flesh and drinks My blood enjoys eternal life and I will raise him up on the last day* (JN 6:54). The Resurrection of our Lord is the pledge of our own resurrection.

St. Paul tells us we have to die daily. A happy death is a masterpiece, and no masterpiece was ever perfected in a day. It took seven years to make the wax model for the celebrated statue of Joan of Arc. One day the model was finally finished and the bronze poured. The statue stands today as a ravishing perfection of the sculptor's art. In like manner, our death at the end of natural existence must appear as a ravishing perfection after years of labor given to its mold and by dying daily through mortification. The principal reason we fear death is because we are not prepared for it. Death is a beautiful thing for him who dies before he dies, by dying daily to the temptations of the world, the flesh, and the devil. There is a very interesting inscription over the tomb of John Duns Scotus in Cologne; it reads, ANTE SEPULTURAM BIS MORIMUR, a double death preceded his burial. There is not one traveler in a hundred who understands the mystery of love behind this quotation.

Once death comes there is no remedy for an evil life; only before it comes, by dying to ourselves. We follow the law of emulation, which is the law of the universe. There's no other way of entering into a higher life except by dying to the lower. There's no possibility of a man enjoying an ennobled existence in Christ unless he is torn up from the old Adam. When one leads a mortified life in Christ, death does not come like a thief in the night, taking one by surprise. We die daily; thus, we rehearse: *It is appointed unto men once to die and after this the judgment* (HEB 9:27). Those are the words of sacred Scripture. As relatives and friends gather around a dead person, they often ask, "How much did he leave?" But the angels will ask, "How much did he take with him?" The only thing we can take with us in death is what we can take with us in a shipwreck; namely, our merits.

Then comes the judgment, and judgment is twofold. We will be judged at the moment of death in the particular judgment, and we will be judged on the last day in the general judgment. You are a person and are individually responsible for your acts. Your works follow you. The second judgment will be because you worked out your salvation in the context of the social order and the Mystical Body of Christ; therefore, you must be judged with all men.

In the general judgment, we take our bodies upon ourselves as by the resurrection. At death, when the soul is separated from the body, it still retains its aptitude for the body. The soul has made an imprint, as if you left your hand on warm wax. One might almost say at death, the soul desires to have the body with it. When the soul leaves the body at death, it does not leave the body forever. The soul does not become an angel; it remains a human soul. The soul contains all of its experiences, happenings, thoughts, and deeds. At the resurrection of the dead, the soul will have a body corresponding to the spiritual condition of the soul.

It will be glorious, if the soul is saved; and miserable, if the soul is lost. Our salvation is the salvation not just of the soul but of our entire personality. Our bodies have shared in the condition of our souls and will share in their glory or shame. If you pour water into a blue glass, it looks blue. In like manner, on the day of resurrection our bodies will shine forth according to the virtues or vices that are in our souls.

What will the particular judgment be like? It will be an evaluation of ourselves just as we really are. As we live, there almost seem to be several persons in us. There are the persons others think we are, then there's the person we think we are, and then there's the person we really are. During this life it is very easy for us to believe our press notices and publicity, to judge ourselves by public opinion rather than by eternal truth. We may and do think ourselves good, because we find neighbors who are so wicked. We sometimes judge our virtues by the vices from which we abstain. If we made our money under a capitalistic system, we think labor organizations are wicked; if we made our money organizing labor unions, we think capitalism is wicked. If we come from the city, we look down on people from the country. We think because a person speaks with an accent he is unimportant; that if he is a different color, he is of less value. Our enthusiasm for the common man may be because we hate the rich, not because we love the common man. We're not always seeing things straight; we are wearing smoked glasses. St. Paul implied that when he said, *We see now through a glass in a dark manner, but then face-to-face. Now I know in part, but then I shall know even as I am known* (1 CO 13:12). We are what we are not by our emotions, feelings, likes or dislikes, but by our choices or decisions.

We are all on the roadway of life in this world, but we

travel in different vehicles. Some are in trucks, jeeps, and ambulances. Others are in twelve-cylinder cars, and others in broken-down old wrecks, but each of us is doing the driving. The judgment is something like being stopped by a policeman. When we are stopped by God, He does not say to us, as the policeman does not say, "What kind of a car are you driving?" God is no respecter of persons. He asks, "How well did you drive? Did you obey the laws?"

At death we leave our vehicles behind, our emotions, prejudices, feelings, our state in life, our opportunities, the accidents of talent, duty, intelligence, and position. It will make no difference to God if we were crippled, ignorant, or hated by the world; our judgment will be based not on our social position but on the way we lived, on the choices we made, on the things we loved. Do not think when you go before the judgment seat of God that you will argue a case. You will plead no extenuating circumstances, you will not ask for a new trial or a new jury; you will be your own judge! You will be your own jury. As Scripture says, *We will be condemned out of our own mouths* (MT 12:37). God will merely seal our judgment.

What then is judgment from God's point of view and from our point of view? From God's point of view, judgment is recognition. Two souls appear before the sight of God in that split second after death; one is in the state of grace, the other is not. Remember grace is a participation of divine nature. Just as by nature you resemble your parents, so by grace we partake in the nature of God. Our blessed Lord looks into the soul and the state of grace. He sees the resemblance of His nature. A mother knows her child because the child shares her nature, so God knows His own children by resemblance of nature as we are born of Him. By seeing in our souls His divine likeness, He says to us, *Come, ye blessed of My Father. I have taught you to pray "Our Father." I am the natural Son, you the adopted son, come into the Kingdom I have prepared for you from all eternity* (MT 25:34).

Let us look at the other soul, which does not possess the family traits of the Trinity. A mother knows her neighbor's son is not her own because there's no sharing in her nature. Our Lord, seeing in the sinful soul no likeness of His own, can only say those terrible words which signify nonrecognition: *I know you not!* (LK 13:25). It is a terrible thing not to be known by God.

From the human perspective, there is recognition of unfitness or fitness. Just suppose a very distinguished visitor is announced one day at your door. You are in working clothes and your hands and face are dirty. You are in no condition to present yourself before such an important person. You refuse to see him until you can improve your appearance.

A soul stained with sin acts much the same when it goes before the judgment seat of God. It sees His majesty, purity, and brilliance. But the soul knows its own sinfulness and unworthiness. It does not entreat, argue, or plead a case. The soul sees from out of the depth and says, "O Lord, I am not worthy." A soul stained with venial sins says, "Give me time to clean up," and goes into purgatory to wash its baptismal robes. But the soul that is irremediably stained, dead to divine life, casts itself into hell just as naturally as a stone released from my hand falls to the ground. The soul full of divine love and without any temporal punishment due to its sins is like a bird released from its cage; it flies to heaven.

Three possible destinies await you at death and judgment: hell, which is pain without love; purgatory, pain with love; and heaven, love without pain.

45

PURGATORY

Once I visited a man in a hospital who had led a miserable life through alcoholism, infidelity, and other gross sins. He had made his wife very unhappy, his children ashamed of his conduct, and the whole family impoverished. On his deathbed we reconciled him to God.

He said to me, "I will not be here much longer. I have no doubt God has forgiven my sins, but I am ready for the strafing I know I shall get and deserve."

Notice the distinction he made between peace and pain. He was at peace because his sins were forgiven; yet he knew he had not fully atoned for all of his sins. He distinguished between forgiveness and making up for the sins, just as the thief did on the right-hand side of our Lord. Our Lord assured him of paradise; and yet, he continued to suffer. While he was hanging there the thief said, *We suffer the due reward of our deeds* (LK 23:41). It is one thing to be forgiven, it is quite another thing to expiate for that sin. If you ever visited a great diamond mine such as Kimberley and saw the diamonds there in the raw, you would be disappointed, because they look so dull and are full of flaws. Each and every one of them would have to be cut and then polished.

Purgatory is a means of reaching excellence by achieving a perfection that otherwise would never be known. It is something like a darkroom for a photographic film, where the film is taken and treated with burning acids so its hidden color and beauty may be revealed. Purgatory is like that. The judgment of God is final, but there is a merciful chance to be cleansed of sin by those who die in a state of grace, but have not yet atoned for all the punishment due to sins. For example, we're forgiven for having stolen, but we haven't returned the stolen goods.

Most of us are not ready to go before the judgment seat of God. Look at how many undone duties there are in our lives, loose ends, and muddling through of responsibilities. There are wrong turns retraced and then taken again lightly, opportunities missed; intentions were good and not wholly carried into action. Most of our good intentions actually were only on the thin upper surface of our souls. They did not always sink down into the depths of our being. Therefore, God will not sentence such souls to eternal loss. A provision was made for making up for our failings if we die in the state of grace after death. We read in the book of the Maccabees that it is a pious and holy thought to pray for the dead that they may be released from their sins (2 M 12:45). Our blessed Lord spoke of forgiveness in the world to come. Remember the parable of the debtors' prison from which there was no release until the debt was paid (MT 18:23-25)? That implied a release from debts in another life. St. Paul says man has imposed poor materials on the foundations which were laid by Christ, and these materials must all be tried by fire (1 CO 3:13).

Purgatory is the place where the love of God tempers the justice of God and where the love of man tempers the injustice of man. The necessity of purgatory is grounded upon the absolute purity of God. In the Apocalypse we read of the great beauty of His pure gold city with its walls of jasper and spotless light, which is not of the sun or moon, but the light of the Lamb slain from the beginning of the world. We also learn of the condition for entering into the gates of heavenly Jerusalem. The Holy Book reads, *There shall not enter into it anything defiled or that worketh abomination or that maketh a lie, but they that are written in the Book of the life of the Lamb* (RV 21:27). Justice demands that nothing unclean, only the pure of heart, shall stand before the face of the pure God.

Suppose there were no purgatory. The justice of God would be too terrible for words! Who of us would dare assert at the moment of death we were pure enough to stand before the immaculate Lamb of God? Do you think you could say it? I know I cannot. There are some, like the martyrs, who sprinkled the sands of the Colosseum with their blood in testimony of their faith; the missionaries, like Paul, who give of themselves for the spread of the Gospel; and cloistered saints, who in the quiet calm of a voluntary Calvary become martyrs without recognition. Souls like that are glorious exceptions. How many millions die with their souls stained with venial sins, who have known evil and by their strong resolve have drawn with them the weakness of their past as a leaden weight? The day we were baptized the Church laid upon us a white garment, saying: "Receive this white garment, which mayest thou carry without stain before the judgment seat of our Lord Jesus Christ, that thou mayest have life everlasting."

Have you kept your garment unspoiled by sin? Have any of us? Have we kept the garment so clean we could say we deserve to enter the white-robed Army of the King of Kings?

How many souls departing this life have the courage to say they left without any undue attachment to creatures, or were never guilty of a wasted talent, a slight stupidity, an uncharitable deed, a neglect of holy inspiration, or even an idle word, for which every one of us must render an account? How many souls are gathered at the deathbed like late seasonal flowers, absolved from sins, but not from the debt of sin? Take any of our national heroes whose names we venerate and whose deeds we emulate. Would any Englishman or American who knew something of the purity of God, as much as he loves and respects a Nelson or a Washington, believe either of them at death was free enough from slight faults to enter immediately into the presence of God? The very nationalism of Nelson and Washington, which made them both heroes in war, might make them suspect of being unsuited after death for the true internationalism of heaven, where there is neither English nor American, Jew nor Greek, barbarian nor free, but where all are one in Christ Jesus, our Lord.

All souls who die with some love of God possessing them are beautiful souls. But if there's no purgatory because of slight imperfections, they must be rejected without pity by divine justice. Take away purgatory and God could not pardon easily, for will an Act of Contrition at the end atone for thirty years of sinning? The infinite justice of God would surely reject those from heaven who resolved to pay their debts, but have not paid. I say purgatory is where the love of God tempers the justice of God. God pardons because He gives time to retouch these souls with His Cross, to recut them with the chisel of purification; thus, they might fit into the great spiritual edifice of the heavenly Jerusalem, where He plunges them into purifying places so they can wash their stained baptismal robes to enter into the spotless purity of heaven. In this place He can resurrect them like the phoenix of old, from the ashes of their own suffering, like wounded eagles healed by the magic touch of God's cleansing flames. They might mount heavenward to the city of the pure, where Christ is King and Mary is Queen. Regardless of how trivial the fault, God does not pardon without tears, and there are no tears in heaven. Purgatory is a place where the love of God tempers the justice of God and the love of man may temper the injustice of man. I believe most men and women are quite unconscious of the injustice, ingratitude, and thanklessness of their lives until they see the cold hand of death laid upon someone that they love. It is then, and only then, they realize with regret the haunting poverty of their love. Among the reasons the bitterest of tears are shed over graves are words left unsaid and deeds left undone.

"The child never knew how much I loved her."

"He never knew how much he meant to me."

"I never knew how dear he was until he was gone."

Such words are the poisoned arrows which cruel death shoots at our hearts from the door of every sepulcher. Then we realize how differently we would act if only the departed one could return.

Tears are shed in vain before eyes which cannot see. Caresses are offered without response to arms that cannot embrace, and sighs stir not a heart whose ear is deaf. Then the anguish for not offering flowers before death had come, and for not sprinkling incense while the beloved was still alive, and for not speaking kind words now must die in the very air they cleave. Oh, the sorrow at the thought that we cannot atone for the stinted affection we gave them, for the light answers we returned to their pleading, and for the lack of reverence we showed to one who was perhaps the dearest thing God ever gave us.

Purgatory is the place where the love of God tempers the justice of God and the love of man tempers the injustice of man. It enables hearts left behind to break the barriers of time and death to convert unspoken words into prayers, unburned incense into sacrifice, unoffered flowers into alms, and undone acts of kindness into help for eternal life. Take away purgatory and the grief for our unkindness would be bitter and our sorrow for our forgetfulness would be piercing. Without purgatory our bowed heads and moments of silence would be empty. With purgatory the bowed head gives way to a bent knee, the moment of silence turns to a moment of prayer, and a fading wreath to the abiding offering of sacrifice in the Mass of that great Hero, Christ.

Purgatory enables us to atone for our ingratitude, because our prayers, mortifications, and sacrifices make it possible to bring joy and consolation to the ones we love. Love is stronger than death; hence, there should be love for those who have gone before us. Shall death cut off gratitude? Certainly not! The Church assures us that not being able to give more to them in this world, we can still seek them in the hands of divine justice and give them the assurance of our love and the purchasing price of our redemption. Just as the man who dies in debt has the maledictions of his creditors following him to the grave, he may have his good name restored by the labor of his son who pays the last penny. The soul of a friend who has gone to death owing a debt of penance to God may have it remitted by us, who are left behind, by knitting the coin of daily actions into the spiritual coin which purchases redemption by praying for these poor souls in purgatory.

Do they suffer? Yes. They can no longer gain merit and are like automobiles that have run out of gasoline, so they must passively undergo some kind of purification. In purgatory we love and are happy because suffering brings us closer to divine love. The fires of purgatory burn away dross; therefore, when a soul is completely purified, there's nothing left to be consumed, and it goes before the throne of God. There is no sense of pain when perfect love is eventually reached.

The suffering of the souls in purgatory is rather difficult for us to imagine; it is a kind of duel. On the one hand it is a suffering because we are separated from God, and on the other hand, it is a suffering because we are so anxious to be with him. Perhaps no one has ever put this better than Cardinal John Henry Newman in "The Dream of Gerontius." He wrote:

> When then—if such thy lot—thou seest thy Judge,
> The sight of Him will kindle in thy heart
> All tender, gracious, reverential thoughts.
> Thou wilt be sick with love, and yearn for Him,
> And feel as though thou couldst but pity Him,
> That one so sweet should e'er have placed Himself
> At disadvantage such, as to be used
> So vilely by a being so vile as thee.
> There is a pleading in His pensive eyes
> Will pierce thee to the quick, and trouble thee.
> And thou wilt hate and loathe thyself; for, though
> Now sinless, thou wilt feel that thou hast sinn'd
> As never thou didst feel; and wilt desire
> To slink away, and hide thee from His sight:

And yet wilt have a longing aye to dwell
Within the beauty of His countenance.
And these two pains, so counter and so keen,—
The longing for Him, when thou seest Him not;
The shame of self at thought of seeing Him,—
Will be thy veriest, sharpest purgatory. (vv. 728–47)

46

HEAVEN IS NOT SO FAR AWAY

There is a line in a popular song that goes "I'm in heaven when I'm near you." To understand heaven, though it is in eternity, we must begin by talking about time. Heaven is outside of time, but we have to use time to get there. It almost seems like a paradox. None of us would really want a kind of endless existence on this earth. If it were possible for us to live four hundred years with some new kinds of vitamins, do you think that we would all swallow them? There would certainly come one moment in our existence when we would want to die. Have you ever been in any one place on this earth you are absolutely sure would be one in which you'd want to spend every day of your life? It is not very likely. The mere extension of time to most of us would probably be a curse instead of a blessing.

Have you ever noticed that your happiest moments have come when eternity almost seemed to get inside of your soul? All great inspirations are rather timeless, and that gives us some suggestion of heaven. Mozart was once asked when he received the inspirations for his great music. He said that he saw them all at once. There was a great heat, warmth, and light, then the succession of notes. When I prepare a talk, telecast, or begin writing a book, a moment comes when the end is seen at the beginning. One cannot write fast enough. Eternity is in the mind, and time is at the end of the pen. Words do not come out fast enough. Jean-Baptiste Henri Lacordaire, the great French preacher, was once asked if he had completed his famous sermons to be given in the Cathedral of Notre Dame. He answered, "Yes, I have finished them. All that I have to do now is to write them."

Everybody experiences some dim intimations of immortality, such as Wordsworth wrote about, in what will happen after death. There are so many men who try to immunize themselves from those thoughts of eternity. They put on a kind of a God-proof raincoat so the drops of His grace will not get through to them. They shut out eternity. I wonder if anybody ever described this better than T. S. Eliot in "The Men Who Turned from God" (CHORUSES FROM "THE ROCK," 3). It is a poem about those who busy themselves with everything in time and never give a moment to the stranger who has been knocking at the gates of their souls almost every day, the stranger who made them uneasy in their sleep, for at night there are dreams of immortality.

This stranger is the one who brings eternity into your soul. Though we live in time, it is the one thing that makes happiness impossible. Simply because you live in time, you cannot combine your pleasures, joys, and happiness. You cannot make a club sandwich of pleasures. By the mere fact that you are in time, you cannot march with Napoleon and march with Caesar. You cannot sit down to tea with Horace, Dante, and Alexander Pope. Because you are in time, you cannot enjoy winter sports and the seashore simultaneously.

Time demands you take all of your pleasures successively. Time not only gives them to you, time also takes them away.

Unless you examine your own psychological intuitions and experiences, you will discover your happiest moments are those when you are not conscious of time at all. When you are in school, or perhaps in your office, you look at the clock. You are not enjoying school or your work. Maybe you are attending a concert or enjoying a conversation with friends, possibly you may be reading, and you say, "Time really passed!" The less conscious you are of the passing of time, the more you enjoy yourself. There is a hint of what heaven must be. It must be outside of time, where you can possess all joys at one and the same full moment.

You have to use time in order to get to heaven. Often we think of heaven as being "way out there," and we draw all kinds of unreal pictures about it. Because we think of heaven, and even hell, as something that happens to us at the end of time, we keep on postponing it. As a matter of fact, heaven is not way out there. Heaven is in here. Hell is not way down there. Hell could be inside of a soul. There is no such thing as dying and then going to heaven or dying and going to hell; you're in heaven already, you're in hell already. I've met people who were in hell, and I'm sure you have. I remember attending a man in a hospital, and I asked him to make his peace with God.

He said, "I suppose you're going to tell me I'm going to hell."

"No," I said, "I'm not."

"Well," he said, "I want to go to hell!"

I said, "I have never met a man who wanted to go to hell, so I think I will just sit here and watch you go."

I did not intend to let time pass without doing something, but I was absolutely sure that if he had a few minutes to himself he would change his point of view; so, I sat alone with him for twenty minutes. I could see him going through a kind of a soul struggle.

He said to me, "Do you really believe there's a hell?"

I said, "Do you feel unhappy on the inside? Are you fearful? Is there dread and anxiety? Are all the evil things of your life coming up before you as specters and as ghosts?"

It was not long until he made his peace with God.

I have seen people with heaven in them. If you ever want to see heaven in a child, look at that child the day of First Communion. If you want to see how much love is related to heaven, just look at a bride and groom at the altar on the day of the Nuptial Mass. Heaven is there because love is there. I've seen heaven in a missionary nun who was giving herself among the lepers. Sometimes you see a virtuous young person and you see heaven there. The beauty of such a person is not put on the outside; it is a kind of imprisoned loveliness from within, as if it were breaking down the bars of flesh in order to find some outward utterance.

Heaven is here just as hell can be in the souls of some. Heaven is very close to us, since heaven is related to a good life like an acorn is related to an oak. An acorn is bound to become an oak. He who does not have heaven in his heart now will never go to heaven, and he who has hell in his heart when he dies will go to hell. Heaven is related to a good and virtuous life in the same way knowledge is related to study; one necessarily follows the other.

Hell is related to an evil life in the same way corruption is related to death; one necessarily follows the other. Heaven is not just a long way off; it begins here, but it doesn't end here. We just get faint glimpses of it now and then. If we postpone the thought of heaven until the moment we die, we will be very much like the Israelites during their wanderings in the desert. The poor Jews were at one time within about eleven days of the Promised Land. It took only three weeks for them to make the journey from Egypt to the Promised Land, but because of their disobedience, failures, backsliding, and rebellions against Moses, it took them about forty years to get into the Promised Land, which represents a pilgrimage in many of our lives. We make progress and then we slip back. Thank heavens we have a merciful Lord, who forgives us seventy times seven!

Time is necessary in order to gain heaven, but the lapse of time itself does not bring us to heaven. What brings us to heaven is how we live, how we die. We are not to think that just one particular act is the sole determinant. We are determined by the habits of our lives. For example, a great pianist may sit down at a piano and strike a wrong note, but you will say, "Well, he usually is a very good piano player." If I sat down to a piano to play, I might hit a right note, but you would say, "He can't play!" I remember once hearing a comedian sit down at a piano and talk to a famous artist. He said, striking one note, "If you know so much about music, tell me what I'm playing!" I would not have the habits, virtue, and goodness of artistry in my soul.

Next we come to what our Lord said about heaven at one moment in His life, the night of the Last Supper. Our blessed Lord gathered all of His Apostles—poor, weak, frail men—and washed their feet. He was facing death, the agony in the garden, that terrible betraying kiss of Judas, and even the denial of Peter himself. One would think all of His

thoughts would be on Himself; certainly when we have trials we think about ourselves. No, He thought about them.
He saw the sadness in their faces and said, *Be not troubled,
do not be sad. I go to prepare a place for you. In My Father's house
there are many mansions* (JN 14:1–2). How did He know about
the Father's house? He came from there; that was His home.
He was the kind of prodigal Son who left the riches and happiness of the Father's house to come to this earth and waste
the sustenance of His life on our salvation.

Preparing to go back home, He told them about the
Father's house, and He said, *I go to prepare a place for you*
(JN 14:3). God never does anything for us without preparation. He made a garden for Adam, as only God knows how
to make a garden beautiful. When the Jews came into the
Promised Land, He prepared the land for them. He said He
would give them houses full of good things, houses which
they never built; He said He would give them vineyards and
oil which they never planted (JOS 24:13). He goes to prepare a
place for us because we were actually not made for heaven;
we were made for earth. Man spoiled the earth by sin, so
God came down from heaven to help us remake this earth.
After having redeemed us, He said He would now give us
heaven, so we got all this earth and heaven, too! Do not say
we work to go to heaven because we are mercenary. Does a
man love a woman and ask for her hand because he is mercenary? I love poetry; there's no money in it. I love tennis; I
play tennis twice a week. Do I participate because I am mercenary? I do it simply because I love these pastimes.

Something we must remember about heaven is that it
is social; it's a fellowship. In some places heaven is called
a country to indicate its vastness and a city to suggest the
number of its inhabitants. Heaven is called a kingdom to

suggest order and harmony, a paradise full of delights, and the Father's house to indicate eternity and the permanence of love and peace. To be perfectly happy after the end of the world, we will have to have our bodies with us. Our bodies have done a great deal for the salvation of our souls. There we will meet, in the communion of saints, all of those who were our friends and mates on earth. It's hard to lose friends; after a time two hearts grow together. Death is not just the separation of two hearts; it's the tearing asunder of one heart.

Cicero wrote a book in his later days entitled *An Essay on Old Age*. It was a poignant story of the loss of his daughter, Tullia. He said that after his death, on his way to the Elysian fields, if he met someone who asked him, "Do you want to go back to earth?" he would say, "No, I do not want to return. I want to go ahead and converse with Plato and Socrates." We have many with whom we would enjoy conversation. I would like to see Plato, Aristotle, Moses, Thomas Aquinas, and the thief on the right. I would like to see you, too, because you have spent so much of your time with me. I ask you to go back and think of some great moment in life when you really enjoyed the thrill of living. Then go back and think of a time when somebody told you a truth or you studied and understood a great mystery. Then go to another moment of your life, when you had the great spiritual ecstasy of love and wanted it to go on and on.

Suppose you could take this moment of life, raise it up to a focal point where it became the Father, take this truth, lift it to infinity until it became the moment of the ecstasy of truth, namely, the Son; and take that moment of love and internalize it so that it became the Holy Spirit. That would be a dim suggestion of heaven.

Heaven is perfect life, perfect truth, and perfect love. I'm not afraid of going to hell; I'm only afraid of losing divine love, which is Christ. The reason I want to go to heaven is because I want to be with love. There'll be many surprises there. People we never expected to see and a number of people absent whom we thought would be there. Finally, there will be one great surprise, the greatest of all—that you and I are there. I will see you in heaven!

47

THE HELL THERE IS

Few today believe in either the devil or hell. Why don't they believe in the devil when so much is devilish? The communists have unsuccessfully tried to convince us there is no God, but they have convinced us there is a devil. We cannot explain all the evil in the world today. Just as they deny the devil, they deny hell. They deny the justice of God because they deny an existence of guilt and of sin. The basic reason why so many moderns disbelieve in hell is that they disbelieve in freedom and responsibility. The existence of hell is one of the strongest arguments in the world for the reality of freedom. God allows us free choice, and He allows us to have our choice to eternity. To disbelieve in hell is to assert that the consequences of good and bad acts are indifferent. It makes a greater difference if your soul drinks virtue or vice. It is just as difficult to make a free nation without judges and prisons as it is to make a free world without judgment and hell. No state constitution could exist for six months on the basis of liberal Christianity which denies what Christ meant when He said, *Depart from Me ye cursed into everlasting fire which was prepared for the devil and his angels* (MT 25:41).

Have you ever noticed saints fear hell but never deny it, and great sinners deny hell, but they do not fear it—for the moment. The devil is never so strong as when he gets a man to deny there is a devil. The modern man who is not living according to his conscience wants a religion without a Cross, a Christ without a Calvary, a Kingdom without justice, and in his church, a soft dean who never mentions hell to polite ears. Why do we praise men for making decisions about whether they will invest in this farm or in that industry, while refusing to give them credit to decide whether they will go to heaven or hell for all eternity? Suppose there were no heavenly Judge or Ledger which recorded our deeds and sins. Suppose we had no conscience to divulge right and wrong and no memory to record our crimes and sins. Suppose there were no formal sentence of a judge. Would something be left within us pointing to a destiny according to the way we lived; I mean our passions, dreads, melancholies, and fears?

Here is a secret world which burns inside coming out in curious ways. Why is there so much mental distress if there is not already a hell within people? Seeds that are buried seek light; trees in a dense forest mount to absorb the light; shells in the sea creep to the shore; a piece of glass in a body works its way out; a murderer returns to the scene of his crime. Unholy deeds are poured out to a psychoanalyst and along with them all the woes, worries, and wounds troubling their doers on the inside. If the stomach cannot keep poison food in it, shall not the poison mind vomit the filth that is already in it? Even though they deny God and judgment, they are attesting to them by the effects of their own lives. Their burdened consciences cannot escape reaping a judgment by excesses and torturing themselves with personal hell. Those who have denied the fruit of love see the children at windowpanes, looking in, denied wombs and bosoms.

And then there are all of the distractions, worries, and fears. For those who are conscious of their own sin, as a poet said, "Even an atheist is half afraid in the dark." All those in this world who are in the state of grace have within themselves the seed of glory. Those who are in the state of mortal sin, even though they deny God, have within themselves the seed of hell. Hell begins here; so does heaven; and neither ends here. Modern literature describes how hell has moved inside as people have denied it outside. Our blessed Lord spoke fifteen times of hell. Eleven times He mentioned eternal fire. Thirty times in the New Testament eternal fire is mentioned. Our blessed Lord said, *Fear ye not them that kill the body and are not able to kill the soul, but rather fear him that can destroy body and soul into hell* (MT 10:28).

Our blessed Lord described hell as the place where *the worm dieth not and the fire is not extinguished* (MK 9:48). Usually, a worm feeds on a decaying body and then dies. On this earth fire consumes full and dies, but our Lord is speaking here of the worm that never dies and the fire that never goes out. That worm that never dies is the memory of the past which is always gnawing at the conscience of the impenitent. Our Lord implied two kinds of destruction: the internal corruption, the worm; and the external consuming force, which is the fire. It may be fires are lighted in this life by rejecting God's love. The poet William Butler Yeats wrote in "Two Songs from a Play," "Whatever flames upon the night, man's own resinous heart has fed" (2.2). Each one of us is locked in our own uniqueness. And Percy Bysshe Shelley, who knew this inner hell well, wrote in "Queen Mab," "And

conscience, that undying serpent, calls her venomous brood
to their nocturnal task" (3.61–62). The worm that dieth not.

Why shouldn't God warn us? What good would another
warning do? That was what the rich man asked. Remember
in the parable of the rich man and the poor beggar Lazarus
(LK 16:19–31)? The rich man asked someone to go back and
tell his brothers how much he was suffering in hell. Suppose God had granted the request and sent Lazarus back
to his five brothers and they recognized him. Do you think
they would change? They probably would demand proof he
had really lived, died, and visited the region of the departing
soul. The point is judgment and hell are things of faith, not
of sight. If the Risen Christ is no proof to the senses, then no
one risen from the dead can be a convincing warning to us.
If the Resurrection of Christ would not convince those who
were witness, then resurrection of a dead man who came
from hell will not. If a messenger came back from the rich
man, the brothers would probably have tried to kill him just
as the Pharisees tried to kill the Lazarus our blessed Lord
raised from the dead.

Why do souls go to hell? Simply because they refuse
to love; that's the only reason. A young man loves a young
woman; he gives her gifts, is faithful, generous, and kind;
she is disloyal, takes gifts, is traitorous. And after being deceived a thousand times, he still continues to love her. Eventually there comes a moment when he will say, "All right, I'm
through now! Love is finished." God, the Hound of Heaven,
pursues us all during life, inviting us to His Kingdom, bid-
ding us sit down at the banquet of the Eucharist, fortifying
us with His grace and His sacraments. We reject, betray, are
disloyal, refuse to love, and eventually, when death comes,
our lives are sealed and that kind of love does not return.

Love is eternal, and so is hell. What is the one thing love cannot forgive? It is hate! What is the one thing life can never forgive? It is death. Why? Because death would mean its destruction. What is the one thing truth can never forgive? Error. And the refusal to love is eternal.

The punishment is twofold; there is a double character to sin. Whenever we commit a serious sin, there is a turning away from God; there is a turning to creatures. Alcoholism is a turning away from God—repudiation of the reason He has given us, and there is the turning to creatures; namely, to alcohol. There is a double punishment corresponding to turning away from God, which is the most terrible of all pains, because that is the loss of God Himself. Then there is the pain of sense; we are punished by the very creatures we abused. The soul in this life refuses to love God and no longer responds to His love just as a magnet cannot have any influence on wood. It never thought of God; in fact, it rejected all of His mercies. When death comes, the soul cannot do without God. But God is not there. It is just as if one had been playing blindman's bluff, takes off the handkerchief and discovers he's gone blind! The godless universe persists, and the soul knows that it cannot be happy without life, truth, and love, which it has eternally rejected, and that is hell.

Take the pain of sense. An alcoholic abuses alcohol; then come the slavery, excesses, and hangover, which are punishments from the alcohol. There are different kinds of punishment in hell. The fiercer the grip pleasures have on a soul in this life, the more fiercely the fires of torment burn in eternity.

Here are three brief ways of describing hell from our

human experiences. First, hell is the hatred of things you love. A sailor lost on a raft at sea loves water. He knows he ought not to drink the water from the sea, but he does. In like manner, the soul was made to live on the love of God, but if a soul perverts that love with sin, then, as the sailor hates the very water he drinks, so the soul hates the perverted love it seeks. Just as the sailor becomes mad because he cannot do without water, so the soul in hell wants love, yet that love has been refused. The wicked do not want hell because they enjoy its torments; they want hell because they do not want God! Hell is eternal suicide for hating love.

A second fact is this: Hell is the mind eternally mad at itself for wounding love. How often during life have you said, "I hate myself for doing that!" You hated yourself most when you hurt someone you loved. The souls in hell hate themselves most for wounding perfect love. Just as you hurt someone whom you love, they can never forgive themselves. Their hell is eternal, self-imposed unforgiveness. It is not that God will not forgive them, but they will not forgive themselves.

Finally, hell is submission to love under justice. We are free in this world. We can no more be forced to love God than we can be forced to love classical music or antiques. Often souls fall out of love. Many a wife is tied to a drunkard or a worthless husband until death do them part. They do not freely love one another, and to be forced to love anyone is hell! But they are forced in virtue of the justice of their contract to love one another until death does them part. The lost souls could have loved God freely, but they chose to rebel against that love and came under divine justice. Justice forces souls in hell to love God, to submit to His divine order. But to be forced to love is the negation of love, that is hell!

Do not think that if a soul went to heaven it would be happy. Suppose you hated mathematics and you had to spend your whole life with mathematicians, and every time you picked up a newspaper or spoke to a friend, they were talking about logarithms and algebra. That would be a hell for you. Suppose you hated perfect life, truth, and love, which is God and His revelation in Christ our Lord, and you were forced to live with perfect life, truth, and love. That would be a hell for you, a greater hell than the one you had.

Do not think God is angry because He sentences us to hell. Remember this, the sun which shines on wax softens it; the sun which shines on mud hardens it. There is no difference in the sun, but only in that upon which it shines. The love of God shining on a soul that loves Him turns to heaven, and the love of God shining on a soul that hates Him turns to hell. Hell is a place where there is no love. Could anything be worse?

48

THE FEMININE PRINCIPLE IN RELIGION

Did you ever think there should be a feminine principle in religion? Suppose there was nothing about womanhood in religion. What a rightful protest we would hear. All religions have a feminine principle. I have a statue on my desk given to me by a former missionary in China. It is a statue of Kwan Yin, who, according to the Chinese legend, was a young princess who lived about five hundred years before Christ. She wanted to dedicate her virginity to God, and her father killed her. According to the legend, a tiger dragged her into hell. She began pleading mercy for all the inmates and so disrupted hell. She introduced charity, and the devil ordered her out of hell. She became Kwan Yin, the goddess of mercy to the Chinese. Probably an Oriental yearning for some great woman in religion.

Mohammed had a daughter whose name was Fatima. She died at a very early age and Mohammed mourned her deeply. He wrote, "Of all the women in heaven she is the most blessed next to Mary." Did you know the Koran of the Moslems has over forty verses concerning our blessed Mother? They believe in the Immaculate Conception and in the virgin birth. There are African peoples who have a tradition that when a son succeeds to a throne, the inauguration ceremonies consist of sitting on the lap of his mother. In other words, he derives some authority from the maternal principle.

The great Latin poet Virgil, in his Fourth Eclogue, which has been called a messianic poem, has these lines:

> Now the last age by Cumae's Sibyl sung
> Has come and gone, and the majestic roll
> Of circling centuries begins anew:
> Justice returns, returns old Saturn's reign,
> With a new breed of men sent down from heaven.
> Only do thou, at the boy's birth in whom
> The iron shall cease, the golden race arise,
> Befriend him, chaste Lucina; 'tis thine own
> Apollo reigns. And in thy consulate,
> This glorious age, O Pollio, shall begin,
> And the months enter on their mighty march.

Then Homer, the great Greek poet who lived a thousand years before Christ, wrote in history the story of a defeated man and a sorrowful woman. While her husband, Ulysses, was away on a voyage, Penelope had many suitors. She said to each of them, "Just as soon as I finish weaving this garment I will consider your plea." Every night she undid the stitches put in during the day until her husband came back. No one understood why this great poet should make history understand a defeated man and a sorrowful woman until a defeated man and a sorrowful woman came.

The real feminine principle in religion is that all love begins with a dream. I think all people have love in their minds and hearts, a composite of memories, thoughts, dreams, ideals, and experiences. Then one day someone appears. It's called love at first sight, but it is love at second sight. Every great love is a dream come true. Did you ever see a dream walking? Well, I did. Love is very much like music. We hear music for the first time and we like it because we already have that music inside of our hearts!

When God became man, or when He willed it from the very creation of the world, He dreamed about a Mother who would decide the time of His birth, circumstances, and all of the details. He thought of her long before she was born: the world's first love. Just suppose you could have made your own mother. Would you have made her the most beautiful, kind woman in all the world? God could make His own Mother in somewhat the same way artists can create. I suppose one of the most famous of all the mother paintings is James Abbott McNeill Whistler's. When someone complimented him about his portrait, he said, "Well, you know how it is; one tries to make one's mummy just as good as one can." Almighty God preexisted His own Mother and made her just as beautiful as He could. That is why she was immaculately conceived.

What does "immaculate conception" mean? It means she was conceived without the stain of original sin. One thing I cannot understand is why people today disbelieve in the Immaculate Conception, because most people today believe they are without sin; therefore, they are all immaculately conceived! The Immaculate Conception does not mean our blessed Lady did not need to be redeemed like you and me; it means that from the moment of her conception she was immune from the stain of sin. But was not this fitting? If you have a distinguished visitor announced at your home, do you sweep the front hall? Well, if God is going to enter this world, do you think that He should come into portals that were rather clean? Look at all the trouble God went through to make a paradise for humanity to celebrate the first nuptials of man and woman.

Here's a new paradise, not the paradise of creation, but the paradise of the Incarnation. Should He make this garden much more beautiful? Should it be a garden in which not a single weed of sin would grow, over whose portals the name of evil could never be written? This paradise of the Incarnation was to be gardened by the new Adam, our blessed Lady, the feminine principle in religion.

When the time came, God sent out an angel from the great white throne of light. The angel descended down over the plain of Esdraelon and came to a humble virgin kneeling in prayer and said, *Hail, full of grace* (LK 1:28), which means the Lord loves you, and asked that chosen woman if she would give to God a human nature. She said, *Be it done to me according to Thy will* (1:38). In Latin it is *fiat*: be it done. There are three great fiats in the world: *fiat lux,* let there be light of creation; *fiat voluntas tua,* suffering on the Cross; *fiat mihi secundum verbum tuum,* be it done unto me according to Thy word. The Annunciation was when Mary in the name of us all said, "I allow you to come into this world. I will be your Eden. I will give you a human nature." So God took a new nature upon Himself in this cloistered garden. And from this woman, Christ was born.

I need hardly tell you there's no such thing as adoration of Mary. We have not made Mary important; it is our Lord who made her important. Notice how He changed her role in relationship to us. Here we go to the marriage feast of Cana. This was at the beginning of the public life. At the marriage feast of Cana, our blessed Lord came from the Jordan and brought all of His disciples along with Him. That is why I think the wine gave out; there were so many gate crashers! You just can't imagine a wedding ceremony in a wine country without providing enough wine. But the wine gave out. Who's the first one to notice it? The blessed Mother. She knows our needs very often before we do. She said simply, *They have no wine* (JN 2:3). He gave a strange answer; He said, *Woman, what is that to Me?* or in the original Greek, "What is Mine is thine"—*My hour has not yet come* (2:4).

Let us analyze this: *My hour has not yet come.* Whenever our blessed Lord used the word "hour," it was always in relationship to His Passion and His death. When they attempted to stone Him on two or three occasions, the Gospel said, His hour was not yet come (JN 8:20). When Judas came down in the garden to betray Him, our Lord said, *This is your hour* (LK 22:53); your hour, the hour of evil. The night of the Last Supper, *Father, the hour has come* (JN 17:1).

Our Lord is saying to His mother, "The hour of My Passion and death has not yet come."

"What do you want Me to do?"

"Do you want Me to work My first miracle?"

"Do you want Me to prove I am the expected Messiah, the Son of the living God?"

"Do you realize if I work this miracle and announce Myself as the Christ and the Son of God, I will be sent to the Cross?"

"Do you want to be a mother who sent her son to the battlefield?"

"My dear Mother, if you want Me to begin My public life now and usher in My death, Passion, and redemption of men, then your relation to Me will change."

"Up to this point, you have been known as the Mother of Jesus, but the moment I begin My redemptive work, you will not just be My Mother, you will be the Mother of everyone whom I redeem."

"Then you will be the Mother of all humanity, the universal Mother of the world."

Three years pass, we come to the Cross. One day in the middle of those three years, the blessed Mother was waiting in a crowd, worrying about His long night prayers and all day preaching.

Someone said, *Your Mother waits.* Our blessed Lord said, *Who is My Mother?* Then He said, *The relationship is not of blood. In the new order the relationship is of the spirit. He that doth the will of My Father in heaven is My Mother, My Father, My brother, My sister* (MT 12:46–50).

Our Lord looks down from the Cross upon the two most precious creatures He has on this earth: John and His Mother. He speaks to His Mother, but He does not call her Mother. This is redemption, the hour has come. He says, *Woman, woman,* and inasmuch as a crowned head could gesture, indicating John, He adds, *This is your son* (JN 19:26–27). He did not call John "John," because if He called him John, he would have been just the son of Zebedee, but being left unnamed, in his anonymity, John stood for all humanity. Our blessed Mother is made the mother of all humanity and not in virtue of a metaphor, but in virtue of the veritable pangs of childbirth. Was she to have other children? Yes, but not according to the flesh. John was the first of that long line in which we are added, millions and millions of sons and daughters. He said to John, *This is your Mother* (19:27). That's why we love our Lady. Our blessed Lord made her our Mother, the feminine principle in religion.

There is no such thing as doing her honor in a way to make us forget our Lord. Suppose I visited your home and refused to talk to your mother. What would you think? You would not entertain me very long. Do you think our blessed Lord is going to think kindly of us if we pay no attention to her? Sometimes we ask her to intercede for us. When we want a favor, we go to the Mother of the one from whom we want the favor. She has some special powers of intercession. We say the Rosary. Yes, a repetition of Our Father and Hail Mary, which means when we love anyone we keep saying over and over again "I love you." Why do we repeat the words "I love you"? It is in a new moment of time, a new location in space, so, in the Rosary we keep saying the Our Father and Hail Mary as a way of telling her, "I love you, I love you, I love you!" Her intercession is tremendous.

One day it seems our blessed Lord was walking through the courts of heaven and saw some souls who apparently got into heaven very easily.

He went to Peter and said, "Peter, I have given you the keys to the Kingdom of heaven. How did these souls gain entry into My Kingdom?"

Peter said, "Don't blame me, Lord, every time I close a door your Mother opens a window!"

Perhaps some of us will get in through an open window. George Bernard Shaw said shortly before he died, "I think maybe His Mother will let me in."

49

PRAYER IS A DIALOGUE

Many look on prayer in the same fashion as an aviator may look at a parachute. He hopes he will never have to use it, but it may come in handy in case he has to bail out. Prayer, as our blessed Lord described and taught, was something quite different. Let us see how prayer was used in His own life.

There are four great headings under which our blessed Lord spoke of prayer. His prayers were at the great events of His life: He prayed at His baptism (LK 3:21); before He chose the twelve Apostles (LK 6:12–13); before Peter made the confession of His divinity (LK 9:18–20); at the Transfiguration (LK 9:28–36); in Gethsemane (LK 22:41–44); and He prayed on the Cross (LK 23:34). In addition to these great events of His life, He prayed in the course of His ministry: before the great conflict with the Temple authorities; before giving the Apostles the Lord's Prayer (LK 11:1); when the Greeks came to Him; and after feeding the five thousand (MT 14:23). He also prayed at His miracles: when He healed the multitudes (LK 5:15–16); when He fed the five thousand (MT 14:19); when He healed the deaf man (MK 7:34); and when He raised Lazarus from the dead (JN 11:41–42). And then there were prayers that He said for others: He prayed for the eleven (JN 17:9); He prayed for the whole Church (JN 17:20); He prayed for those who nailed Him to the Cross (LK 23:34); and in a very special way, He prayed for Peter (LK 22:32).

What is prayer? The best definition of prayer is that it is a lifting of the mind and the heart to God. Prayer is a dialogue. Man breaks silence in two ways: a dialogue with his fellow man, and a dialogue with God. My dialogue with others is proof we are both persons. The same is implied in a dialogue with God. These dialogues are fulfilled in the two Commandments: love God, and love neighbor. Turn over the pages of sacred Scripture, what do you find? You find a record of people to whom God has spoken, and you'll also find a record of people who listened to Him. Scripture is fulfilled in concrete, living dialogues.

We do not always want that dialogue with God. Sometimes we seek it, other times we flee from it. Adam was afraid when God called him in the garden. Cain was afraid when God spoke to him. Moses was afraid before the burning bush. When you and I have a dialogue with God, what does it consist of? One thing that makes it up is a consciousness of our own sin, and the other is the voice of God urging us to confess it, to seek His mercy. One voice crushes, the other delivers life. One of the most beautiful examples of dialogue in Scripture is that between St. Paul and our Lord, the Risen Christ, on the road to Damascus (AC 9:3-6). Everything St. Paul wrote after that was nothing but a dialogue in which he was thereon engaged, and God's answer always was *My grace is sufficient for thee* (2 CO 12:9).

Prayer is a lifting of the heart and mind to God; notice we said nothing about the emotions. Prayer does not have very much to do with sensations, emotions, or feelings. It's not a feeling in the stomach just as it is not a pain in the stomach;

it is not a capricious feeling, something that makes us purr on the inside. It has nothing to do with the animal part of us. It is not in the glands. Prayer is in the intellect, in the will, and in the heart, as embracing a love of truth with a resolve and determination to grow in love through an act of the will.

We do not pray because we feel like it. Sometimes our prayers are better when we do not feel like praying. St. Francis de Sales said, "An ounce of desolation is of greater worth than a pound of consolation." Often in prayer we do not have a deep sense of God's presence. We are very much like children carried in a mother's arms. If we are carried in our Lord's arms, we rarely see His face, but we know He is there. Prayer is an interaction between the created spirit and the uncreated Spirit, which is God. It is a communion, a conversation, an adoration, a penance, a happiness, a work, a rest, an asking, a submission.

Prayer has many forms, some belonging to beginners and others to great saints. Vocal prayer is said with our lips; then there is meditation, which is a kind of a reverie; and the higher contemplation of saints, which is in effect a union with God. In vocal prayer we go to God on foot; in meditation we go to God on horseback, and in contemplation we go to God in a jet.

It may be asked, "Why should we pray?" Why breathe? We have to take in fresh air and get rid of bad air; we have to take in new power and get rid of our old weaknesses. We pray because we are orchestras and always need to tune up. Just as a battery sometimes runs down and needs to be charged, so we have to be renewed in spiritual vigor. Our blessed Lord said, *Without Me you can do nothing* (JN 15:5). We can eat, drink, and sin, but we cannot do anything for our supernatural

merit and heaven without Him. We happen to live in a con-
ditional universe; when we fulfill certain conditions, certain
effects are produced.

There are millions of favors hanging from heaven on
silken cords, and prayer is the sword that cuts them. Our
real strength comes from without, not within. Light is not
in the eye; it is in the sun. Sound is not in the ear; it is in
something outside of us. The sun uses the eye, music uses
the ear, and God uses us in prayer. When we pray we get into
a new environment of love. It is something like the difference between a child in a nice family and a waif who has no
guarantee of security, food, clothing, and shelter. This child
is not in an environment of love such as the child in a family.
When we pray, we put ourselves under God's love; hence, we
receive blessings which otherwise would not be ours. This
is something to keep in mind in family life. Those who are
raising children and never put themselves in God's care by
providentially trusting Him are not receiving the blessings
of those who know God provides when He gives a child.

The following are suggestions about prayer. In prayer, do
not do all the talking. If you went into a doctor's office, you
would not rattle off the symptoms and then rush out. How
did you learn to speak the English language? You learned
to speak by listening. How does a scientist learn the laws
of nature, by imposing laws upon nature? No, he sits down
before nature and says, "Now you reveal your secrets to me."
We are not to be constantly yapping in prayer. Sacred Scripture says, *Speak Lord, thy servant heareth* (1 s 3:9). We often say,
"Listen, Lord, thy servant speaketh!" Prayer is not a one-way
street; it is a boulevard. In prayer we must speak and listen.
God talks to us more in meditation than in vocal prayer.

Petition is a very valid form of prayer, but do not make all your prayers ones of petition. Don't let your attitude before God be "Give me! Give me this! Give me that!" What would a young man think of a girl who constantly said, "Give me this mink coat. Give me this ring. Send me these flowers!" Isn't it true that when you love, you are embarrassed when anyone asks, "What do you want?" In a certain sense, the more you love the less you want. This does not mean to say we may not pray for certain favors from God. Petition is an essential part of prayer, but it is not the perfect prayer. Think of other forms besides asking.

When you pray, do not think God is reluctant about giving you favors. You must not think God acts toward you like some people act toward a beggar. They see a beggar on the other side of the street and will sometimes turn a corner to get rid of him. God is a loving Father. As soon as we begin praying, He does not turn a deaf ear to us. Our relationship with God is like the relationship of a child to a father. Our blessed Lord told us to pray the Our Father, which contains seven petitions (MT 6:9–13).

There are liturgical prayers and indulgence prayers. They should always be favored. In your private devotions you should try to remember your prayers ought to be out of your own heart. Do not let all of your prayers be like circular letters. When you get a circular letter, do you sometimes put it in a wastebasket? Pray out of your own heart. Your heart has problems like no one else in the world. It has certain worries, hopes, agonies, fears, and weaknesses that constitute the content of your prayer. Your prayer will come out of them; you will be a person who is praying. Our blessed Lord said He called His sheep by name; in other words, we are individual before Him. Our blessed Lord turned to the thief and addressed him in the second-person singular, "thou": *This day thou shalt be with Me in paradise* (LK 23:43). Let your prayer be personal, and even when you say certain indulgences and liturgical prayers, be attentive to God. If you are not attentive to Him as a person, how can you expect Him to hearken to you? Pray out of your own heart.

Every now and then cut out the deadwood of prayer. Over a long period of time you will fall into certain habits and routines, becoming so used to them that they lack fervor. Do not be afraid to say, "All right, I'm going to get out of this jungle. I'm going to start all over again!" God will not be angry with you. Such an attitude may freshen your prayers and make you much more personal.

Always let the motive of your prayer be love. St. Augustine once said, "Give me a man who has loved and I will tell him what God is." Whatever lovers say to one another, you say to God. Do not think of your relationship to Him as being one of a servant to a Master, but as a lover to the Beloved.

Keep all of your prayers fresh by praying out of your heart with the inspiration of love. Then they will be something like these words of the fourth-century poet Ausonius, who wrote, "Wife, let us live as we have lived nor ever lose the little names that were the first night's grace." Marriage takes a great deal of effort. Sacrifices have to be sprinkled through a marriage to keep up the freshness of love. Every now and then when love becomes routine, we freshen it by a sacrifice. No one ever rises to a higher level of love without a death to a lower one.

Do not let all of your prayers be like blueprints which you bring to God and then ask Him to rubber-stamp. Remember God has intelligence and a plan for your own life which is far better than the one you have. A little baby cries for taffy, but the mother will not give the baby taffy. A six-year-old boy wants a shotgun, but the father will say "No." There are some things that are not good for us, so God's answer to prayer is sometimes "No." A little girl once prayed for a thousand dolls for Christmas, and her unbelieving father said, "God didn't answer your prayers, did He?" The little girl said, "Yes. God said, 'No.'" When you pray in petitionary prayer, say something like this:

> Dear Lord, there is something I want, I need badly. I hope I want it for Thy glory and it's best for my salvation. You know what I wish. Maybe it is not good for me or you would have given it to me long before this. Just in case You are waiting for me to ask again, well, I am. You know best what to do. Thanks.

In conclusion, may we suggest two special forms of prayer: the Rosary and silent meditation. The Rosary is almost like words with music. It combines the physical by moving the beads through our fingers; the mental in meditation on the Joyful, Sorrowful, and Glorious Mysteries of our Lord and His blessed Mother; and something vocal, saying our prayers with our lips.

Once a young lady said to me, "I think a Rosary is monotonous and I don't think God likes us to say monotonous prayers."

I inquired who the man was with her.

She said, "He is my fiancé."

I asked, "Do you love him?"

She responded, "Yes."

"How does he know?"

She said, "I told him 'I love you.'"

"When did you tell him?"

"Last night."

"Did you ever tell him before?"

She said, "Yes, I told him the night before."

"Don't you think he tires of it? Isn't it a bit monotonous?"

Saying we love is never monotonous, because we repeat it in a new moment of time and in a new place; thus it is with our Rosary.

Finally, silence. Take at least a half an hour a day to live above yourself and live within yourself. Have an inward solitude, fulfill the words of John the Baptist, *He must increase, I must decrease* (JN 3:30). In the language of St. Paul, you will say your life is *hidden with Christ in God* (COL 3:3). Through prayer and contemplation you can say what St. Bernard said to Pope Eugenius, *Tuus esto ubique:* always belong to yourself and then you will belong to God.

50

WORLD, SOUL, AND THINGS

We have come to the end of our Catholic encyclopedia. I'm sure you have noticed how many imperfections there were in the course of these topics. I'm not satisfied with this work, but I wish you would regard it just as a kind of a piece of carbon. Perhaps, if the light and fire of your own charity shine through the carbon, then it might turn into a diamond. In conclusion, everything poor is mine; everything good is the Lord's.

If you have followed the meaning, I perhaps have led you step by step like our blessed Lord led the woman at the well. You will remember that when He met her at noon, there were a number of steps that she took in coming to know Him. Initially, she was rather discourteous and she said to Him, *How is it that Thou, a Jew, speak to me, a Samaritan?* (JN 4:9). The Jews and the Samaritans did not speak. That was all our Lord was to her at first, just a member of another nationality with whom the Samaritans had no relations. Then as she talked a little longer to Him, she perceived He was a gentleman, for she called Him "Sir"(4:11). A few more minutes and He began to put His finger onto her soul and to stir it into a kind of uneasiness, and particularly, to tell her that she had five husbands and the man with whom she was living was not her husband. Then she said that He was a prophet (4:19). This was a step further in getting to know Him. Then she went a little bit further and said, *I know that the Messiah is coming* (4:25). Think of how surprising it must have been to her when He said, *It is I, the Christ, the Messiah, who speak to you* (4:26). She was so excited that she left her water pot at the well and ran back into the village. A short time later she returned with a number of village people, and then comes the last name, He is called the Savior of the World.

I may have led you to some understanding of our blessed Lord. First, He was a Jew; then the great Gentleman; and then the Prophet; then Christ, the Messiah; and finally, Savior of the World. That is really what He is, the Savior of the World. We never know Him until we know that truth. He's Savior because He died on the Cross for us. May I bid you to look at the world and then at your own soul. It is our world, and we are responsible for it, and on the last day we are going to be judged in the context of that world. Our blessed Lord said, *I was hungry and you gave Me to eat, I was thirsty and you gave Me to drink, I was naked and you clothed Me* (MT 25:35–36). We who are saved will ask, "When did we see You hungry and give You to eat, thirsty and give You to drink, and naked did we clothe Thee?" He will say, *When you did it to the least of these My brethren, you did it unto Me* (25:40).

In other words, there is the *Christus incognitus,* the unknown Christ in the world, in the poor, and in the slums. We cannot know Christ apart from them. I know there are many who are predicting disaster for the world, particularly in this atomic age of ours. Even in the close of the last century there were some who were dimly envisioning this disaster. One day two great French scientists, Claude Bernard and Emil Boutroux, paid a visit to a French publisher whose name was Jean Quer. They said to Quer, "We have just begun to list the alphabet of destruction, and in the next century we will have completed the alphabet." Quer said, "And when that day comes, I think that God will come down from heaven like a night watchman rattling his keys, and He will say, 'Gentlemen, it's closing time,' and we will have to start all over again!"

This is the pessimistic view of the world. There are those who think of communism and its dangers, which are very real, but we are never to be without hope. Remember the great Russian writer of the nineteenth century who was a kind of a prophet? He saw communism coming in Russia long before it was thought of or existed. But he also saw communism ending in Russia. He foresaw a day when the devils would come into Russia and possess it, body and soul. He called for the Gospel and picked up that particular passage where our blessed Lord drove the devil out of a young man into the swine, and they were drowned in the sea (MT 8:28–32). Dostoyevsky said, "That's my Russia, my beloved Russia. It will one day be filled with devils, but the devils will be driven out and pushed back into the sea. There they will be drowned, and Russia will sit at the feet of Christ and learn His Gospel."

Yes, there's hope even in the midst of all our trials, disasters, and darkness, for we are never without God. If we return to Him, all can be changed. Do you remember the English poet Swinburne, who wrote, "Glory to man in the highest, for man is the master of things" ("HYMN OF MAN," 200)? The English essayist Alfred Noyes, before his conversion, visited Swinburne at his paternal home in Bonchurch, England. Swinburne took him into the library, where he wrote his atheistic poetry. They began talking about Christianity, and Noyes said he literally spat out his words.

Years passed. Swinburne went to meet the God whom he denied and Who was his Judge. Later on Noyes was received into the Church. Noyes went back again to Bonchurch, walked up the same long line of lilac trees, and before him saw children clothed in white. They dropped flowers as they walked. He followed them into the home, which was now the Convent of the Sacred Heart. On the day of the Feast of Corpus Christi, the Feast of the Body of Christ, Noyes went into the chapel, which was the old library. At the moment of Benediction, when Noyes raised his eyes to look at our Lord and the blessed Sacrament, his eyes also fell upon the great window which he had seen on his first visit. Immediately above the monstrance on that window were the initials of the paternal Swinburne, "I.H.S." which is the Greek abbreviation for the name of Jesus. All things can be changed by the power of God so sweetly and so gently.

As regards your soul, may I discuss some intimacies of love? There are three degrees of intimacy. The first one is speech. We would never know anyone loved us unless we were told. A word is the summation of a character, all a person is and will become. We need only hear a person speak and can tell if he's a kind, cruel, or educated man. The first intimacy of all love is we must be told, we must hear it. God has spoken about that revelation. Open up your Scriptures, you hear the Word of God. It is not enough to hear the voice of the beloved; we want to see the beloved. We want to see words borne on human lips; we want to see the earnestness of a visage and the flash of an eye. If God really loves us, He must not only be heard, He must be seen. One day an angel came out from the great white throne of light to a humble

Virgin kneeling in prayer and said, *Hail, full of grace* (LK 1:28). These were not words; they were the Word, and the Word became Flesh and dwelled among us. God was seen in the form of Man. You'll see Him in the blessed Sacrament with the eyes of faith. You see Him in His Church, the continuation of His Incarnation. You see Him in the poor.

I might say this speech on the vision of God is like the relationship between radio and television. The Old Testament is radio—we hear the voice of God but do not see Him—and the New Testament is television, where we not only hear but see God. Is there another intimacy of love more sacred and profound? There is one so delicate that the greatest insult anyone who does not know us can show us, and that is the intimacy of touch. If our blessed Lord is to exhaust all the intimacies of love, He must touch and be touched. He was touched by Thomas (JN 20:27–29), by the woman with the flow of blood (MT 9:20), and He touched the leper and the sick (MK 1:41). As for you, if the gift of faith comes, you will have this gift of touch, which is reserved only for the intimates, the ecstasy of Holy Communion. Just as in marriage the peak of love is the unity of two in one flesh, so in the Eucharist the peak of love is the unity of two in one spirit. It is my fervent prayer to God that this third and most beautiful of all intimacies may come to each and every one of you.

Every single action in your daily work, whether sweeping the street or teaching classes, can be made a prayer. Every action is a kind of a blank check that has value only if the name of our Lord is signed to it. That is why St. Paul said, *Whether you eat or drink, or whatever you do, do it in the name of Christ* (COL 3:17). The tiny little actions of your daily life—as a mother, father, workman, teacher, nurse, or secretary—can be divinized and sacramentalized provided you bring the divine intention, a prayer of action to them. Down in the gutter of a city street there was a drop of water, soiled, dirty, and stagnant. Way up in the heavens a gentle sunbeam saw it, leaped out of the azure sky down to the drop, kissed it, thrilled it through and through with new, strange lives and hopes, lifted it up higher beyond the clouds, and one day left it as a flake of immaculate snow on a mountaintop.

Your humdrum, routine, workaday world can be transmuted and changed just on condition that you do it all for the name of Christ. It is not important what you do in this world, but how you do it. Shakespeare said, "All the world's a stage" (*As You Like It* 2.7). Why should he, who plays the part of a king, glory in his tinsel crown and tin sword, think that he is better than the one who plays the role of a peasant? When the curtain goes down they're just actors! When the curtain of our life goes down, we will not be asked what role we played; we will only be asked how well we played the role that we were assigned.

It will not be hard to save your soul; however, being a Catholic will never prevent you from sinning, but it will take all the fun out of it, because once you have loved, you know what love is. Sin in the Scriptures is always called adultery because it is a false love. I know you will find people who cut corners, play loose, cheat, commit adultery, avoid paying their taxes, and ruin their neighbors' reputations. They do not seem to have any bumps on their consciences, but they have no peace. If we are to love, we have to have the Cross of Christ. We cannot escape it though we try.

I must take leave of you now. I have enjoyed being with you and hope you have profited. Perhaps our hearts have grown a bit together; they do in long conversations. May I remind you that your heart and mine are not perfect in shape and contour like a valentine. There is a small piece missing out of every human heart, which may be to symbolize a piece torn out of the universal Heart of humanity on the Cross. I think the real meaning is that when God made your heart, He found it so good, so lovable, He kept a small sample in heaven and sent the rest into this world, where you would try to be happy, but could not be perfectly happy, because you did not have a whole heart to love with. He has always reminded you that to be truly peaceful, happy, and wholehearted, you must go back again to God to recover the piece He has been keeping for you from all eternity. Your heart will be there in heaven, and please God, so will mine. I will see you in the Heart of God. Bye now, and God love you!

REFLECTION AND STUDY GUIDE

BY MAURA POSTON ZAGRANS

In *Your Life Is Worth Living* Fulton Sheen hopes to guide us through a succession of insights into Jesus as a Jew, a Gentleman, a Prophet, the Messiah, and, finally, Savior of the World. For Sheen, the reason these insights are important is that they illuminate the core of existence as well as the purpose of life, both of which can be summed up in a word. The word is "love."

As you consider the personal journey you have made in reading this book, return to this scaffolding by which Sheen wrote his book and to his stated motivation for writing it. Do the individual chapters help the book accomplish the author's stated goals for you? Does each section build toward an ultimately successful reading experience in you? Try to remember the kind of person you were when you began the book. Try to recall the questions you held in your mind, the holes you felt in your heart. Did this book answer your questions? Did it fill any of those holes? What did you learn? How did you grow?

As we proceed through this guide, try to articulate your answers to these questions. This articulation of reactions and responses is itself a whole new journey.

PART I: GOD AND MAN

1. Sheen wastes no time in tackling the two biggest questions in all of existence. Right away, in chapter 1, he asks: What is the purpose and meaning of life? Strictly from the point of view of a reader, why might Sheen have chosen this as his opening salvo? Having posed such dramatic questions, does Sheen leave us hanging? Does he leave us suspended and confused, or does his two-step solution for existential ennui hold promise as a way toward finding those answers?

2. Why do you think he suggests a method of discovery rather than explicit answers? Do glimmers of wisdom make you want to turn the pages?

3. Just as a scientist would do, Sheen sets the stage for the arguments he will mount by giving us some operational definitions in chapter 2. First up is conscience. Keeping his eye on the notion of purpose, Sheen asks us to think about the purpose of a conscience. The conscience can be viewed as magnificent or as a pest. Why? How do you think about your conscience? Are you glad for it, or have you developed self-destructive behaviors in an attempt to ignore or suffocate what Sheen calls "this unbearable repartee"?

4. Is Sheen convincing when he links conscience and freedom? Do you agree that having a dialogue with our conscience is a choice? Who among us has not wondered why there is evil in the world? In chapter 3, it is Sheen's contention that the type of world God chose to make is precisely right because the juxtaposition of good and evil

allows us to prove our character. Here again, even when considering evil, Sheen finds divine purpose. Are you able to embrace this notion of evil as an opportunity?

5. In chapter 4, Sheen draws a distinction between being bad and being evil. He also explains that there are two types of grace and three primary desires inherent in the human heart. How do these ideas relate to your philosophy of life? Have you thought about what it is you most desire out of life? Once you have articulated those desires, what will you do to get from what you have or where you are to what you wish to have or where you want to be? Sheen introduces us to an obscure poet, Francis Thompson. Judging from the primacy accorded to Thompson in this chapter, it is apparent that he and his work are important to Sheen. By sticking with Sheen until this point, you have in effect entered into sort of a friendship with the author. Since friends care about whatever is important to the other, this would be a good time to take a break and conduct a little research on Thompson. Read his poems and study the life of the poet. Give fresh consideration to Sheen's arguments in the light of what you have learned about Thompson.

6. What is it about Christ that sets Him apart from all other prophets and messengers of God?

7. In chapter 7, Sheen places doubters and believers side by side. He writes, "Persons do not suffer for what they believe to be false." Have you ever suffered for something that you knew you did not believe in? Does this simple observation help you understand the Resurrection? In our world, doubters often delight in stumping those who believe in miracles with the ultimate challenge: Make the

amputated limb reappear and I will believe in miracles. Does Sheen's discussion of what is a miracle help you answer such challengers?

8. Consult your Bible as you read through chapter 8. Read and reflect upon each of Sheen's Scripture references.

PART II: CHRIST AND HIS CHURCH

1. What does it mean to be human? What does it mean to be divine? What does love look like? In chapter 9, Sheen writes, "Love knows no limits. The only way to prove perfect love is by a surrender of all one has." Consider what surrender feels like. In the past, when you surrendered, were you rewarded with love?

2. Sheen makes a case for the unlimited humanity of Christ in chapter 10. His portrait of the human Christ is both thorough and scientific and, at the same time, passionate and tender. When you think of Jesus as human, are you reassured, terrified, or both?

3. The Trinity is the most difficult aspect of Catholicism to explain. Approach the material in chapters 11 and 16 as if you will someday be faced with the challenge of explaining the Trinity, because chances are that you will. Study and practice the arguments in chapter 12 so that you can do a better job of explaining the "tremendous encircling love" that is God the Father, God the Son, and God the Holy Spirit.

4. Catholics are often accused of "worshipping" the Blessed Mother, Mary. Do Sheen's observations and arguments provide helpful tools for the defense of Mary's promi-

nence and role in our prayers and in the Church? Does seeing Mary as the mother of us all enable you to feel closer to her? If so, how might this new relationship find expression—perhaps with greater trust in her, or more sincere respect for her, or in a more authentic honoring of her Son?

5. Chapters 13, 14, and 15 are devoted to sketching Jesus's life. By presenting the key events in pairs of opposites, Sheen deftly shows the fullness, the completeness of Jesus's accomplishments. Go through these chapters with an eye toward finding all the ways that beginnings wrap around to endings, to the ways in which every aspect of Jesus's life is a closed and perfect circle. Sheen advises, "If you ever want good counsel, go to someone who has suffered." Consider this in relation to your life. Would you give this advice to someone you love?

6. Chapters 17 through 20 deal with Christ's legacy to the world. After His Ascension, what we were left with can be summarized by *We are all in this together*. Christ charged us with responsibility not only for our own lives but also for the lives of others. If we are to be His Church, what does this require of each one of us? Sheen contends, "Right is right if nobody is right, and wrong is wrong if everybody is wrong." What are the consequences if we fail as Christ's Church? If Sheen is correct when he asserts, "There's a map to the truth of Christ in the Church," then what is sacrificed when we wander, lose our way, and become disconnected from His Church?

PART III: SIN

1. Basically, everything about Christ comes down to Love. Even sin. Sheen writes, "The only way we really prove love is by choice. Every act of love is not only an affirmation; every act of love is also a negation." In choosing Christ, what must be forsaken? Sheen observes, "The tragedy of life is not so much what people suffer; it's what they miss." Do you know someone who is missing out on life? On love? What could you do to help?

2. What do you risk by becoming involved? What might you gain?

PART IV: SACRAMENTS

1. Throughout the book, Sheen shines as a teacher with his masterful use of analogy. Time and again we have seen him offer unusual analogies to explain difficult concepts. Here, Sheen dispels confusion and sets the stage for understanding his discussion of the purpose of the seven sacraments in this memorable line: "A kiss is a kind of sacrament: it is something visible, and at the same time something invisible, namely, the communication of love." Think about this for a minute. Do you agree that receiving the sacraments is like being kissed by God?

2. How will this perspective on sacraments change the way you keep the sacraments? The way you parent?

PART V: WORLD, SOUL, AND THINGS

1. If the world is to reflect a robust Body of Christ, then all of us have a part to play in what goes into the daily soup of life. We are the microcosm that creates the macrocosm. This means that the depths of depravity in our world are a reflection of what is inside us. "The essence of all obscenity is the turning of the inner mystery into a jest." How are we able to prevent base instincts from interfering with our pathway to the Lord?

2. How can we use the tensions of love to strengthen our relationships, our marriages, our families?

3. Does it help to view discontent and dissatisfaction as a tap on the shoulder from God?

4. How can we reconcile ourselves to stay the course, to love better, even as we accept that we will never be fully satisfied in love because "God keeps something back," and because "The heart was made for the infinite, which only the infinite can satisfy"?

5. What does it mean to die daily? How does practicing daily deaths help us make our way to the Lord?

6. When you pause to consider what actually will happen after you die, what changes will you make in the way you live?

7. In chapters 45 and 46, God's creation reflects a beautiful symmetry. First, Sheen shows why purgatory is necessary. Then, he shows that purgatory is important. Finally, he shows how we can minister to our hurting hearts and burnish our souls by praying for those souls that are

being purged in the crucible of this place. All is circular, nothing is wasted. The system has been designed to help the deceased as well as the living get closer to God. How does this conception change the way you will pray in the future? What do you think will bring us to heaven? What is your motivation for wanting to go to heaven? What do you think will bring you to hell? Do you agree with Sheen that souls go to hell because they refuse to love?

8. What is prayer? Why pray? Why should we make ourselves utterly vulnerable when we communicate with God?

9. Here on earth, it is not unreasonable to expect that our beloved answers "I love you" with "I love you, too." How is prayer like telling God "I love you," and what is the necessary action we must take so that we can hear His response?